Popular Culture Review

Also from Westphalia Press

westphaliapress.org

The Idea of the Digital University

Dialogue in the Greco-Roman World

The Politics of Impeachment

International or Local Ownership?: Security Sector Development in Post-Independent Kosovo

The Role of Theory in Policy Analysis

ABC of Criminology

Non-Profit Organizations and Disaster

The Idea of Neoliberalism: The Emperor Has Threadbare Contemporary Clothes

Donald J. Trump's Presidency: International Perspectives

Ukraine vs. Russia: Revolution, Democracy and War: Selected Articles and Blogs, 2010-2016

Iran: Who Is Really In Charge?

Stamped: An Anti-Travel Novel

A Strategy for Implementing the Reconciliation Process

Issues in Maritime Cyber Security

A Different Dimension: Reflections on the History of Transpersonal Thought

Contracting, Logistics, Reverse Logistics: The Project, Program and Portfolio Approach

Unworkable Conservatism: Small Government, Freemarkets, and Impracticality

Springfield: The Novel

Lariats and Lassos

Ongoing Issues in Georgian Policy and Public Administration

Growing Inequality: Bridging Complex Systems, Population Health and Health Disparities

Designing, Adapting, Strategizing in Online Education

Secrets & Lies in the United Kingdom: Analysis of Political Corruption

Pacific Hurtgen: The American Army in Northern Luzon, 1945

Natural Gas as an Instrument of Russian State Power

New Frontiers in Criminology

Feeding the Global South

Beijing Express: How to Understand New China

Demand the Impossible: Essays in History as Activism

Journal of the Far West Popular and
American Culture Associations

POPULAR
CULTURE
REVIEW

· ·

volume 30 number 1 winter 2019

Felicia F. Campbell, editor

Heather Lusty, associate editor

Westphalia Press
An Imprint of the Policy Studies Organization
Washington, DC
2019

Far West Popular Culture Association

Popular Culture Review gratefully acknowledges the contributions and support by the University of Nevada, Las Vegas: College of Liberal Arts, and the University of Nevada, Las Vegas: Department of English.

Popular Culture Review: Vol. 30, No. 1, Winter 2019

Westphalia Press
An imprint of Policy Studies Organization
1527 New Hampshire Ave., NW
Washington, D.C. 20036
info@ipsonet.org

ISBN-10: 1-63391-769-X
ISBN-13: 978-1-63391-769-9

Table of Contents

Book Reviews

From the Editor's Desk

· ·

As I write this latest "From the Editor's Desk, I am struck once more with the power of popular culture to influence all of our lives. From the media we consume all day, every day, to the public figures who dominate our lives, even the most reclusive of us find ourselves exposed to and dominated by popular and celebrity culture. Public affairs have gone beyond satire, and comedy skits often seem tamer than events in the news. "You couldn't make this stuff up," as I am fond of saying.

Sometimes, breaking into the public consciousness can help raise awareness and prompt empowerment. Scooter Pegram explores the political disenfranchisement of women in France and the importance of a perhaps unlikely avenue to equal representation in a look at the fame and reputation of female hip-hop artists in France. Resistance needs a call to arms, and music can be the perfect vehicle to find the pulse of the common citizen, as explored in "Feminizing the Rhymed Narrative: Women Rappers and Gender Empowerment in French Hip-Hop."

In "A Conversation with Nanette: A Not-So-New Proposal for an Invitational Rhetoric," Nanette Hilton describes how Hannah Gadsby's 2018 comedic sensation scapegoats previous women writers for societal ills, making the point that studying writers from Margaret Fuller to Rita Felski may teach us a better way.

Of course, public figures have always had a mystical ability to become timeless icons. Kathy Merlock Jackson's article speaks to the relevance of so many important figures from the past, including Patty Duke and Marlo Thomas. While visual media like cinema and television programs have preserved the charm of those celebrities, other heroic female characters have faded from the public consciousness with time.

Marcus Axelsson's "War, Patriotism, and Nationality in the Norwegian and Swedish Translations of *Cherry Ames*" takes a look at the representation of the once quite popular protagonist in different cultural contexts: sometimes she is intrinsically tied to a patriotic war movement in her military nursing career, whereas in other translations her character is the primary emphasis. (The last few years should have taught us how important character is in our heroes.)

Brian Mosich's article is perhaps one of our most pragmatic. Title VI prohibits discrimination on the basis of race, color, or national origin, but what happens when those in positions of power find ways to work around it that seem to be completely legal at first glance? Can justice be maintained in such an atmosphere? Speaking of crime, Daryl Malarry Davidson takes a look at crime and sexuality between 1951 and 1984. The topic might be serious, but it is often those things which draw us in most strongly.

While our waking world might seem increasingly nightmarish, the surreal fantasies of the past are as relevant as ever. Daniel Ferreras Savoye examines one of the most haunting short stories of all time in Guy de Maupassant's once famous and now perhaps neglected "Le Horla," which he calls "Dracula's older French cousin." Whether it is the Horla or not, something invisible is certainly watching us even now.

Tammy Wahpeconiah explores the human need for another invisible presence in conceptions of God in "'The Wrong Side of Heaven, the Righteous side of Hell': Religion, Faith and Belief in Ted Chiang's *Story of Your Life and Others*."

Whatever your personal beliefs, if the current state of the world is driving you to existential despair, then perhaps it is good news that we have Graeme J. Wilson's look at a controversial television series which runs the risk of glamorizing suicide in "None of You Cared Enough: The Problematic Moralizing of *13 Reasons Why*." It seems the second season of that show has taken up a more preventative and responsible representation of suicide and the resources available for those struggling with suicidal thoughts, and in an era of constant negative images and decaying mental health, this message is more important than ever.

Finally David Monod and his fellow authors offer us a new resource into vaudeville, a website containing 30,000 reviews of vaudeville performances for the 1900-1920 period.

When a reality television star can rise to the heights of world authority, we see how popular culture affects the globe. What then must we do? What are our responsibilities in providing for the best future? Are we in a position where our entertainments might destroy us, or can we spread positive messages of hope and understanding through the media which connects all of us?

Let us hope for the latter.

Felicia

"The Horla,"
Dracula's Older French Cousin

by Daniel Ferreras Savoye

ABSTRACT

Although both Guy de Maupassant's "Le Horla" and Bram Stoker's *Dracula* have benefited from a great deal of scholarly attention, their striking similarities in terms of form and content have been so far ignored by the critics. The comparative analysis of both texts not only sheds new light upon the influence Maupassant's short story assuredly had on Stoker's novel, but illustrates as well fundamental mechanisms of the fantastic mode, such as familiarization and scientization, which allow us to better define it against the ever-elusive notion of gothic literature.

Keywords: The fantastic, Maupassant, Stoker, "The Horla," Dracula, vampire, gothic

"Le Horla", el primo mayor de Drácula

RESUMEN

Aunque tanto "Le Horla" de Guy de Maupassant como *Drácula* se han beneficiado de una significativa atención académica, sus marcadas similitudes en cuestión de forma y contenido han sido hasta ahora ignoradas por los críticos. El análisis comparativo de ambos textos no solo arroja una nueva luz sobre la influencia que el relato de Maupassant tuvo en la novela de Stoker, sino que también ilustra mecanismos fundamentales del modo fantástico, como la familiarización

1

y la cientificación, que nos permiten definirlo mejor contra la noción escurridiza de la literatura gótica.

Palabras clave: The fantastic, Maupassant, Stoker, "Le Horla," Dracula, vampiro, gótico

"奥尔拉"——德古拉的法国表兄

摘要

尽管居伊·德·莫泊桑所著的《奥尔拉》和布莱姆·斯托克所著的《德古拉》都受到了相当多的学术认可，这两部作品在形式和内容上惊人的相似度却一直以来被评论家所忽视。对这两个文本进行比较分析不仅能阐明莫泊桑短篇小说对斯托克作品所产生的影响，同时还能阐述怪诞模式的根本机制，例如通俗化和科幻化。与一直以来哥特文学中难以解释的概念相比，通俗化和科幻化有助于更好地定义怪诞模式。

关键词：怪诞，莫泊桑，斯托克，《奥尔拉》，德古拉，吸血鬼，哥特式

· · · · · · · · ·

There is another vampire before Dracula, just as disturbingly modern, and that is the maleficent, intangible entity that destroys the protagonist's life and sanity in Guy de Maupassant's classic fantastic tale "The Horla" ("*Le Horla*"). Originally published under the name "Letter of a Madman" as early as 1885 in the French newspaper *Gil Blas*, "The Horla" was further developed throughout two consecutive versions, in 1886 and 1887, the last one being the most well known and that which is usually read. Although all agree in considering "The Horla" as a masterwork of fantastic literature, starting with the author himself who felt the need to keep on improving it in form and content by rewriting it twice, its striking similarities with *Dracula* have gone unnoticed, in spite of the considerable amount of scholarship devoted to both works. "The Horla" is only occasionally mentioned and in a peripheral way as one possible literary antecedent of *Dracula*, along with William Polidori's *The Vampyre*, Thomas Prest's *Varney the Vampyre*, and far behind Sheridan le Fanu' *Carmilla*, which provides some of novel's most obvious tropes, such as the friendship between two young women or the character of Baron Vordenburg, a clear inspiration for that of professor Van Helsing. However, when it comes to the treatment of the supernatural in the fantastic mode, *Dracula* is much closer to "The Horla" than to *Varney the Vampyre* or *Carmilla* and it is not a coincidence if Maupassant's creature remains to this day more well known that any other vampire that preceded Dracula.

Chronologically speaking, the first English translation of "The Horla" appeared in *Modern Ghosts*, a compilation of supernatural stories published by Harper & Brothers in 1890, that is seven years before *Dracula* was published in 1897, which would have given Stoker ample time to appreciate and assimilate Maupassant's fine story telling. Not only are Stoker's first working papers regarding *Dracula* dated "8/3/90" (Frayling 339), the very year "Le Horla" appeared in English, but some specific details, both formal and referential, lead us to conclude almost irrefutably that not only Bram Stoker was very aware of "The Horla," but that he also left some clues behind, either willingly or unwillingly, regarding the direct influence Maupassant's story had upon his creation.

Given their many similarities, a comparative analysis of these two masterworks of fantastic literature will naturally further our understanding of the fantastic mode by revealing some of its more characteristic structural patterns and recurrent narrative motifs, allowing us, among other things, to distinguish it from the often misused and confusing notion of "gothic genre." To better contextualize my demonstration, I will use the 1890 English translation of "The Horla," that which, according to all probabilities, Bram Stoker read the same year he began to conceive *Dracula*.

THE THREE FACES OF "THE HORLA"

"The Horla" tells the story of a man who feels progressively possessed by a mysterious being as his reality is suddenly subverted by the irruption of unexplainable occurrences. The first version, "Letter of a Madman," presents relatively little action, leaving more room to the protagonist's considerations regarding the natural limitations of human perception and our incapacity to see beyond the surface. By reflecting upon those matters, the protagonist progressively sharpens his senses until he perceives indeed an invisible presence lurking about which frightens him to the verge of madness, and leads him to address this letter to his physician: "My dear doctor, I place myself in your hands" (*"Mon cher docteur, je me mets entre vos mains"* (233)). Whether "Letter of a Madman" is logically presented in an epistolary form, the second version of the story, and first to be entitled "The Horla," is a framed narration, in which the narrator is invited by an eminent alienist to hear the story of one of his patients, who in turn tells the tale in the first person. This particular version adds several instances of supernatural manifestation to the story, such as the protagonist's sensation of a deadly weight on his chest that sucks his breath as he sleeps, water and milk

4

disappearing overnight from the nightstand, a rose floating in the middle of an alley in the garden, and the pages of a book turning by themselves, without however sacrificing the intellectual considerations that compose most of "Letter of a Madman." It also includes external witnesses, for it is revealed at the end of the story that three of the patient's neighbors have apparently fallen prey to this strange being for they claim identical symptoms, a fact which is corroborated by the physician. The patient finishes his story by pointing out a newspaper article which reports a similar epidemic in Brazil, and stating that he indeed saw a Brazilian boat on the Seine a few days before he began feeling that strange and threatening presence around him; he then concludes that the mysterious creature was most likely hidden aboard.

The third and final version of "The Horla"—the very one that was translated by Jonathan Sturges and published by Harper & Brothers in 1890—is presented under the form of a diary, which gives a day-to-day account of the protagonist's battle with the invisible creature, climaxing in a tragic scene, where the narrator, attempting to eliminate the mysterious creature that has invaded his vital space and his consciousness, burns down his house and his servants along with it, to no avail since he senses that the creature is still alive, and finishes his diary contemplating suicide as the only way to escape its terrifying grip. This version uses most of the same motifs as the previous one albeit in a slightly different arrangement in order to improve their narrative efficiency: the narrator is no longer committed to a mental institution and appears on the contrary perfectly at ease at the beginning of the story, which shows him enjoying the view of the Seine from his garden and saluting a Brazilian boat which he finds particularly handsome, a gesture whose significance will not be revealed until the article describing the mysterious epidemic in Brazil is mentioned toward the end of the story. The news regarding the apparent invasion of mysterious creatures in some villages in Brazil, which corroborate the narrator's tale and hence contribute to the fantastic effect by turning a subjective adventure into an apparently objective reality, is itself more precisely presented than in the previous version, in order to accentuate its realistic dimension: it is no longer a random piece from some anonymous newspaper but a scientific report published in the fictitious albeit prestigious sounding *Revue du Monde Scientifique*, the name of which is reminiscent of the *Revue des Deux Mondes*, one of the most respected publications of the time.

The form of the diary allows naturally for a more direct identification with the receiver, as we experience the progression of the action at the same time as the narrator, whose discourse becomes increasingly fragmented, hence strengthening the relationship between form and content. Unlike the letter of the madman in the first version and the exposition of the patient in the second, which are stylistically static, the diary from the third and last version formally documents the increasing fear of the narrator by linguistically reproducing his mental breakdown. This last version also distances the narrative voice from the immediate neighborhood of psychiatrists and lunatic asylums, hence further removing madness as a possible explanation: whereas "Letter of a Madman" is addressed to a physician, hence implying that the protagonist has accepted the possibility that he might have gone mad, as suggested by the title itself, and the first version of "The Horla" is framed within the walls of a mental institution, the final version only introduces the possibility of madness insofar as the protagonist doubts his own sanity, which paradoxically could be considered as a sign of mental health, for true madness does not doubt itself.

In spite of these noticeable differences, all three versions, however, preserve one specific narrative motif, which constitutes the only true instance of a supernatural occurrence in "Letter of a Madman," as well as the final and climactic confrontation with the mysterious entity in the two versions of "The Horla": one evening, as he strongly feels the presence of the mysterious being around him, the protagonist looks at himself in the mirror and is unable to see his reflection. As his reflection slowly reappears, emerging from behind a diffuse mist, he deduces that the mysterious creature was between him and the mirror, and that it absorbed his reflection. The Horla having no reflection at all should naturally remind us of Dracula himself, and as to confirm our suspicions, the word "vampire" appears at the end of the last two versions in relationship to the epidemic which is forcing the inhabitants of entire villages in Brazil to leave their homes, claiming that they have become possessed by a mysterious creature who steals their breaths and drinks their milk and water during the night.

LE DRACULA

Maupassant's Horla thus seems to already possess most of the same characteristics of Stoker's Dracula and to function in comparable ways. Its relationship with light and darkness, for instance, is similar to that of the vampire, since it is most maleficent at night but can still exist in the daylight, just as Dracula, who, contrary to popular belief, does not spontaneously combust when exposed to sunlight, but only loses most of his powers. The Horla can also manifest himself during the day, as in the episode where the narrator, strolling through his garden, sees a rose being cut by invisible hands, suspended in the air and apparently kissed by invisible lips. Although doubtlessly frightening, for it signifies the irruption of the unexplainable in a very mundane setting, this instance of the supernatural in the protagonist's formerly quietly arranged life does not imply any direct physical threat—it would almost seem an amicable gesture. It is the night that turns the Horla into a monstrous predator, who sucks the breath of the narrator during his sleep, just as the vampire sucks the blood from his victims. The Horla also drinks the water and the milk that the narrator leaves on his nightstand; although definitely less fulfilling than blood, both water and milk still signify life at primordial and essential levels, for water is the fundamental condition for life as we conceive it, and milk is directly and universally related to motherhood. In Stoker's novel, breath, water, and milk are fused into one single element, blood, which is both life and liquid.

The definitive version of "The Horla" also reworks the encounter of the narrator with the Brazilian ship aboard which the mysterious creature is supposed to have arrived by introducing it at the beginning of the story, as the narrator is but a happy, worry-free fellow, so enchanted by the view of the beautiful three masts that he feels compelled to salute him. Naturally, he will not realize the significance of his gesture until the end of the story:

> Ah! Ah! I remember, I remember the beautiful Brazilian three-master which passed up the Seine under my window on the 8th of last May! I thought it was so beautiful, so white, so gay! The Being was aboard it, coming from that distant country where his race was born! (42-43)

This handsome ship aboard which the Horla allegedly arrived from Brazil to Normandy naturally reminds us of the ship Dracula used in order to travel from his native Transylvania to the city of London. Furthermore, the protagonist's gesture of salutation could be interpreted as an invitation to invade his home and his consciousness. Just like Dracula, the Horla travels by sea from a distant, exotic place to what can be considered as familiar surroundings—the outskirts of Rouen or different districts of London—and needs to be previously invited in order to invade his victim's homes. The last revision of "The Horla" therefore adds an element which has since become one of the most well-known staples of the vampire's narrative universe, the need for the monster to be invited in by his prey who therefore become involuntarily responsible for their own demise. This confers a truly tragic dimension to the characters' ordeal, as they appear prisoners of their actions, just as Oedipus was of his.

On the formal front, *Dracula*, interestingly enough, reunites the three types of narrative we find in the successive versions of "The Horla": the epistolary format ("Letter of a Madman"), the testimony ("The Horla," first version), and the diary. However, the latter, which corresponds to that of the final version of Maupassant's tale, overwhelmingly dominates the economy of the narration in terms of both quantity and significance, since the most important developments are presented through Lucy's and Mina's respective journals, Dr. Seward's diary and, of course, Jonathan Harker's journal, which opens the novel and first introduces the ominous Count Dracula. Jonathan Harker's diary progresses in the same manner as that of the nameless narrator of "Le Horla," starting by recording rather ordinary information, such as trite details regarding local cuisine and inadequate transportation until the final leg of his journey and his arrival to Dracula's castle. However, in spite of the uncanny atmosphere of the castle, Jonathan Harker's diary does not start to express fear openly until the end of the second chapter, precisely after he realizes that count Dracula has no reflection in his shaving mirror:

> Suddenly I felt a hand on my shoulder, and heard the Count's voice saying to me, "Good-morning." I started, for it amazed me that I had not seen him, since the re-flection of the glass covered the whole room behind me. [...] Having answered the Count's salutation, I turned to the glass again to see how I had been mistaken. This time there could be no error, for the man was close to me, and I could see him over my shoulder. But there was no reflection of him in the mirror! The whole room behind me was displayed; but there was no sign of a man in it, except myself. (30-31)

Jonathan Harker searches then for a way to escape the castle and concludes that it is "a veritable prison, and I am a prison-er!" (32).

This particular episode is the first supernatural occurrence in the novel, a truly fantastic moment, for the unexplainable is presented in a most mundane context—Jonathan Harker is shaving. It also introduces what has become one of the most distinctive and exploited features of the vampire, his absence of reflection, which he shares with the Horla in all three ver-sions of the story. However, whereas the moment when the narrator is unable to see himself in the mirror is the last, most extreme iteration of the supernatural in "The Horla"—and the only one in "Letter of a Madman"—it is on the contrary its first real irruption in *Dracula*, as if Dracula started precise-ly where the Horla ends.

As to underline this symmetry, this entry in Harker's journal is dated May 8th, which is the exact same date as the first entry in the narrator's diary in "Le Horla." This particular date might seem innocuous enough outside of a close circle of friends, for it is the day on which Gustave Flaubert, Maupassant's friend and mentor, passed away. From a strictly biographical standpoint, May 8th had naturally ominous connotations for Maupassant, which explains why he chose it as the beginning for a dark fantastic tale. In *Dracula*, this day marks the first true confrontation between Harker and the supernatural, that is the moment when the novel becomes fantastic. This parallelism of dates and narrative motifs leaves little doubt regarding the influence "The Horla" had upon *Dracula*, for the choice of the 8th of May to present the episode of the mirror, whether conscious or unconscious, is an undeniable reference to the vampire's older French cousin.

THE UN-GOTHIC

From a generic point of view, "Le Horla" and *Dracula* are both exemplary illustrations of the modern fantastic. Although *Dracula* is often presented as a "gothic" novel, the term proves rather misleading for it describes a narrative category—a set of narrative motifs—rather than a particular narrative mode, that is the way the narrated universe relates to our reality. This common confusion explains why the gothic usually includes an almost infinite variety of authors, ranging from Edgar Allan Poe and Ann Radcliff to Howard Philip Lovecraft and Stephen King, enthusiastically overlooking the fundamental differences and specific intentionality of their respective works. Whereas many of Poe's tales are uncanny rather than fantastic, for they do not present any supernatural element in their narrative universe, i.e., "The Purloined Letter," "The Gold Bug," "The Cask of Amontillado," those by Lovecraft, on the contrary, generate their narrative authority from the direct opposition between what is rationally acceptable and what is not. Whereas Ann Radcliff's novels present a strange reality where the apparently supernatural is often explained, those by Stephen King present an utterly normal reality suddenly subverted by the irruption of the unexplainable, which will remain unexplained, i.e., *Christine*, *Needful Things*, or *The Shining*. This last example does include its share of gothic elements, such as the old fashioned hotel and the isolation of the mountains; however, the interest of the narration resides in the progressive subversion of an acceptable reality rather than in the exploration of its protagonists' familial conflicts and romantic interactions, as in Radcliff's novels. The paradigms we usually conceive as "gothic," such as ancient ruined castles, crypts, skulls, ghostly apparitions, monsters, and strange noises in the night are not enough to create the fantastic mode, which depends upon the organization of the paradigms rather than upon the paradigms themselves: the fundamental narrative authority of the fantastic stems from the confrontation between the very possible and the utterly impossible, a confrontation which all but disappears with Ann Radcliff's conception of the "explainable supernatural." Furthermore, in the case of *Dracula*, it could be argued that the narration quickly sheds its gothic trimmings, first of all by introducing the narration from the perspective of a rather unexciting fellow, whose preoccupations are more practical than romantic:

> The time I waited seemed endless, and I felt doubts and fears crowding upon me. What sort of place had I come to, and among what kind of people? What sort of grim adventure was it on which I had embarked? Was this a customary incident in the life

> of a solicitor's clerk sent out to explain the
> purchase of a London estate to a foreigner?
> Solicitor's clerk! Mina would not like that.
> Solicitor—for just before leaving London I
> got word that my examination was success-
> ful; and I am now a full-blown solicitor!
> (21)

Jonathan Harker's conceptions of life and love appear rather bourgeois and dull, very much like his excitement at having passed the examination to become a real solicitor, which correspond perfectly to the pragmatic rather than emotional tone of his journal's initial entries.

The atmosphere of the Carpathian mountains and the general appearance of Dracula's castle do belong among the most recognizable paradigms of gothic literature, however, not only are they presented from the point of view of a very ordinary individual, they are also quickly left behind, as the narration moves to more recognizable surrounding, such as London and its vicinity, where most of the action takes place: what makes *Dracula* an authoritative narration does not reside in its gothic elements but in the constant confrontation it presents between an acceptable reality and the supernatural.

We find as well our share of gothic elements in "The Horla," although it is not usually considered a gothic tale, such as the visit of the protagonist to the Mont-Saint-Michel, which describes the site's tormented gothic architecture and relates a strange conversation with a monk who expresses our inability to see all that surrounds us in rather mysterious if not mystical terms. However, just as it happens in *Dracula*, where the narration has to move away from Transylvania to a more familiar environment in order to preserve its fantastic dimension, this visit to the Mont-Saint-Michel occurs early in the tale, as the narrator, believing that he is only temporarily ill, has decided to take a trip in order to restore his health and has apparently succeeded, as stated in the following entry: " June 2nd: At home again. I am cured. And besides, I have made a charming excursion. I visited the mont Saint-Michel [sic] where I had never been" (9). In actuality, the beginning of this quote in the French original, "*je rentre*," is better rendered in English by "I'm on my way back home," hence further dissociating the gothic from the fantastic: the Horla does not manifest itself within the recognizably gothic environment of the Mont-Saint-Michel but only within the familiar space of the narrator's house.

Both texts, Dracula and "Le Horla," therefore separate the fantastic from gothic motifs, which, rather than enhancing the fantastic effect tend to dilute it by connoting a less realistic environment, where specters and apparitions are accepted by common folks, as are the superstitions the natives share elliptically with Jonathan Harker at the beginning of his journey or those told to the narrator of "The Horla" during his visit to the Mont-Saint-Michel, which involve a ghost shepherd with an invisible head herding a he-goat and a she-goat with human faces. It is precisely when they are cut off from these superstitions and fairy tales that "The Horla" and Dracula gain their statures of terrifying monsters, as they materialize in a reality we can identify as our own, further suggesting the real possibility of the unthinkable.

WEIRD SCIENCES

In order to enhance the suspension of disbelief, the supernatural has to be wagered against an utmost rational, if not scientific conception of reality, which tends to push away the matters of the heart, and so, rather than developing Lucy's or even Mina's romantic matters, which soon fade into the background, *Dracula* concentrates upon the investigation of its main protagonists, in particular Dr. Seward and professor Van Helsing—both men of science—as they search first for possible explanations and then for the means to destroy the vampire in a very lucid, scientific fashion. Similarly, the narrator of "The Horla" experiments in a highly rational manner with the different liquids he leaves on his nightstand in order to determine if they are indeed being drunk by the invisible creature during the night; in one instance, he wraps up the bottles of water and milk with white muslin and rubs his lips, his beard, and his hands with black-lead before going to sleep, as to demonstrate to himself that he is neither sleepwalking nor going mad.

Since the narrative tension on which the fantastic mode relies is most of all epistemological, it naturally plays upon the limitations of sciences within sciences themselves, which tend to be represented in their more enigmatic modalities, raising more questions than providing solutions, as to challenge our very means of apprehending the world. Just as the narrator of "The Horla" started by questioning our perception and understanding of what surrounds us, Dr. Seward and Professor Van Helsing often discuss the validity of human perception and understanding of reality, and underline their fundamental flaws by presenting apparently unexplainable yet verified facts:

> Can you tell me how the Indian fakir can make himself to die and have been buried, and his grave sealed and corn sowed on it, and the corn reaped and be cut and sown and reaped and cut again, and then men come and take away the unbroken seal and that there lie the Indian fakir, not dead, but

> that rise up and walk amongst them as be-
> fore? (172)

Scientific demonstrations hence only demonstrate the inad-
equacy of our epistemological apparatus, which echoes the
doubts repeatedly expressed by the narrator of "The Horla"
regarding our understanding of reality.

Some sciences tend to exhibit their own limitations more
than others, and hence remain objectively mysterious, paradoxically functioning as links between reasonable compre-
hension and what remains incomprehensible. Among them,
psychiatric medicine occupies a place of choice, for it deals
directly with one of the areas of human understanding that
remains irreducible to rational terms by definition, madness,
and is logically a recurring theme in the fantastic mode. Although the last version of "The Horla" eliminates all direct
mentions to psychiatrists and lunatic asylums, it still retains
the constant interrogations of the narrator vis-à-vis his sanity, as madness is the most evident and rational explanation
for the irruption of the impossible in real life. In *Dracula*, the
character of Dr. Seward, director of a lunatic asylum, represents the rational view of madness, which allows the supernatural to exist by opposing it to the most extreme manifestations of the human psyche; as a physician, Dr. Seward
constitutes a privileged witness of the incomprehensible for
he is professionally trained to distinguish the strange possibilities of mental illness from the true manifestations of the
supernatural.

One medical practice in particular, hypnotism, which in the
nineteenth century used to be regrouped, along with telepathy, thought transmission and such, under the loose category
known as "magnetism," allows both "The Horla" and *Dracula* to represent the reality of the incomprehensible in an

allegedly scientific manner, albeit in slightly different ways. In "Le Horla," the narrator, feeling sick again, goes to Paris, and while having dinner with his cousin, Mme. Sablé, meets a physician who introduces him to the modern medical advances regarding hypnotism and suggestion. As the narrator and his cousin remain incredulous, the physician offers to hypnotize Mme. Sablé:

> At the end of ten minutes she slept. "Put yourself behind her," said the physician. And I seated myself behind her. In her hands he placed a visiting-card, saying: "This is a mirror; what do you see in it?" She answered: I see my cousin" "What is he doing?" "He is twisting his mustache." "What now?" "He is taking a photograph out of his pocket." "A photograph of whom?" "Of himself." It was true! [...] So then she saw in this card, in this white card, as well as she would have seen in a glass! (22-23)

The physician also plants in Mme. Sablé's subconscious the need to go to see the narrator on the next day in order to ask for a sum of money that she does not need. After the experiment succeeds, the narrator concludes: "The wise man says: 'It may be '" (29). The original French text adds a question mark to the sentence (*Le sage dit: peut-être?*) to better emphasize the uncertainty of sciences when it comes to fully understanding our environment.

In *Dracula*, hypnotism becomes the ally of the vampire hunters, as Mina, having been contaminated by the unclean blood of Dracula is able, when under hypnosis, to inform the search party regarding the monster's whereabouts in order to guide their quest. Although the reality of hypnotism has been demonstrated in terms of behavioral suggestion, its representation in both texts "Le Horla" and *Dracula* goes well beyond its proven capacities, for it is merged with telepathy, which, unlike hypnotism, remains scientifically indemonstrable. Just as Mme. Sablé appears to be able to read the narrator's mind after being put under hypnosis, Mina becomes telepathically connected to Dracula when hypnotized by Van Helsing. Hypnotism is therefore used by both narrations as a reasonable gateway into the unreasonable, all the more justified that it benefits from a legitimate scientific reputation sanctioned by a historical figure, French pioneer neurologist Jean-Martin Charcot, whose name is invoked by Dr. Seward during a conversation with professor Van Helsing and whose lectures at the prestigious Hôpital Salpêtrière in Paris were occasionally attended by one Guy de Maupassant.

FRENCH CONNECTION

Beyond their uncanny correspondence of dates, either historical (1890) or literary (May 8th), "Le Horla" and *Dracula* can be considered as transatlantic twin illustrations of the modern fantastic, which leave behind the narrative trappings of the gothic tradition in order to concentrate upon the rational understanding of the irrational, for the fantastic is not about ruined castles in faraway lands but on the contrary about our familiar surroundings being invaded by the impossible, which is why Dracula has much more to do with his French cousin from Normandy than with Vlad the Impaler himself.

WORKS CITED

Frayling, Christopher. "Bram Stoker's Working Papers for *Dracula.*" *Dracula.* Norton, 1997, pp. 339-50.

King, Stephen. *The Shining.* Anchor, 2012.

———. *Needful Things.* Signet, 1992.

———. *Christine.* Signet, 1983.

le Fanu, Joseph Sheridan. *Carmilla.* Minerva Publishing, 2018.

Maupassant, Guy de. "The Horla." *Ghost Stories.* Translated by Jonathan Sturges, Harper Brothers, 1890, pp. 1-55.

———. "Le Horla." (1st version) *Contes Fantastiques Complets.* Edited by Anne Richter, Marabout, 1978, pp. 271-80.

———. "Le Horla." (2nd version) *Contes Fantastiques Complets.* Edited by Anne Richter, Marabout, 1978, pp. 281-308.

———. "Lettre d'un fou." ("Letter of a Madman.") *Contes Fantastiques Complets.* Edited by Anne Richter, Marabout, 1978, pp. 233-39.

———. *Contes Fantastiques Complets.* Edited by Anne Richter, Marabout, 1978.

Poe, Edgar Allan. "The Cask of Amontillado." *Complete Tales and Poems.* Barnes and Noble, 1992, pp. 666-71 .

———. "The Purloined Letter." *Complete Tales and Poems.* Barnes and Noble, 1992, pp. 593-607 .

———. "The Gold Bug." *Complete Tales and Poems*. Barnes and Noble, 1992, pp. 449-76 .

Polidori, John William. *The Vampyre*. CreateSpace, 2016.

Prest, Thomas. *Varney the Vampyre*. CreateSpace, 2016.

Stoker, Bram. *Dracula*. Norton, 1997.

Various. *Ghost Stories*. Harper Brothers, 1890 .

"The Wrong Side of Heaven, the Righteous Side of Hell": Religion, Faith, and Belief in Ted Chiang's *Stories of Your Life and Others*

by Tammy Wahpeconiah

ABSTRACT

In this article, I argue that Chiang addresses questions surrounding faith, religion, belief, and the nature of God. He questions whether God has a role in our lives, what that role may look like, and the ability of religion to provide meaning. I further argue that Chiang's stories are apocalyptic in nature and have a certain similarity to the apocalyptic writings of John because they reveal our disillusionment with the world and our inability to find meaning in religion alone.

Keywords: Chiang, Ted; Ted Chiang; Stories of Your Life and Others; Religion; Apocalypse; Science Fiction; Tower of Babylon; Hell Is the Absence of God; Division by Zero

"El lado equivocado del cielo, el lado correcto del infierno": religión, fé y creencias en *Historias de tu vida y otras*

RESUMEN

En este artículo argumento que Chiang aborda temas que tienen que ver con la fé, la religión y la naturaleza de Dios. Se pregunta si Dios juega un papel en nuestras vidas, cómo podría ser este papel y la habilidad de la religión para dar un sentido. Adicionalmente argumento que las historias de Chiang son de naturaleza apocalíptica y tienen cierta similitud con los textos apocalípticos de John porque revelan nuestra desilusión con el mundo y nuestra falta de habilidad para encontrar sentido exclusivamente en la religión.

Palabras clave: Chiang, Ted, Ted Chiang, Historias de tu vida y otras, Religión, Apocalipsis, Ciencia ficción, Torre de Babilonia, El infierno es la ausencia de Dios, División por cero

"天堂之过、地狱之功"：宗教、信念和信仰在特德·蒋作品《你一生的故事》中的体现

摘要

笔者主张，特德·蒋研究了围绕信念、宗教、信仰和上帝本性的相关问题。蒋就上帝是否在人的生命中产生了作用、产生了何种作用、以及宗教在赋予人意义一事上的能力提出了质疑。笔者进一步主张，蒋的作品在本质上是预示大灾变的，并且在一定程度上和约翰对启示录的描写相似，因为二者都揭示了人类对世界的幻灭以及其无法仅从宗教中发现意义。

关键词：Chiang, Ted，特德·蒋，《你一生的故事》，宗教，启示录，科幻小说，《巴比伦塔》，《无神之地即是地狱》，《除以零》

· · · · · · · · ·

How is God in the world? Is He, according to Christian theology, both transcendent and immanent? In other words, is He distant and separate from the world and humanity while at the same time working within both? Or, did He create the universe and then remove Himself from it? Are we able to comprehend certain aspects of God through our understanding of the order and beauty of the universe? Or, do humans seek a God who is no longer interested? Many science fiction writers have asked and responded to such questions including Ted Chiang in his collection, *Stories of Your Life and Others*. Several of his stories deal directly with these questions and we can read them as a critique of faith, religion, belief, and the nature of God. Chiang questions whether God has a role in our lives, what that role may look like, and the ability of religion to provide meaning. Furthermore, these stories are apocalyptic in nature, especially if we think of apocalypse as "revelation," the Greek definition.

Frederick Krueziger further defines apocalypse as "an unfolding; hence a revelation through unfolding" (5). Such unfolding always takes place within a story; thus, we must consider the inherent connection between apocalypse and story. As Krueziger says, "Apocalypse as story first of all reveals story as that which shapes our search for meaning" (5). The revelation, the unfolding, therefore *is* the story itself as well as *what* the story means. We can read Chiang's stories as apocalyptic because they reveal our disillusionment with our world and our inability to find meaning in religion alone. For Krueziger, science fiction as apocalypse illustrates our disillusionment with "the failure of the promise of technology and science to deliver the world from poverty, ignorance, disease, war, famine, plague, and death ...." (6). Although I agree that many science fiction works address these particular disillusionments, Chiang's stories, I would argue, have a certain similarity to the apocalyptic writings of John. People disappointed at the failure of the Second Coming to occur during their lifetime lost faith in the promise of God. John's writings deal with crises of both history and faith. Thus, Chiang's stories are similar to John's writings in that they deal with the disillusionment and failure of faith and religion.

Before discussing the stories, it may behoove us to consider the definitions of faith, religion, and belief. Although we may feel we know what these words mean, and may even think they are synonymous, the distinctions among them are of importance to this essay. As John Bishop states, "... at its most general, 'faith' means the same as 'trust.'" Greg Popcak defines faith more narrowly, asserting that faith "is merely the innate drive to search for meaning, purpose and significance." Religion, at its most basic, can be defined as a specific form of human activity as a means of achieving spiritual or material improvement. However, this form of human activity is often cultural because it is a system of behaviors and praxes uniting a community. Belief, according to Eric Schwitzgebel, refers "to the attitude we have, roughly, whenever we take something to be the case or regard it as true." Interestingly, many define faith as belief without proof. Although many use these three terms interchangeably, Chiang employs them in specific ways in his stories.

In the "Tower of Babylon," Chiang uses the biblical story of the tower of Babel as his premise. His focus is not on God's creation of various languages as punishment for defying Him, but on humanity's desire "to see what lay beyond [the earth's] borders, all the rest of Yahweh's creation" (5-6). This story juxtaposes science with faith and religion as the Babylonians are building the tower so they can break into the vault of heaven. They desire knowledge about their world, but also desire knowledge about God, believing that the tower will enable them "to ascend to see the works of Yahweh" while allowing Yahweh to "descend to see the works of man" (6). In this story, Ted Chiang combines the above definitions of religion as a "search for meaning, purpose and significance" as well as the desire for material and spiritual improvement (Popcak).

In addition to religion as a thematic focus, Chiang also incorporates geocentrism: a specific, albeit outdated, "scientific worldview" (Smith). As Alexander Robishaw explains:

> The envisaged structure is simple: Earth was seen as being situated in the middle of a great volume of water, with water both above and below Earth. A great dome was thought to be set above Earth (like an inverted glass bowl), maintaining the water above Earth in its place. Earth was pictured as resting on foundations that go down into the deep. These foundations secured the stability of the land as something that is not floating on the water and so could not be tossed about by wind and wave. The waters surrounding Earth were thought to have been gathered together in their place. The stars, sun, moon, and planets moved in their allotted paths across the great dome above Earth, with their movements defining the months, seasons, and year. (60)

Chiang brilliantly describes the geocentric worldview through the protagonist of the story, Hillalum, who is an Elamite miner, contracted to dig into the vault of heaven. He, along with other Elamite miners, spends four months climbing to the top of the tower. Along the way, he discovers how his world and his universe functions. He comes to know that night is "the shadow of the earth itself, cast against the sky" ("Tower" 11). He and the others reach a point on the tower where they see "storms from above and from below" and where people "[harvest] crops from the air" (14). After climbing a number of weeks, the miners find themselves "at precisely the same level as the moon when it passed; they had reached the height of the first of the celestial bodies" (14). When they reach the level of the sun, the intense heat forces them to travel at night. Passing this level, Hillalum finds that the sun shines "*upward,* which [seems] unnatural to the utmost" (15, emphasis in original). When they are level with the stars, the miners discover that a star has hit the tower, leaving "a knotted mass of black heaven-metal, as large as a man could wrap his arms around" (16). Finally, they reach the vault of heaven itself, "a solid carapace enclosing all the sky" (16) that "[seems] to be made of fine-grained white granite, unmarred and utterly featureless" (18-19). Hillalum's travels to the top of the tower allows him to discover both the meaning and significance of the physical world, not through religion or faith, but through his own observation.

Since, in the geocentric view, the Earth is "situated in the middle of a great volume of water," the Babylonians and the Elamite miners fear that breaking into the vault of heaven will release another Great Flood (Robishaw 60). They believe Yahweh caused the Great Flood, or the "Deluge," by releasing "the waters of the Abyss ... from the springs of the earth, and ... [from] the sluice gates in the vault" (19). Concerned that they may hit one of these reservoirs, the Babylonians enlist Egyptian masons who design a system using large blocks of granite that will "slide down until [they] rest in the recess of the floor" and will completely block any opening (22). Using this design, they are able to safeguard the world from another flood when their worst fear is realized and the miners accidently dig into a reservoir. Hillalum and two others are trapped within the vault, but only Hillalum survives. The rising water forces him upward and the current of water carries him until "the walls [open] out away from him" (25). He awakens in a tunnel, but is able to see light ahead. He comes out of what he discovers is a cave and finds himself in the land of Shinnar, which is south of Babylon. Hillalum's return to earth from the vault of heaven forces him to realize that the world is shaped like a seal cylinder, "wrapped around in some fantastic way so that heaven and earth [touch]" (28). Thus, Hillalum's journey is in itself apocalyptic—as his story unfolds, the world reveals itself through his experience.

The scientific worldview Chiang incorporates is fascinating; yet, what is even more fascinating is the way the inhabitants view God and their attempts to connect with Him. The people fear God's displeasure and Hillalum feels uneasy at the thought of breaking open the vault of heaven (4). Standing at the base of the tower even Hillalum's senses rebel, "insisting that nothing should stand so high" (6). He and the others continually wait for a sign from God "to let men know that their venture was approved," yet God is silent (14). When the star mentioned above first hit the tower, "everyone descended .... , waiting for retribution from Yahweh for disturbing the workings of Creation. They waited for months, but no sign came" (16). God never acknowledges their efforts, either blessing or damning them for their attempts. Their overwhelming desire for knowledge of God's workings cause them to give "thanks that they [are] permitted to see so much" while at the same time they "beg forgiveness for their desire to see more" (18). Their reactions show lack of surety regarding their purpose as Yahweh fails to respond.

The inhabitants debate how God may perceive their attempts to reach Him. Qurdusa, one of the tower's bricklayers, argues that "if the tower were sacrilege, Yahweh would have destroyed it earlier" causing one of the Elamites to counter: "If Yahweh looked upon this venture with such favor there would already be a stairway ready-made for us to use in the vault" (19). Hillalum, however, takes a more Deistic viewpoint, saying, "Yahweh may not punish us, but Yahweh may allow us to bring our judgment upon ourselves" (19). The God in this story creates the world but does not actively intervene. When Hillalum and the others hit a reservoir, he believes "his fate had come at last. Yahweh had not asked men to build the tower or to pierce the vault; the decision to build it belonged to men alone, and they would die in this endeavor just as they did in any of their earthbound tasks. Their righteousness could not save them from the consequences of their actions" (24). In this world, the focus is on the choices one makes and the consequences one must pay for those choices. Yes, God exists, but He does not intervene in human lives, nor does He care if they are virtuous or sinful, or if they worship or ignore Him.

Hillalum's realization of how the world is structured leads him to an understanding of why God never responds to humanity's attempts to reach him:

> It was clear now why Yahweh had not struck down the tower, had not punished men for wishing to reach beyond the bounds set for them: for the longest journey would merely return them to the place whence they'd come. Centuries of their labor would not reveal to them any more of Creation than they already knew. Yet through their endeavor, men would glimpse the unimaginable

> artistry of Yahweh's work, in seeing how
> ingeniously the world had been construct-
> ed. By this construction, Yahweh's work
> was indicated, and Yahweh's work was con-
> cealed. Thus men would know their place.
> (28)

Hillalum comes to understand that faith does not provide meaning or significance to his life. He glimpses "the unimaginable artistry" of the world through human endeavor, not through worship or religious ritual. As Alan Gregory states, while all "apocalyptic texts reveal human life in its precarious contingency," apocalyptic "science fiction finds the contingency of life before immanent powers" (161). The inhabitants of this world find "a sense of wonder at the complexity of creation" that comes from their own exploration of the world (Smith). Yahweh does not open their minds or increase their understanding of their world and their place in it, only an individual's desire for knowledge does so. Chiang's story is apocalyptic in that it is the story itself that reveals our search for meaning. We do not need religion to achieve spiritual or material improvement; what we need is our continuing desire to discover and understand the physical world.

The "Tower of Babylon" is a story illustrating the existence of God through the reasoning and observation of its characters, but not by supernatural manifestations. Such is not the case in "Hell Is the Absence of God." In the world of the story, the idea of faith as belief without proof is not an issue. Angels make frequent appearances and inhabitants witness the dead ascending into Heaven or descending into Hell. Hell itself becomes visible on occasion, allowing the living to see a place very similar to their world as going to Hell means "permanent exile from God, no more and no less" ("Hell" 208). Angelic manifestations can lead to miracles but can also lead to indiscriminate death and birth defects because of the destructive power of their visitations. Furthermore, anyone caught in "Heaven's light," which appears "only when an angel [enters] or [leaves] the mortal plain," goes to Heaven, even if they are wicked or evil (226).

The protagonist of the story, Neil Fisk, believes in God (as do all in this world since there is no question of God's existence), but he does not love God. Neil views "God's actions in the abstract," believing that "circumstances were fully capable of unfolding, happily or not, without intervention from above" (206). Because Neil is devoid of either positive or negative feelings about God, he fully expects to go to Hell since, "for people like him, Hell was where you went when you died" (209). Permanent exile from God holds no fear for Neil as it means "living without interference" (209). His wife, Sarah, however, is devout, a fact that surprises Neil since "there weren't many signs of her devotion" such as church attendance. Yet, he sees in her "the best argument for loving God that he had ever encountered. If love of God had contributed to making her the person she was, then perhaps it did make sense" (218). The years spent together even improved Neil's view of God and given time, Neil "probably would have reached the point where he was thankful to God" (218). However, he is not given that time.

Unfortunately, Sarah is one of eight casualties during a visitation from the angel Nathanael; she is "hit by flying glass when the angel's billowing curtain of flame [shatters] the storefront window of the café in which she was eating" (206). Witnesses see her ascension to Heaven, and while Neil "could have seen Sarah's death as a wake up-call," he instead becomes "actively resentful of God" (218). He wants to be reunited with Sarah, and the only way to achieve this reunion is for Neil to learn to love God. However, he finds himself in a paradox: "Sarah had been the greatest blessing of his life, and God had taken her away. Now he was expected to love Him for it? For Neil, it was like having a kidnapper demand love as a ransom for his wife's return. Obedience he might have managed, but sincere, heartfelt love? That was a ransom he couldn't pay" (218-19). He joins a support group of those who witnessed the visitation but is bothered by the suggestion that he should "[accept] his role as one of God's subjects" (208). Unlike those who have discovered a "newfound devotion to God," Neil is unable to accept his loss and make peace with God (208).

Unable to find a way to love God, Neil finds a loophole when "Barry Larsen, a serial rapist and murderer who, while disposing of the body of his latest victim, witnessed an angel's visitation and saw Heaven's light. At Larsen's execution, his soul was seen ascending to Heaven, much to the outrage of his victims' families" (225-26). Neil decides to become a "light-seeker," one of those who go to sites where angels either arrive or depart the mortal plane. When the angel Barakiel appears, Neil attempts to follow him but ends up crashing his truck into a boulder. However, a shaft of Heaven's light passes over Neil, blinding him. At that moment, "the light revealed to Neil all the reasons he should love God" (232). As he now loves God "with an utterness beyond what humans can experience for one another," he confidently assumes that he will go to Heaven since "he [is] truly worthy of salvation" (232-33). Yet, "God [sends] him to Hell anyway" (233). In Hell, Neil's sight is restored and he has a perfectly formed body; nonetheless, he experiences "more anguish than was possible when he was alive, but his only response is to love God .... He knows his being sent to Hell was not a result of anything he did; he knows there was no reason for it, no higher purpose" (234). His love for God, the narrator tells us, "is the nature of true devotion" (235).

In "Hell Is the Absence of God," Chiang brilliantly critiques a fundamental tenet of those who espouse a religious belief: that God rewards those who love Him. Chiang forces the reader to grapple with a deeply philosophical question: why would a loving God impose suffering on the innocent? Chiang believes this "is one of the fundamental problems of religion," accepting and making peace with "all the terrible things that happen in the world" (Solomon). Faith Mendlesohn reads this story as "Chiang's consideration of an ontological world in which the miraculous is a daily event [that] directly challenges the comfortable assumptions of the religious Right that miracles are always good things" (274). While I do not agree that it is just the religious Right who believe miracles are always positive, I do agree that many who would define themselves as religious have such beliefs. In the world of the story, supernatural visitations can have both profoundly negative and profoundly positive effects on people.

However, we see characters on whom these visitations have no effect at all. Ethan Mead, a witness to the angel Rashiel's visitation, believes God has a purpose for him and longs for "an encounter with the divine to provide him direction" (214). However, Rashiel's visitation does not change Ethan either spiritually or physically. He witnesses Neil Fisk's death and descent to Hell, which leads Ethan to a recognition of God's ambivalence: "He tells people that they can no more expect justice in the afterlife than in the mortal plane" while encouraging them to worship God, just not "under a misapprehension" (234). Whether one worships God or not seems to have no effect on whether one ends up in heaven or hell. Therefore, the reader is forced to question the benefits of religious faith.

In many ways, "Hell Is the Absence of God" is a commentary on Pascal's Wager. In the world of the story, the inhabitants know God exists; therefore, there is no infinite gain or infinite loss in choosing to believe or not to believe. The infinite gain or infinite loss is situated in the love one has or does not have for God. If one loves God and goes to heaven, then one receives infinite gain. However, if one loves God and goes to hell, as does Neil Fisk, then one experiences infinite loss. There is no "best bet" in this world as one cannot trust God to reward the righteous.

Rudy Busto argues that "Chiang is asking us to take a religious belief and make it a real, statistically measurable thing-in-the-world, and by so doing, he forces us to think about ways religion can be so abstracted and 'unreal' in our lives" (398). Many of us feel comfortable pronouncing certain events as either a blessing or a scourge from God, yet few of us would feel comfortable definitively pronouncing a birth defect, for example, as one or the other. Chiang brings us into a world where the inhabitants do not have such options, a world where "God is not just, God is not kind, [and] God is not merciful" ("Hell" 234). This God is the God for those who do not see religion as a means of achieving any kind of spiritual improvement. Chiang lays bare the mystery and the incomprehensibility of God's purpose. We never know why God sends Neil Fisk to Hell and Barry Larsen to Heaven. "Hell Is the Absence of God" is an apocalyptic story that reveals a crisis of faith, the disillusionment of those who no longer (never?) believe in the promise of God to reward the faithful.

The disillusionment of faith affects those who do not see God as a way of improving their lives. If belief is, as Eric Schwitzgebel defines it, something we regard as true, what happens when one proves that something incorrect? To return to Pascal's Wager, what if one can prove that God does not exist? Moreover, what happens when the one to prove it is the one for whom religious belief fundamentally structures one's life? In "Division by Zero," math professor Renee and her husband, Carl metaphorically represent what happens when the devout seek and find unexpected answers to the questions surrounding religious belief.

Renee's understanding of herself and the universe centers on her certainty of the consistency of mathematics. For Renee, mathematics "is the sacred language of the high priests, the scientists and the technicians. As a sacred language, mathematics ... is all-inclusive, timeless, transcendent, and incapable of being misinterpreted .... To think and speak the sacred language of mathematics is to think and speak the truth" (Kreuziger 38). Math has always provided Renee with a "sense of rightness"; she discovers this "rightness," when she is a child and the epiphany grounds her understanding of the universe (74). However, Renee's research leads her to a theorem that proves mathematics is inconsistent and thus meaningless. She discovers "a formalism that lets you equate any number with any other number," thus proving that any two numbers are equal (80). Her discovery, which disproves "most of mathematics," engenders in her the same sense of rightness that has structured her world up to this point, but this sense of rightness leads to her realization that the language of mathematics is neither sacred nor true (81). Her encounter with apocalypse reveals that mathematics can no longer provide meaning or structure to her life and she attempts suicide.

Carl's understanding of himself and the universe centers on his certainty that "compassion [is] a basic part of his character" (87). Carl's suicide attempt 20 years earlier allows him to become a person who knows "the difference between sympathy and empathy" and he finds his identity in his ability to "offer comfort in similar situations" (87). Just as mathematics provides "rightness" to Renee's world, helping others, "[sitting] in the other seat, and [playing] the other part" provides rightness to Carl's world (87). Therefore, Carl is stunned to discover he has no empathy for Renee's predicament: "Whatever was bothering Renee, it was something he couldn't fathom" (79). In fact, he feels "no more than a sense of duty toward her" (74). Similar to a devout person when faith and religion no longer provide structure and meaning, both Renee and Carl lose their bearings when they discover that what they have always taken as the truth of themselves and their world can no longer be trusted.

Chiang's structure of "Division by Zero" adds further context to the effects of loss of faith. The story is laid out in eight numbered tripartite vignettes, with the exception of the last one, which only contains two sections ("9" and "9a=9b"). The first section is numbered one through nine and provides a mathematical concept; the other two sections are based on either Renee's perspective (the "a" section) or Carl's perspective (the "b" section). Each initial section details a discrepancy in mathematical logic and we can read each one as a metaphor for faith and belief.

For example, in Section 6, the narrator tells us that "In 1931, Kurt Godel demonstrated two theorems. The first one shows, in effect, that mathematics contain statements that may be true, but are inherently unprovable .... His second theorem shows that a claim of the consistency of arithmetic is just such a statement: it cannot be proven true by any means using the axioms of arithmetic" (79). In other words, mathematical truth and mathematical proof are not the same thing:

we can know certain things to be true while not having the ability to *prove* they are true. Such is one of the definitions of faith: belief without proof.

Chiang provides us with an intimate look at what happens when what we believe "[imposes] meaning onto the universe" is proven false and the proof comes, not from the outside, but from ourselves (86). As Renee tells Carl, the fact that she develops this theorem is analogous to a "theologian proving that there was no God. Not just fearing it, but knowing it for a fact" (88). For Renee, mathematics was something she "believed deeply, implicitly" and she is "the one who demonstrated" that it is not true (88). At the same time, Carl discovers his ability to empathize, his belief that imposes meaning onto his understanding of the universe, does not extend to Renee for whom "he couldn't feel anything" (85). He feels exactly as she does, that he, too, has discovered the falsity of something he "believed deeply, implicitly," which is why the last section of the story is titled "9a=9b." However, this empathy, this connection, Carl feels for Renee divides rather than unites. Both Renee and Carl lose their faith and both do so through their intellect and insight.

Ted Chiang's apocalyptic stories are commentaries on our own search for meaning. Many science fiction writers often consider "what religion may become under vastly altered circumstances" (Reilly 6). Chiang, however, creates places and characters where religion and faith are somewhat altered, while at the same time appearing familiar to the reader. As the stories unfold, we recognize our own disillusionment and loss. Like many of us, the characters in the "Tower of Babylon" are forced to ask themselves whether they put "ultimate trust in knowledge or faith" (Frisch and Martos 18). Hillalum's discovery and understanding of the world reveals to him that meaning is found in scientific exploration, not ritual or faith. Neal Fisk, on the other hand, lives in a world where proof of God is a given fact, yet he comes to know that God dispenses justice, kindness, and mercy arbitrarily. We, too, may question why God, like the God in "Hell Is the Absence of God," rewards the unrighteous and damns the righteous seemingly without rhyme or reason. In "Division by Zero," religion is, for Carl and Renee, "the audacious attempt to conceive of the entire universe as humanly significant"; yet, they find their universe not only insignificant but false (Berger 28). Chiang's story speaks to those whose belief structure has crumbled under intense scrutiny and whose search for meaning leads them not to a structured and orderly universe, but only leads them further into chaos.

As with all science fiction, Ted Chiang's stories reveal more of our present than our present reveals to us. We are not given definitive answers to God's role in our world; instead, his stories force us to question our own beliefs. Chiang's apocalyptic literature is born out of our own profound disillusionment that is centered "not on the world, but on the promise of God ... which has dimmed, flickered, and for some expired" (Krueziger 11). Yet, these stories do not leave us with, or lead us to, despair and nihilism. Ted Chiang's apocalypse reveals and reaffirms that meaning and therefore, life, come out of death—the death of falsely held beliefs.

WORKS CITED

Berger, Peter. *The Sacred Canopy*. Doubleday, 1967.

Bishop, John. "Faith." *The Stanford Encyclopedia of Philosophy*. Fall 2010. Web. 9 Feb. 2016 .

Busto, Rudy. "Religion/Science/Fiction: Beyond the Final Frontier." *Implicit Religion,* vol. 17, no. 4, 2014, pp. 395-404. Print.

Chiang, Ted. Division by Zero. *Stories of Your Life and Others.* Small Beer Press, 2002, pp. 71-89. Print.

———. "Hell Is the Absence of God." *Stories of Your Life and Others.* Small Beer Press, 2002, pp. 205-35. Print.

———. "Tower of Babylon." *Stories of Your Life and Others.* Small Beer Press, 2002, pp. 1-28. Print.

Frisch, Adam J., and Joseph Martos. "Religious Imagination and Imagined Religion." *The Transcendent Adventure: Studies of Religion in Science Fiction and Fantasy,* edited by Robert Reilly, Greenwood Press, 1985, pp. 11-26.

Gregory, Alan P. R. *Science Fiction Theology: Beauty and the Transformation of the Sublime.* Baylor UP, 2015. *ebrary.* Web. 8 Feb. 2016.

Krueziger, Frederick A. *The Religion of Science Fiction.* Bowling Green State University Popular Press, 1986. Print.

Mendlesohn, Farah. "Religion and Science Fiction." *The Cambridge Companion to Science Fiction,* edited by Edward James and Farah Mendlesohn, Cambridge UP, 2003, pp. 264-75. Print.

Popcak, Greg. "Faith, Spirituality, Belief, Religion ... What's the Difference?" *Patheos.* 5 May 2014. Web. 8 Feb. 2016.

Reilly, Robert. "Introduction." *The Transcendent Adventure: Studies of Religion in Science Fiction and Fantasy,* edited by Robert Reilly, Greenwood Press, 1985, pp. 3-8.

Robishaw, Andrew. *The Esoteric Codex: Dynamics of the Celestial Spheres.* Lulu Press, 2015. Web. 22 Feb. 2016.

Schwitzgebel, Eric. "Belief." *The Stanford Encyclopedia of Philosophy.* Summer 2015. Web. 10 Feb. 2016.

Smith, Jeremy. "The Absence of God: An Interview with Ted Chiang." *InfinityPlus.* September 2002. Web. 27 Jan. 2016.

Solomon, Avi. "Ted Chiang on Writing." *BoingBoing.* 22 Jul. 2010. Web. 18 Feb. 2016.

Patty Duke, Marlo Thomas, and Mary Tyler Moore—Three Stars, Three Iconic Shows, and a Young Generation of TV-Watching Females

by Kathy Merlock Jackson

ABSTRACT

Today when people look back at television in the 1960s and 1970s, they cringe at its portrayals of women and see that messages that seemed to be progressive at the time were merely smokescreens in a patriarchal world view. Nevertheless, changes in culture had to begin somewhere, and for an audience of post-World War II baby-boom females, television provided a lens for growing up. Prime-time network television programs targeted different segments of the population, but very little was available for baby-boom girls growing up and looking toward their futures. However, three popular prime-time television sitcoms, *The Patty Duke Show*, *That Girl*, and the *Mary Tyler Moore Show*, aired when few shows were built around the lives of young single women, demonstrated for their time agency, ambition, and professional aspirations of females. Although antiquated by today's standards, each of these shows--driven by an attractive woman with a flip hairstyle, lots of warmth, and endless determination--was groundbreaking. Collectively, they comprise a single narrative of female maturation from high school student, to job seeker, to young professional, showing steps a woman can take to navigate a male-dominated world, achieve independence, and establish an identity and career.

Keywords: The Patty Duke Show, That Girl, The Mary Tyler Moore Show, baby-boom females, television portrayals of women, prime-time sitcoms

41

Patty Duke, Marlo Thomas y Mary Tyler Moore—tres estrellas, tres programas icónicos y una generación joven de mujeres televidentes

RESUMEN

Hoy en día, cuando las personas recuerdan la televisión en los años sesenta y setenta, se estremecen ante sus representaciones de las mujeres y ven que los mensajes que parecían ser progresivos en ese momento eran simplemente cortinas de humo en una cosmovisión patriarcal. Sin embargo, los cambios en la cultura tenían que comenzar en algún lugar, y para una audiencia de mujeres nacidas en la posguerra de la Segunda Guerra Mundial, la televisión proporcionó una lente para crecer. Los programas de televisión de la hora de mayor audiencia se dirigían a diferentes segmentos de la población, pero había muy poca disponibilidad para las niñas que crecían y miraban hacia su futuro. Sin embargo, tres series populares de televisión en horario estelar, *The Patty Duke Show*, *That Girl* y *The Mary Tyler Moore Show*, se emitieron cuando había pocos programas alrededor de la vida de mujeres solteras jóvenes, demostradas por su agencia de tiempo, ambición y aspiraciones profesionales. Aunque anticuados para los estándares de hoy, cada uno de estos shows, impulsado por una mujer atractiva con un peinado tipo flip, mucha calidez y una determinación infinita, fue innovador. En conjunto, comprenden una sola narrativa acerca de la maduración femenina desde la secundaria, pasando por la solicitud de empleo, hasta la profesional joven, mostrando los pasos que una mujer puede tomar para navegar en un mundo dominado por los hombres, lograr la independencia y establecer una identidad y una carrera.

Palabras clave: *The Patty Duke Show, That Girl, The Mary Tyler Moore Show,* mujeres nacidas después de la posguerra, mujeres baby boomers, representaciones televisivas de las mujeres, comedias de la hora con más audiencia

帕蒂·杜克、马罗·托马斯、玛丽·泰勒·摩尔——三位明星、三部标志性节目、和观看电视剧的年轻女性

摘要

如今当人们回顾二十世纪六七十年代的电视剧时，会为当时对女性的刻画感到难为情，人们认为，在当时看起来似乎是进步性的信息却仅仅只是父权世界观下的烟幕形象而已。尽管如此，文化总会在某处发生改变，且对于在二战后婴儿潮出生的女性观众而言，电视陪伴了她们的成长。黄金时段的网络电视节目将不同人群作为目标观众，但很少有节目考虑到在婴儿潮时期出生的女性的成长和未来。然而就在这时，三部热门的黄金时段电视情景喜剧相继播出，即《帕蒂杜克秀》、《那个女孩》和《玛丽·泰勒·摩尔秀》。这三部情境喜剧展示了婴儿潮女性的时代性、志向和抱负。尽管从今天看来，这三部剧显得有些过时——每部剧的主演都是一位有魅力的女性，她们有着看似轻率的头发、以及充足的热情和决心——但在当时却极具突破性。整体看来，三部剧都讲述了女性从高中生到求职者、再到年轻专业人士的成熟过程，展示了女性能在由男性主导的世界里通过努力获得一席之地、实现独立、建立身份和事业。

关键词：《帕蒂杜克秀》，《那个女孩》，《玛丽·泰勒·摩尔秀》，婴儿潮女性，电视对女性的描绘，黄金时段情景喜剧

INTRODUCTION

Today when people look back at television in the 1960s and 1970s, they cringe at its portrayals of women. A popular advertising campaign for Virginia Slims cigarettes claimed, "You've Come a Long Way, Baby," but like that slogan, messages that seemed to be progressive at the time were merely smokescreens in a patriarchal world view. Nevertheless, changes in culture had to begin somewhere, and for an audience of post-World War II baby-boom females, television provided a lens for growing up. In America between 1946 and 1964, roughly seventy-six million babies were born, about half of them female, with the high-water mark for births occurring around the mid 1950s, which was also a key period for the expansion of the television audience. Prime-time network television programs targeted different segments of the population, but very little was available, in the early age of the Barbie doll, for baby-boom girls growing up and looking toward their futures. Beginning in 1959, Mattel Toys took to the air waves to advertise Barbie directly to girls on children's television. In the words of its creator, Ruth Handler, Barbie assured little girls that they would someday grow up, enabling them to imagine their future selves and truly dream their dreams (Stern).

So too did three popular prime-time television sitcoms, *The Patty Duke Show*, *That Girl*, and the *Mary Tyler Moore Show*, which aired in an era when few shows were built around the lives of young single women who, for their time, demonstrated agency, ambition, and professional aspirations. *The Patty Duke Show*, which ran on ABC from September 18, 1963, to April 27, 1966, became the first television show to be named after a teenage girl. In it, Duke played identical cousins Patty and Cathy Lane, high school students in Brooklyn

Heights, New York. The show centered on teen girls, showing that their lives, concerns, and hopes are important. Just five months after *The Patty Duke Show* ended, Marlo Thomas debuted on ABC in *That Girl, featuring television's first young, single independent female. She* played the role of struggling actress Ann Marie, who moves out of her parents' home in Brewster, New York, and tries to make it on her own in her early twenties in New York City. The show ran for nearly five years until it ended on March 19, 1971, just six months after another female-focused show, *The Mary Tyler Moore Show*, appeared on CBS, featuring thirty-year old Mary Richards leaving town after the break-up of a two-year relationship to begin a new life and career in Minneapolis The show followed Mary for seven years, wrapping up on March 19, 1977.

Although antiquated by today's standards, each of these shows—driven by an attractive woman with a flip hairstyle, lots of warmth, and endless determination—was groundbreaking for its time. Collectively, they comprise a single narrative of female maturation from high school student, to job seeker, to young professional, showing steps a woman can take to navigate a male-dominated world, achieve independence, and establish an identity and career. In so doing, these shows, which share patterns of goofy sidekicks and madcap capers, fill an important role not only in the evolution of prime-time television but also in the lives of young females, demonstrating that they have agency, abilities, and life choices aside from love and marriage. Considering the shows in this manner constitutes a new way of looking at television characters and their sequential influence on the mindset of a youth audience, dovetailing with what Melissa Ames and Sarah Burcon describe in *How Popular Culture Shapes the Stages of a Woman's Life* as studying the "impact that popular culture products marketed toward girls and women have on

their development through various ages and 'stages' of life"
(5).

Patty Duke, who at the age of sixteen won the 1962 Academy Award for Best Supporting Actress for her role as Helen
Keller in *The Miracle Worker*, plays a very different part in her
namesake series, *The Patty Duke Show*. Entertainment writer
Ramin Setoodah, who claims the show was her favorite when
she was growing up, calls Duke's character "a high-school version of Lucy Ricardo, except she didn't have Ethel. She had
something better: an identical cousin." As Setoodah reflects,
"*The Patty Duke Show* spoke to me as a kid because it was like
a serialized version of *The Parent Trap*. But ... I also realized it
was one of the first TV shows to feature a strong, single, opin-
ionated young woman. You could say that it paved the way
for *The Mary Tyler Moore Show, Rhoda, Murphy Brown, 30
Rock*, even *Hannah Montana*" (Setoodah). Although Patty
has an affable boyfriend Richard, she does not center her life
on pleasing him. Instead, she functions as a force in her high
school. In one episode, Patty, whose father is a New York
journalist, becomes editor-in-chief of her high school newspaper and has her own ideas about news; in another, Patty
plans celebrity musical events for her high school prom and
even sings with the band. However, Patty's aspirations take
her beyond Brooklyn Heights High as she explores many career options. Other endeavors include starting a babysitting
business (even though she has no babysitters), marketing
one of Cathy's popular handmade dresses to the masses, selling stocks for a company she calls Patty Lane, Inc., campaign-
ing for a family friend's bid for a Congressional seat, writing
a novel, and joining the Peace Corps. Cathy, Patty's quiet,
reserved, and serious cousin, succeeds in school, appreciates
the arts and travel, and provides a different role model for
tween and teen viewers. She is tapped for student of the year,

hosts a classical musical program, writes a fiery letter to the editor of her local newspaper, and works behind the scenes to solve problems when Patty's schemes go awry. Sometimes Patty's and Cathy's styles clash, such as when they unknowingly nominate one another for President of the Girls League or both want to be student of the year, leading to audiences identifying with Team Patty and Team Cathy and acknowledging their different approaches to leadership and conflict. It might be easy to pass off *The Patty Duke Show* as a silly 1960s sitcom in which most of Patty's and Cathy's escapades fizzle; however, for a young female audience watching and talking about this show, it cracked open the door for new roles and possibilities, aside from being someone's girlfriend. It showed that girls' lives mattered.

That Girl debuted the same year that *The Patty Duke Show* left the air, picking up where the earlier sitcom left off. In it, Ann Marie, played by Marlo Thomas, has all the energy of an older Patty Lane. A young woman in her early twenties from a small town in New York, she has just moved away from her parents' home to her own apartment in New York City in order to launch an acting career. Thomas, a political activist who advocated for feminist causes and the Equal Rights Amendment, served as a creator and producer of the show, paving the way for female creative power in *The Mary Tyler Moore Show, Laverne and Shirley, Kate and Allie,* and *Murphy Brown* (Newman 286). In her article on Marlo Thomas as a feminist icon, Emily L. Newman regards the show as "more than just the sweet little sitcom" and asserts that although there was increasing pressure for Ann and her boyfriend Donald not only to get engaged but married, Thomas resisted. "It was her producing role," Newcomb writes, "that allowed Thomas so much control over the program and helped provide a space for women in television to just appear or even star on a program" (286). This control contributed to the Ann Marie persona. Although Ann's father is over protective and her boyfriend Donald is a big part of her life, she forges ahead with her own ambitions, confronting the difficulties of doing so. Making it in acting is not easy, as evidenced by Ann's grueling auditions and roles she plays: gagged hostage, mop, dancing chicken, elf in a department store, villain in a soap opera, dancer in a gypsy revival, model wearing chinchilla, and caterer in a cave girl outfit, all of which made her appear totally ditzy. Still, Ann is committed to building her own self-identity and career, and the series ends not with Ann's marriage to Donald but instead with the duo attending a gathering of feminists (Mitchard).

In 1970, just before *That Girl* ended, *The Mary Tyler Moore Show* appeared, with Mary Richards seeming much like an older and more sophisticated Ann Marie. Like *That Girl*, *The Mary Tyler Moore Show* featured women behind the scenes, including Moore as producer, Treva Silverman and Pat Nardo as writers, and Ethel Winant as talent and casting director. They created what Hope Reese regards as "the first time in television history when a woman's perspective was not only highly regarded, but crucial to the success of the show" or, in essence, "TV's first truly female-dominated sitcom" (Reese). The series begins with Mary Richards leaving her boyfriend, whom she has been putting through medical school, to move alone across country to Minneapolis, where she and old friend Phyllis and new friend Rhoda become confidantes. She rents her own apartment in the same building as the two, interviews for a secretarial position at a local broadcasting station, and lands a job as an associate producer of a television news show after her new boss, Lou Grant, asserts, "You have spunk. I hate spunk." Mary is unsure of herself but proud of her position, mustering up enough courage to ask her boss Lou Grant why she is making less than the man she replaced even though she is doing a better job. She grows into her role, developing news sense and good judgment, solving problems, becoming a valued member of the team, and representing the aspirations and lifestyle of the modern woman. Jacquelyn Michard regards the *Mary Tyler Moore Show* as the "cultural-watershed sitcom that brought us the unsinkable Mary Richards, a single career woman over 30 who didn't need a man to support her." "Demure but sexy," Michard adds, "Mary was one of TV's first women to let a boyfriend sleep over" (Mitchard). Ending in 1977, the series lasted seven seasons, during which time Mary is put in charge of the newsroom while Lou is away, gets arrested for refusing to name a source, is promoted to producer, plans and writes many news shows, and ultimately, along with others in the newsroom, is laid off at the age of thirty-seven when someone new buys the station. The show, which grappled with more serious issues such as prejudice, sexual mores, gender inequities, and news ethics, struck a balance between Mary's work life and personal life, providing a favorable portrait of the modern professional woman.

Beginning in their tweens and teens, baby-boom girls gravitated to *The Patty Duke Show, That Girl, and The Mary Tyler Moore Show* over a span of fourteen years, and decades later, still recall their catchy theme songs and the window on the world that they provided. Audiences seek from television what they need, and young females discovered a trifecta of sequential sitcoms that pushed, ever so slightly, the gender boundaries of the 1960s and 1970s and described what would become for many of them their own trajectories. In their personalities, Patty Lane, Ann Marie, and Mary Richards were bubbly, relatable, girl-next-door types rather than aggressive trailblazers, and their comedy sometimes depended on acting silly or differential. Nevertheless, the situations in which they placed themselves, outside of the traditional domestic sphere of earlier television shows, offered new possibilities, especially in the realm of communication and media, for a young audience caught up in a changing world, and over time, Patty, Ann, and Mary matured, developing new independence and strength. As Hope Reese asserts, "America was in the middle of the women's rights movement; *The Feminine Mystique*, released in 1963, urged women to envision work outside the home, touching a nerve for housewives. The Pill became available to all women, regardless of marital status, in 1972. And more and more women were earning degrees and setting off to find jobs" (Reese). Patty Lane may have made some missteps as a newspaper editor, Ann Marie may have had to play a gagged hostage, and Mary Richards may have heard her own voice quaver when she demanded a raise (Armstrong 183), but these characters nevertheless planted the suggestion that it was desirable for a female to strike out on her own, set goals, pursue interesting work as perhaps an editor, actress, or associate producer, and not worry about getting married and starting a family.

The shows also created an aspirational lifestyle. What Jennifer Keishin Armstrong writes about *The Mary Tyler Moore Show* could really be applied to each of these shows: as its "audience grew, advertisers and thus TV networks, were scrambling to cater to the new consumer group known as 'Life Stylers': women who embraced liberation in their everyday lives without necessarily identifying as feminists. These women *were* Mary Richards. And they needed fabulous clothes, beauty products, and furniture to feel like the independent women they wanted to be. The rise of the young empowered woman on television had at least as much to do with marketing as with feminist ideals. Products such as

Charlie perfume, Breck shampoo, and Aqua Net hair spray now had the perfect place to advertise their wares" (Armstrong 132). Young females identified with Patty, Ann, and Marlo, and although it would still be many years before the majority of American women moved beyond familiar gender stereotypes, these three characters provided a starting point for young females to think, act, and look differently and to navigate their lives and careers on their own terms. Although never the intent of their producers, *The Patty Duke Show*, *That Girl*, and *The Mary Tyler Moore Show* arguably present the same character growing up for the same demographic; they offer a seamless portrait of a post-World War II baby boom female in America maturing from age sixteen to age thirty-seven against a backdrop of social change. Looking at other popular sequential shows in this way may reveal key developmental and aspirational messages that young audiences, seeking and finally finding meaningful role models in television, may have responded to and ultimately absorbed.

WORKS CITED

Ames, Melissa and Sarah Burcon. *How Pop Culture Shapes the Stages of a Woman's Life: From Toddlers-In-Tiara to Cougars-On-The-Prowl*. Palgrave, 2016.

Armstrong, Jennifer Keishin. *Mary and Lou and Rhoda and Ted: And All the Brilliant Minds Who Made* The Mary Tyler Moore Show *a Classic*. Simon and Schuster, 2013.

Mitchard, Jacquelyn. "Twelve Amazing Women Who Changed TV Forever." *AARP*, 2014. https://www.aarp.org/entertainment/television/info-2014/women-tv-boomer-stars.html#slide3.

Newman, Emily L. "From *That Girl* to *Girls*: Rethinking Ann Marie/Marlo Thomas as a Feminist Icon." *The Journal of American Culture* 93:3 (September 2016): 285-297.

Reese, Hope. "The Real Feminist Impact of The Mary Tyler Moore Show Was Behind the Scenes." *The Atlantic*, 16 May 2013. https://www.theatlantic.com/sexes/archive/2013/05/the-real-feminist-impact-of-i-the-mary-tyler-moore-show-i-was-behind-the-scenes/275875.

Setoodah, Ramin. "Q+A: Patty Duke Remembers '*The Patty Duke Show*." *Newsweek*, 29 September 2009. http://www.newsweek.com/qa-patty-duke-remembers-patty-duke-show-220752.

Stern, Susan. *Barbie Nation: An Unauthorized Tour*. El Rio Productions. 2007.

Respectez-nous as We Feminize the Rapped Rhyme: Women Rappers and Gender Empowerment in French Hip-Hop

by Scooter Pégram

ABSTRACT

French women have long been in a subordinate position as compared to men, and females are underrepresented in nearly every sector in France (*including in pop culture*). Moreover, this sort of gender discrimination is even worse for women of color in France, as they are nearly invisible aside from the menial service jobs that they usually occupy. Owing to their lack of a voice in France, one of the only outlets available for women of color to express their frustration, communicate with one another, or uplift themselves is the medium of hip-hop music. This paper introduces readers to the subject of female-led resistance to gender inequality in France via the contemporary medium of French-language hip-hop. This paper analyses lyrical educational empowerment by women in French "rap" by discussing a few examples of this ever-evolving thematic concept of positive resistance via the rhyme as we briefly deconstruct a few popular songs released by the four major female rap artists in France over the past 20 years.

Keywords: French women, Female rappers, Female empowerment, Women of color in France, Hip-hop education, Racism in France, Music as protest, French hip-hop, Lyrical resistance, Rap as protest

«Respectez-nous» mientras feminizamos la rima del rap: mujeres raperas y el empoderamiento en el hip-hop francés

RESUMEN

Las mujeres francesas han estado durante mucho tiempo en una posición subordinada en comparación con los hombres, y las mujeres están subrepresentadas en casi todos los sectores de Francia (incluso en la cultura pop). Además, este tipo de discriminación de género es aún peor para las mujeres de color en Francia, ya que son casi invisibles, aparte de los trabajos de servicio que suelen ocupar. Debido a su falta de voz en Francia, uno de los pocos medios disponibles para que las mujeres de color expresen su frustración, se comuniquen entre sí o se animen a sí mismas es el medio de la música hip-hop. Este artículo presenta a los lectores el tema de la resistencia liderada por mujeres contra la desigualdad de género en Francia a través del medio contemporáneo del hip-hop en francés. Este artículo analiza el poder educativo lírico de las mujeres en el "rap" francés al discutir algunos ejemplos de este concepto temático -que está en constante evolución- de resistencia positiva a través de la rima mientras deconstruimos brevemente algunas canciones populares lanzadas por las cuatro artistas de rap más importantes de Francia en los últimos 20 años.

Palabras clave: mujeres francesas, raperas, empoderamiento femenino, mujeres de color en Francia, educación a través del Hip-Hop, racismo en Francia, música en forma de protesta, resistencia lírica, el rap como forma de protesta

请对说唱押韵的女性化予以尊重：法国嘻哈音乐之女说唱和性别赋权

摘要

法国女性与男性相比长期处于次要地位，同时女性在法国几乎各个部门都无法完全展现其能力（包括流行文化）。此外，这类性别歧视对有色女性而言更为严重，因为她们几乎从事的都是报酬低的服务工作，在其他行业很少看到她们的身影。由于缺少话语权，法国有色女性用于表达沮丧、相互交流和鼓舞自己的有限方式之一则是通过嘻哈音乐这一媒介。本文以当代法语嘻哈媒介为例，为读者介绍了由女性领导的抵抗性别不平等主题。本文通过探讨一些关于这类用歌词进行抵抗"性别不平等"（一个不断发展的主题）的例子，分析了法国说唱女性赋权的抒情性和教育性，同时笔者简要解构了过去20多年间4位法国主要女说唱艺术家发行的部分流行歌曲。

关键词：法国女性，女说唱，女性赋权，法国有色女性，嘻哈教育，法国种族主义，音乐抗议，法国嘻哈，抒情抵抗，说唱抵抗

· · · · · · · · ·

This is for the ladies, pour les ladies.
Pour les ladies je demande du respect, quoi qu'on en dise.

This is for the ladies, for the ladies.
For the ladies I demand respect, whatever they say about it.[1]

—Lady Laistee, *"For the Ladies"*

55

INTRODUCTION

The most recognizable national icon of France is that of *Marianne*. No matter where one goes in the country, it is hard to miss see the image of Marianne because she is represented on postage stamps, money, and she appears on all official government documents. Additionally, Marianne has long been featured as the subject of statues, illustrated on paintings, and shown in every imaginable way. No matter how the iconic image is described, she is always depicted as a defiant and strong woman who symbolizes the strength and revolutionary resilience of the *République française*. However, despite the enduring presence of the radical allegoric female figure that Marianne represents, French women have been in a subordinate position as compared to men for centuries, and they remain underrepresented in nearly every sector of the country. A recent report published by the World Economic Forum places France in the 57th position internationally in terms of gender equality, which ranks it in second to last place in Western Europe. When the data are further broken down by specific category, the findings are even worse. In terms of women's economic opportunity, France ranks 64th internationally. In terms of equality for legislators/senior management positions, the country ranks 61st globally. Even worse, if one were to look at statistics in regard to wage equality for similar work, the country finds itself in the 134th position. Although the French government routinely adopts legislation to equalize the playing field in terms of gender equity and issues, numerical findings like these illustrate a different reality for women in the country.

Despite the fact that females remain in a subordinate position in France when compared to men, they find ways to challenge sexism that extend beyond the more traditional way of protesting in the streets. Over the past century and far beyond, women in France have expressed their frustrations by using the very French tradition of resisting authority and educating the masses via the written word. In other words, the old adage that suggests a "pen" being something that is "mightier than a sword" carries merit. Female authors, such as Simone de Beauvoir, Colette, and George Sand, used literature and the written word in order to discuss various discriminatory morals and codes facing women, and this type of educational and pedagogical approach has continued as subsequent generations of feminist writers take up the cause. Although once limited to women of an elevated social status, in recent decades Francophone women authors of color (e.g., Maryse Condé, Assia Djebar) have also employed this literary resistance strategy within their narratives as they highlighted various issues relating to gender while focusing on subjects pertinent to their unique cultural experience.

Adolescents and young women from visible minority groups are also increasingly turning to this old French style of protest, but with a small twist: Instead of writing, they are rapping their rhymes in hip-hop songs. Thus, the more contemporary medium of rap music is used as a pedagogical tool to educate and inform, and young women of color are the motivators of this movement because they do not feel that their needs are being discussed by women's rights groups or politicians in France. In other words, as traditional feminist organizations in France continue to fail when it comes to addressing issues affecting young females from visible minority groups, the use of rap as a weapon of pride and defiance becomes more important. In other words, this new form of rapped *résistance* is occurring due to a non-response from Women's Rights groups in France to concentrate on issues that pertain to the unique needs of young females of color. Duchen (11) discusses his when she states that French feminist organizations "have the reputation of paying more attention to theory than to practical questions." Owing to this narrow approach furthered by more established feminist organizations, those issues relating to females living in disadvantaged communities are nearly non-existent in the national discourse. Moreover, young women of color are also made invisible by the official policy of State secularism that does not acknowledge gender as a defining national statistic in France. Because these two paradigms marginalize females from visible minority groups, hip-hop is an effective manner in which to bring their issues to the masses.

Although hip-hop culture in France and elsewhere has been dominated by males since its embryonic stage, French women of color have left their own distinct marks on the genre. In terms of content, female rappers tend to focus their attention more on education, immigration, social issues, gender inequality, and quality of life themes in their songs. Moreover, women artists usually give little to no lyrical emphasis on street violence and the type of male posturing/positioning that one often associates with hip-hop music (Rose, "The Hip-Hop Wars"). However, despite this softer thematic approach than the images promoted amongst male rappers, the record industry in France has not always been kind to females. For example, as is often the case in mainstream American hip-hop, rap lyrics in general often portray women ambiguously, usually in oppressive, sexist, or negative ways.

This often-misogynistic portrait motivates the representations put forth by female artists and separates their thematic approaches from males as they shape the genre of hip-hop to fit their unique needs in hip-hop music in the United States and in France. Thus, the goal of many women rappers is to inform listeners about humanistic themes that affect females, and to discuss how social discrepancies in regard to gender affect society at large. This very subject of *résistance* is worthy of our attention and analysis. Thus, after a brief overview of the origins of hip-hop in the United States and France, as well as a discussion on issues as they relate to females of color in the latter country, we introduce and examine a few songs that have a mission to educate listeners on topics concerning women of color by the four most popular female French rap artists over the past two decades. In doing so, we illustrate how this quartet of *rappeuses lyriques* also acts as hip-hop philosophers who use the public platform of the microphone as a pedagogical tool in which to discuss divisive subjects that minimize or ignore the role of ethnocultural women in France.

RACE, SPACE, AND HIP-HOP PHILOSOPHY

Researchers such as Prévos, Forman, Chang , and Rose (*The Hip-Hop Wars*) have long argued that the base rubric of hip-hop music is formed by the rapper's spatial and social construct. Famous rapper-activist Chuck D of the group Public Enemy once echoed that sentiment when he labeled rap lyrics as being *"Black America's CNN."* This was the case because early American hip-hop educated listeners about the numerous social, racial, and economic realities and discrepancies that were occurring in minority neighborhoods in the 1970s, 1980s, and early 1990s. Forman (78) builds upon this sentiment when he argues that a rapper's location, or "place" serves as a "lens of sorts that mediates one's perspective on social relations," and that it "offers familiarity" that provides artists with a certain "perspective" in which to evaluate their spatiality. This concept of speaking truth to power as a way to educate people is constant throughout early American hip-hop culture, as the movement was founded on the fours principles of using rap music as a non-traditional pedagogical tool (i.e., *"peace, love, unity, and having fun"*). Early rappers in New York composed lyrics in ways that would bring to life issues that others in more elevated societal positions were afraid to discuss (Chang; Rose, "Black Noise," "The Hip-Hop Wars"). Thus, the MC who spoke into the microphone had to "drop science" (i.e., teach) the audience how to consume the given message. In this way, hip-hop has much in common with the African narrative tradition of the village *griot*, a person whose job as the village librarian of sorts was/is to educate citizens about their history and culture. Early hip-hop artists in the United States have continued this legacy of *"griot education"* in regard to their lyrics.

The origins of the entire hip-hop movement can be traced to rhythms popular in Jamaica during the 1960s and 1970s. During those decades, the Jamaican musical style known as dancehall served as the primary motivator for the birth of hip-hop in the United States. Dancehall was created by youths from "the Yard" (socioeconomically marginalized areas) of cities like Kingston. Dancehall arrived to New York City via immigration, and it was there that younger Jamaicans, street gangs, melded with other individuals with direct immigrant origins in the Bronx and produced a sound mixed with African-American soul and R&B that would soon be called "rap." Popular street DJs such as Kool Herc, Africa Bambaata, and Grandmaster Flash pioneered this new musical genre in 1970s New York City, and from this nascent stage of street parties, a larger hip-hop movement that consisted of four elements was born. In its embryonic period in the United States, hip-hop culture and the vocal art of rapping were viewed as effective ways in which to discuss topics facing people of color living in what was referred to as the "inner city" (Hebdige; Rose, "The Hip-Hop Wars"). For example, in 1982 a song by Grandmaster Flash's entitled *"The Message"* was one of the first tracks to teach listeners about a myriad of negative social issues emanating from the 'hood. Perhaps, the most well-known artist to juxtapose hip-hop with pedagogy was (and remains) the artist known as KRS-One, a rapper whose very name is broken down as *"Knowledge reigns supreme over nearly everything."* Each of his albums is rooted in subjects involving social justice, and many of his tracks deconstructed controversial subjects such as misogyny, gang violence, drug use, educational deficiencies, and so forth. KRS-One is not the only artist to be labeled as a *"Hip-Hop Philosopher,"* but he is one of the originators of the concept and his popularity remains intact.

Although song lyrics that address similar themes are not limited to hip-hop and have been present in all musical genres for decades (e.g., the protest music of the 1950s, punk rockers in the 1970s-forward, "World" artists from developing countries), rappers were the loudest in terms of effectively defining and mass marketing themselves as "teachers" and "philosophers" with educational messages. However, this sort of pedagogical approach in rap music did not last beyond the early 1990s. The same record companies that once promoted a more positive and socially based thesis in hip-hop lyrics changed course and started favoring and embracing a more aggressive-style in the mid-1990s that came to be known as *"Gangsta Rap."* Instead of discussing social issues faced by African-Americans and others in marginalized communities, the focus shifted in terms of reacting to one's subordinate status by lyrically promoting violence and deviant behavior. Gangsta Rap became a financial success for hip-hop record labels, and a more conscious style music is yet to return to the broad commercially supported acclaim that rap music enjoyed in its early years. Although a socially based hip-hop lives on, it exists without much major support from the record industry.

The use of rap music as pedagogy is also gaining traction among American educators, as it is increasingly seen as being an effective teaching method in classrooms. Tobias argues that because hip-hop music represents a social and cultural practice, the genre critically expresses and socially considers a variety of important subjects that are necessary curricular topics in schools, especially where students of color form the majority of students. Lesson plans that use examples from hip-hop songs that feature themes such as one's representation, agency, place, space, and identity are all valuable ways to understand and teach issues that otherwise may not be discussed in official school curricula. Further elaborating on this subject, Tobias (22) maintains that the use of hip-hop in education enacts and increases critical pedagogy in classrooms, as it provides opportunities for "students to consider themselves and their community in terms of who they are and collectively." Despite this, American hip-hop remains an industry that promotes misogyny and sexual exclusion as profit and the French model differs little from this trope.

RACISM, MARGINS, AND MISOGYNY

In terms of academic investigations on subjects relating to racism and misogyny in France, research on those topics is not easily accessible. Officially, the country is secular and "colorblind." This means, even a minor census or academic study, that might examine an issue as it affects one's race or gender will not be sanctioned by federal Ministries or statisticians, and they are generally discouraged or non-existent (Bleich; Fleming). Fleming argues that the French government has abdicated its responsibility for dealing with racism in terms of official policy. Additionally, Fleming further states that "French 'anti-racism' has not succeeded in changing racist attitudes towards France's ethnocultural communities. For example, instead of formulating anti-racist policies and collecting anti-discrimination statistics, the country "contents itself with anti-racist discourse and magical thinking."[2] In short: From a federal government point of view, it is better for France not to revisit colonialism and other divisive subjects in favor of national unity, as a way in which to protect and preserve a cleaner collective memory. Kokoreff argues that issues facing populations of color are rarely discussed at all anywhere in France, unless one concentrates on deviance and other sociological ills that take places in areas where minority populations reside in large numbers (such as in the Paris suburbs). As for women from ethnocultural or visible minority communities, Fleming states that their stories are rarely heard at all. That said, French youths of color have found a unique niche in terms of talking about their "space" and any issues relevant to them: Via Hip-hop music, songs, and rap lyrics.

Even though global hip-hop culture is assumed to be the domain of young men, women have also played a major role in rap, and gender motivates the topics and subjects that are discussed in their songs. Berry and Rose (*Black Noise, The Hip-Hop Wars*) posit that males in hip-hop usually rhyme about social dichotomies such as racism and other issues that focus solely on the masculine urban experience (e.g., police harassment, crime, street violence). This means that the thematic material in their songs is spatially limited, because men rap by using language associated with power and dominance. However, female rappers also breach social issues in their lyrics, but their narrative tends to focus less on the above-mentioned themes and more on equality and social issues. Strausz and Dole argue that the subjects that are heard in songs released by women seek to produce a broader dialogue concerning different ideologies, topics, and communities that are not spatially limited to urban areas. These include topics like domestic abuse, gender bias, sexual discrimination, and misogyny. Rose (*Black Noise*: 147) supports these points by arguing that one tactic employed by female rappers of color is their desire to work "within and against the existing dominant sexual and racial narratives" in order to conceptualize and educate listeners on issues that are important to them. Furthermore, Rose ("Black Noise," "The Hip-Hop Wars") also posits that women rappers use their pulpit to speak to the importance of the female voice and sexual freedom. In other words, women in hip-hop educate their listeners on themes such as autonomy, the importance of gender unity, and the resistance to all types of violence and dominance affecting females across racial lines. Perhaps for some, rap music is not something that would consider as being inherently feminist. That said, female artists employ specific and simple generic qualities of the genre to promote themselves and their unique lyrical message. Because hip-hop music represents extreme self-promotion, women rappers are able to use this public platform to their advantage in order to express female power without being accused by critics as being self-centered feminist radicals who are anti-establishment, thereby dismissed by mainstream pop-culture outlets and being spatially limited to the academy.

Although women have influenced the rap genre stylistically and technically, their overall contributions are often downplayed or ignored in favor of men (Layli, et al.). Since hip-hop music is usually framed as being a representation of life as experienced by "urban" males of color, it has not always been easy for young females to create spaces outside of the pre-conceived sexual and misogynistic tropes and stereotypes found in many rap lyrics and videos (Weekes). More-over, the appearance of women in the hip-hop industry is often one of an outsider or a bystander rather than as what Guevara (51) labels as a "participant," since females and their contributions to the genre are largely unrecognized or downplayed. Guevara (51) further states that whenever women take leading roles in commercialized visual presen-tations of hip-hop culture (especially in film), they enter the scene as "exotic outsiders" who make their mark via some sort of romantic involvement with a male protagonist. In this sense, hip-hop remains a male-dominated industry or privi-lege. Industry executives and even some consumers may re-fer to rap as being the *music of the streets*, a place where female artists are seen as interlopers (Rose, "The Hip-Hop Wars"). Adams and Fuller argue that in a world where negative social constructs such as sexism, misogyny, and hatred are institu-tionalized, observations of this sort of patriarchal ideology and attitude in hip-hop culture as promoted by the commod-ification of the genre by the record industry are extensions of outer negative societal parameters that go beyond music.

In light of these realities, to gain acceptance and credibility in hip-hop culture, women often borrow or adopt mascu-line attitudes and personalities when they rap, dance, or tag graffiti. Faure and Garcia state that this type of appropriation of male behavior is intended to mask signs of femininity, and it is often manifested by language, fashion, or personal-ity changes that mirror those as seen amongst male artists. Therefore, female rappers take style cues from men in the industry and visually or lyrically appear as "tough" or "hard" in their appearance and delivery, even when many women artists outpace males in overall sales and popularity. More-over, stylistic changes assumed by female rap performers are not just limited to one's look, behavior, or sound. Troka (87) argues that the experiences of women of color in hip-hip are made invisible since they are neither male, nor a member of the dominant culture, which are traits that she labels as being the two "prized markers of neutrality" in the United States. Misogynistic lyrics, songs, and video presentations further demonstrate the dominance of males in rap by ignoring, dismissing, subjugating women, or outright discriminating against them. According to Guevara (56), female rappers are restricted when they perform, and hip-hop music is oppressive and discriminatory because women artists are "expected to act differently" than males when they appear in front of a crowd. For example, it is acceptable for men in rap to be sexually suggestive and even misogynistic on stage or in visual presentations. At the same time, with a few exceptions, female rappers refrain from doing anything similar when they present themselves to the public. That said, this is starting to change. For example, contemporary artists such as Cardi B, Lil Kim, and Nicki Minaj seem to present more of a "female in control" narrative in lyrics. However, the sort of feminist presentation promoted by these same rappers is often given from the perspective of the male gaze (again, pushed by record companies), as suggested by the sexist imagery in their video-clips. Because industry insiders and executives are cognizant that young males are the major consumers of hip-hop in the United States, Hollywood's concept in regard to the involvement of women in rap focuses more on *fantasy* (i.e., focusing on the appearance of female artists) than *reality* (i.e., the creative talent/art of females). Although rap music is promoted as mere entertainment, representations of women within hip-hop culture does little aside from perpetuating existing gender and sexual objectifications and stereotypes, all of which endorse a society where females are the subordinate objects of men (Quinne).[3]

Similar to hip-hop cultural presentations in the United States, rap music has been no less limiting and misogynistic towards women. What is known in France as *le rap français* is also traditionally dominated by men and geared towards male consumers and females are by and large marginalized by record companies. Strausz and Dole (12) argue that women who are present in French rap have been more "tolerated than accepted," and in order to gain respect, female artists have been forced to struggle against hardened patriarchal attitudes that have been pervasive in the industry. However, when given support, a handful of women rappers have been major money makers in the genre, whilst earning massive fame and esteem amongst hip-hop's consumers. This sort of popularity suggests that the opinions of the purchasing public in France do not reflect the assumed male-dominated aesthetic of the larger market as seen, forwarded, funded, and promoted by record labels.

EARNING RESPECT VIA RESISTANCE

Despite the many limitations that they face, women in French hip-hop have a long history with the music, dating to the very beginning. Even though there is a lack of equilibrium in rap music in France in terms of gender, the first ever hip-hop song to be issued on vinyl in was the song *"Une sale histoire"* by the female artist Beside, which appeared on the B-side of New York rapper Fab Five Freddy's 1982 hit, *"Change the Beat."* However, following this initial groundbreaking contribution to rap music in France, women largely disappeared from the scene and remained non-visible players until the late 1980s. The first female hip-hop artist to receive album recognition after Beside was Saliha, a *rappeuse* (a female rapper) who entered rhyming competitions across France. Throughout the late 1980s, Saliha recorded singles that appeared on the numerous best-selling *"Rapattitude"* compilations, which featured the major artists of the day. Saliha later followed up this sort of exposure with a complete album of her own in 1994. However, following her tepid success, no other woman would attract much interest from record companies or producers in terms of a large commercial perspective. Other artists (such as Princess Aniès) occasionally appeared and released albums that featured feminist-empowered lyrics, some of which at times enjoying moderate airplay. That said, a sustainable female presence in the hip-hop game was lacking throughout the 1990s. Regardless of these sorts of challenges, over time things would change as a newer and younger group of women rappers emerged to challenge male dominance in rap music. This fresh group of female artists would eventually start to reverse the misogynistic imagery as presented in hip-hop culture up until that point.

One of things that help expedite the serious arrival and visibility of female rappers in France in the late 1990s was the sudden rise of women in American hip-hop. Artists such as Lauryn Hill and Missy Elliot were breaking sales records and winning multiple Grammy awards as they changed the sound and redirected the landscape of rap music in the United States. The emergence of American female rappers was hardly a new concept, as earlier popular artists paved the way in the late 1980s. Female rappers such as Queen Latifah helped to diversity the genre with empowering songs such as *"Ladies First,"* a track whose lyrics and Afrocentric feminist narrative celebrated the contributions of women in hip-hop and in society, as this example shows (from Berry: 193):

> Who said the ladies couldn't make it, you must be blind
>
> If you don't believe, well here, listen to this rhyme

> Ladies first, there's no time to rehearse
>
> I'm divine and my mind expands through-
> out the universe
>
> A female rapper with the message to send
>
> The Queen Latifah is a perfect specimen.

Stimulated by this new wave of women artists gaining prominence and respect in American hip-hop, things started to evolve in France as well. In the late 1990s, a rapper from the French-Caribbean island of Guadeloupe named Lady Laistee (née: Aline Farran) emerged onto the scene. Her last name "*Laistee*" means "*style*" when the word is reversed and restated in Verlan, which is a linguistic code that is spoken by urban youths in France. After working alongside one of the pioneer groups of French hip-hop (NTM) and issuing a few songs on compilation albums (notably "*Respecte mon attitude*," which appeared on the release entitled "*Cool Sessions 2*"), Lady Laistee enjoyed popular success not previously seen for a female performer. Following this small bit of initial visibility via her contributions on those male-dominated compilations, Lady Laistee put forth a few successful albums of her own, two of which deserve denoting. For example, the first of these releases, entitled "*Black Mama*," became a top selling record in France, a first for a woman rapper. The most popular track of this groundbreaking album was the song "*For the ladies*." As its title suggests, the song's lyrics challenged everyone in France who dismissed females as second-class citizens, as shown here:

> Lower your arms, my status as a woman
> makes me excluded
>
> The closed universe, past up, let's share the
> monopoly (...)

> No machismo. Step off, keep your weak-
> ness, brother,
>
> Get back and between us all, I represent all
> proud sisters.[4]

The above excerpt echoes familiar themes as manifested in many songs by Lady Laistee, such as a demand for equal rights and female empowerment. This technique was previously used by artists in the United States. Weekes (147) maintains that American rappers such as Queen Latifah and later Missy Elliot were re-appropriating hip-hop music and producing their own responses to the "masculinized containing of femininity" by using hip-hop to educate the masses and create a place where women could portray themselves on their own terms. It is from these established American female artists that their French *cousines* (female cousins) would draw their inspiration. The song "*For the ladies*" as well as several others from Lady Laistee's album *Black Mama* received massive airplay in France, making her the first French female artist to rise up and challenge male dominance on a large commercialized scale; whether in the industry or French society in general. In addition to rapping about the subject of sexism from the point of view of a woman of color, Lady Laistee also followed the usual thematic trends as established by male hip-hop artists in France. For example, subjects such as racism, acculturation, exclusion, and marginalization form the traditional rubric of *le rap français* and Lady Laistee also discussed these topics in several of her songs. The following excerpt from the song "*Black Mama*" (a track that addresses the disparities and exclusion facing French-Caribbean migrants in France) demonstrates this point:

> Born in the tropics, my domain is the
> DOM-TOM

Until I was taken far from my home sweet
home

I took an eight-hour flight to become
metropolitan

Métro, police hatred, suburbs, hardly had it
better (...)

We used to play with those who insulted
us, I stood up for myself

It was from all of that where I became con-
scientious of the color that I am.[5]

The discussion of one's ethnocultural identity and marginalized social position is a frequent topic found in French hip-
hop. The above lyrical example shows that Lady Laistee also
used rap music in order to protest against majority society
or send out a social message, albeit from a women's perspective. Further lyrics throughout the song *"Black Mama"*
address the realities of downward mobility and exclusion as
faced by immigrant women in France in particular, including
those residents coming from the overseas *départements* and
territoires (known as the DOM-TOM). Despite their lack
of traditional immigrant status (they are French citizens in
full), people from the Caribbean and Indian Ocean colonies
are frequently marginalized in mainland France. Similar to
immigrants from French-speaking regions of Africa, Caribbean residents also tend to live in the socially disadvantaged
suburbs of Paris and other cities where they are faced with
racism, low educational attainment vis-à-vis the majority
culture, as well as constant suspicion by the police. Unemployment figures amongst youths of color aged 15–25 years
old in many Paris suburbs are estimated to range upwards to
85 percent, with women being the most underrepresented in
terms of jobs and upward mobility (Kokoreff; Mallière).

Unlike the few female artists who came before her, Lady Laistee was able to sustain her fame for a few years. Her follow-up album to *Black Mama* was entitled "*Hip-hop Therapy*" and this new release featured several songs promoting the empowerment of women, as well as discussing the lack of rights concerning females of color in general. The two most popular tracks of this new album were the songs "*Diamant noir*" ("Black Diamond," a track where she reflects on the nostalgia of growing up in as a woman of color in the downtrodden Paris suburbs) and "*Un peu de respect*" ("A little bit of respect"). Both songs received considerable airplay in French radio. The track "*Un peu de respect*" was intentionally modeled after the famous 1960s feminist anthem "Respect" by Aretha Franklin, even going as far as to sample its background music and beat. This enabled Lady Laistee's single to be immediately recognizable to listeners. Moreover, lyrics from "*Un peu de respect*" follow the exact same trajectory as the earlier empowering song by Aretha Franklin. In other words, respect for females is both demanded and expected in a society where women should be treated as equals. Throughout the entirety of the track, female listeners are instructed to stand up, speak loudly, and believe in one another, as shown here:

> We're asking for a little respect
>
> Come on, we're going to teach you how to stand tall
>
> In our world, don't expect us to wait any longer to be heard
>
> Because we believe in ourselves (...)
>
> The stone age is over, we're precious gemstones,
>
> That will break things apart, we hit hard (...)

Let us sisters talk.[6]

Later parts of the song further echo this sort of powerful re-frain of shaking and breaking up this system as a means of appealing for female unity and empowerment. For example, Lady Lastee reminds her listeners to let "the haters hate when it comes to our future" (*"On laisse baver les bavards sur no-tre futur"*) and to allow women to talk for themselves (e.g. *"laisse parler des soeurs"*). The premise of this song is to de-mand true equality for all women, because they are setting their sights on new goals in order to create a female-centered history that will be as good as that of their forefathers. This is highlighted when Lady Laistee raps *"on vire nos repères pour égaler nos pères"* (we'll be as good as our fathers). There are good reasons for this sort of demand. In a country with such intense gender inequality and imbalance, empowering lyrics such as are intended to resonate with female listeners and in-form them that despite the positive developments of recent decades, much more work needs to be done.

Similar to Queen Latifah in early American hip-hop, Lady Laistee's massive success opened the door for future female rappers. Other artists soon followed in her footsteps as the genre further developed during the first decade of the 2000s. However, not all women rappers would receive the same type of popular and critical acclaim. The most famous female *"rappeuse"* who immediately followed Lady Laistee was an artist known as Bams. Born in France of Cameroonian par-ents, Bams (née: Rita Bamsoukoisant) was an outstanding scholar and athlete in her adolescent years who later became attracted to hip-hop as a teenager. Similar to previous female rappers, Bams also appeared on compilations that featured emerging artists, and she was the only woman who with a track on the *hardcore* rap album entitled *"Hostile hip-hop."*

Bams differed from other women rappers in the sense that her lyrical narrative was more radical in form, which mimicked the approach used by popular male *hardcore* artists at that time. This was not surprising considering that she released songs under the tutelage of the same management company that worked with artists such as NTM, a frequently banned hardcore group who has made a career out of tackling controversial issues dealing with race and class in France, often with very forceful and direct language. Bams' debut album "*Vivre ou mourir*" ("Live or Die") did exceptionally well in regard to radio airplay, and from this release came the powerful song "*Douleur de femme*" ("Women's' Pain"). The thematic approach of this track focuses on direct and explicit feminist militancy; one that is far greater in scope than what was stated by Lady Laistee and others. In this track, Bams raps "*je fais mes thèses bien exposées*" ("I expose my theses well"), and further lyrics explicitly delineate sexism as they concern the male-described historical role of women in society, as shown here:

> Nothing has changed, history repeats itself
>
> Violated, all (women/stories) has been perpetuated
>
> No matter the offense, women are the star (i.e. to blame)
>
> Eve's sin due to a very stupid husband
>
> Who was an idiot, too stupid, with a gluttonous taste
>
> (And) that so-called evil magnetized (influenced) everyone (...)
>
> Women at the dawn of 2000: The marks the history leave indelible traces

Whatever the decade, we are treated the
same way

Always more beautiful, yet more servile.[7]

In addition to the above example, later lyrics from *"Douleur
de femme"* further elaborate on subjects of rape and violence
against women. Female listeners are instructed to understand
that firm resistance to these things is not solely their duty, but
one that is the responsibility of all of humanity, when Bams
raps: *"ce n'est pas un geste, ni une cause feministe, juste un sentiment de devoir humaniste"* ("it's neither a feminist cause nor
gest, just a feeling of humanist obligation"). An additional refrain from this song aims to unite all women together as one
in order to resist the uneven and subordinate categorization
of females everywhere on Earth: *"unis, l'ensemble des femmes,"*
or "united, all together as women." The song *"Douleur de
femme"* fared very well commercially, and its accompanying
videoclip visually showed viewers that is not just male artists
who could take a more militant approach to rhyming about
negative societal ills. Bams made sure to remind everyone
who listened that women also have something to say on the
matter their subordinated position.

Additional tracks from the album *"Vivre ou mourir"* such as
"Pas cool" feature lyrics that address sexism and gender imbalances directed towards women: *"J'veux pas être jolie, fais
chier d'être une fille"* ("I don't wanna be pretty, it sucks to be a
girl"), whilst other releases on the same album such as (*"Moi,
ma violence"* or "My Own Violence") take a more direct approach. In the latter song, Bams suggests that working-class
females of color (about whom she raps as those women being
"on the bottom, those women who have nothing") should
revolt and resist against the systematic discrimination they
face. Direct, hard-hitting tracks such as these made Bams

the first true *hardcore* female rapper, and her approach has been further copied and emulated by others in recent years, notably by the contemporary Marseille-based radical artist Keny Arcana. Bams was a very popular and *rappeuse* whose lyrics were far more revolutionary than the time when they were released in the 1990s, when women in French hip-hop avoided confrontational thematic subject matter. In other words, despite the fact that male artists had been addressing themes of social resistance to the political order for years, Bams was the first female rapper to cast away any reluctance to tackle these subjects in the same fashion as men in French hip-hop, which was atypical for a woman artist. Although she received critical acclaim for her work, Bams' popularity was short-lived and she did not enjoy the same amount of sustained commercial success as Lady Laistee. After Bams' success waned, she moved to other educational-type projects that have had a lasting impact. Amongst other things, Bams became the co-founder and later editor of *Respect Magazine*, which is a popular bi-monthly magazine whose target audience is youth of color in France. Several years would pass until another female would gain any sort of popular visible prominence in French hip-hop.

TEACHING FROM THE PLATFORM OF A *MÉGASTAR*

The immediate years following Bams' success did not see the emergence of any notable female rap talent on a grand scale, though a little-known rapper by the name of Diam's (née: Mélanie Georgiades) started gaining notoriety for her unique rhyming, smooth lyrical delivery, and stylistic technique. Diam's would soon become the highest-grossing female rapper ever seen in French hip-hop to date, and one of the best-selling Francophone musical artists of all time. Born in Cyprus of a French mother and a Cypriot father, Diam's moved to Essone in the Paris suburbs when she was very young. She came of age up in the disadvantaged "*banlieues*" (urban–suburbs) at the same time when French rap started to explode in popularity in the early 1990s. When she was an adolescent, Diam's started writing and performing and she was quickly noticed by small record labels. Similar to other artists who came before her, Diam's would also be first gain acclaim after she was featured in tracks or albums released by male rappers (in her case by Les Neg Marrons and Black Mozart). After a few solo releases that were mildly received by the public in terms of their very modest sales and airplay, Diam's finally evolved from the rap underground in 2003 with her own album entitled "*Brut de femme*," ("*Crude Woman*"). This particular release was autobiographical in nature and one that tackled many women's issues head on, such as domestic violence, marital problems, and gender discrimination in employment, amongst others. Once the album hit the airwaves, "*Brut de femme*" became one of the top selling French hip-hop releases of all time, and its crossover appeal helped Diam's win a "*Victoire*" award for "*Best Rap Album of 2004*" (a first by a female artist). This sort of visibility and commercial success enabled Diam's to cement her status as a major player in the French hip-hop scene.[8] However, despite her preliminary success, even greater things lied ahead for her. For example, it was her next album, entitled "*Dans ma bulle*" ("In my Bubble") that would set a new standard, not only for female artists, but for French hip-hop in general. The subject matter of this new release did not shy away from discussing contentious matters as they affect women and others from ethnocultural communities. The thematic matter of her newest songs addressed, discussed, and deconstructed divisive topics such as racism and sexism in France. Diam's was fully cognizant of her growing popularity and she used this public platform as a lectern in which to educate the entire

French public about the status of women and young people of color living in disadvantaged and marginalized communities across the country.

Upon its release, "*Dans ma bulle*" quickly rose up the charts where it quickly became the top selling album in France in 2006 (of all musical genres). In addition to gender, Diam's takes on the subject of one's identity and social position in France since these topics are repetitive refrains amongst nearly all artists in *le hip-hop français*. Several songs from "*Dans ma bulle*" addressed the marginalization of immigrant youths, albeit from a feminist and humanist perspective, as this excerpt from "*Ma France à moi*" ("My France") demonstrates:

> This is not my France, this deep France
>
> The one that shames us and wishes that we submerse ourselves
>
> My France does not live in the lie
>
> With heart and rage, we're in the light, not in the shadows (...)
>
> My France is all mixed together, yeah, it's a rainbow,
>
> My France bothers you, I know, because it does not want you as a model.

France is a country that is deeply divided by race. High concentrations of immigrants and people of color reside in the impoverished suburban areas surrounding Paris, cramped into small apartments located in high-rise complexes known as "*cités.*" Kokoreff, Marlière, and Thomas state that youths from these areas suffer from institutional discrimination, low educational attainment, high unemployment, all of which contribute to feelings is disillusionment and malaise. All of these issues are the primary themes featured in the song "*Ma France à moi*," albeit from a female perspective. What separates female artists from their males is their broader focus on issues that go far beyond the usual lyrical tropes that center on racial and cultural discrimination as the central thematic refrain. According to Rose (*Black Noise, The Hip-Hop Wars*), women rappers tend to discuss social issues from a far less revolutionary perspective than is often the case with male rappers, choosing instead to focus on more humanistic themes. Diam's is no exception to confronting personal and social issues, and she does so by rapping empowering messages in her songs and their accompanying videos. This sort of pedagogical and philosophical narrative was previously used successfully by Queen Latifah and Lauryn Hill, amongst other female rappers in the United States (Rose, "Black Noise," "The Hip-Hop Wars").

The second major release by Diam's also tackled a broad range of social issues, many of which had never before been discussed so openly in French music, no matter the genre. Topics such as teen suicide, relationships, anxiety, dating, eating disorders, and body image were featured as major themes in many songs, all of which were accompanied by popular music videos. Additionally, more radio-friendly feminist topics were also covered on this new album, such as what one hears in the song "*Jeune démoiselle cherche mec mortel*" ("Young Lady seeks Cool Dude"), a song whose subject matter revolves around women looking for an ideal partner, but with a small twist: Females seize and maintain control of the power dynamic of mate selection and dating (not males, with this theme being further emphasized visually in the track's official video). In the single and videoclip, the men to whom Diam's makes reference are told to be courteous towards women and to treat them well, as illustrated in this line: "*Mon mec a des valeurs et du respect pour ses soeurs*" ("my guy has values and respects his sisters").[9] Further lyrics from "*Jeune démoiselle*" echo similar points when Diam's raps: "In my dreams, my guy speaks to me very low, when he writes letters to me he writes like Booba" (Booba is a famous artist in French hip-hop). The song and video presentation were both extremely popular on French music charts, where they remained for several weeks.

Other tracks from "*Dans ma bulle*" contain similar lyrics that demand a reconfiguration of gender imbalances. For example, lines from the popular song "*La Boulette*" proclaim "*y a comme un goût de boum boum dans le coeur de mes soeurs*" ("there are exploding feelings in the hearts of my sisters") that serve to pay homage to the growing unity amongst women of color in France.[10] Furthermore, the song goes on to address some of the dangers facing females in the disadvantaged suburbs of Paris, as this example shows:

> Kinda tastes like rape when I walk around my city.
>
> Kinda tastes like fear for us chicks in the 2000s
>
> Kinda tastes like pot in the oxygen we breathe,
>
> Don't ask me what breaks your balls.
>
> I ain't like 911, I'm just a young girl who hustles well.[11]

After first naming some of the distractions that affect women of color in poor neighborhoods on a daily basis (e.g., rape, fear of walking freely without being harassed, drugs), Diam's states how she is able to navigate the contours of her environment because she "hustles well" as a means to survive. All of the subject matter discussed in *"La boulette"* serves as an educational rallying point that call for other women to mimic this sort of aggressive reactionary approach (i.e., hustle and fight back). Further lines from the song go on to get to the cause of the sexist and racist social ills that plague marginalized communities. Diam's asks her listeners to reject the educational curricula in France that minimizes any contributions that deviate from a Euro-linear narrative when she raps: *"nan nan c'est pas l'école qui nous a dictée nos codes"* ("no no, school hasn't taught us how to be"). The "us" in this excerpt makes reference to women of color in particular, as they are often in a triple or quadruple minority position vis-à-vis majority society (e.g. language, status, race, and gender). Additional lyrics from *"La boulette"* highlight generational differences in France when Diam's describes the rebelling adolescents of her contemporary era as belonging to *"la génération nan-nan"* ("generation no-no," which is a repetitive and continual refrain throughout the track). On other words, *Génération nan-nan* rejects the usual schematic norms of France as dictated by adults from previous eras, as they prefer to rewrite the rules of French society in a way that benefits youths within it.

What makes Diam's stand out from earlier female artists such as Lady Laistee has been her mass appeal across gender, class, and racial lines. At her peak during the first decade of the 2000s, her popularity was unrivalled (to date), and record sales and chart dominance of all of her releases reflected this reality. However, constant touring and endless hassling by the French media forced her to retreat from recording and take a two-year sabbatical until 2009 when she released *"S.O.S."* Similar to her previous releases, the new album by Diam's also featured tracks that addressed controversial and contemporary themes in France, but with some new twists. For example, in addition to gender, race, and class, religious differences were included in many songs. Perhaps, the most famous track from this album is "*Lili*," a song that discusses the organization of female immigrants and Muslim women in French society:

> France for me is nothing but a very large hospital,
>
> I spend my life in isolation since they told me I'm wrong sick (e.g. negative media coverage)
>
> I do not deserve that because they kept me from my studies, from my education
>
> This (i.e. France) is not a secular nation, it is one that fears getting ill (...)
>
> So, because I am a converted woman, and I wear the veil.

This song confronts the Islamophobia that divides France, a fact that Diam's labels as societal "illness." Kokoreff argues that youths of color in France (and Muslims in particular) have few prospects of success, and thus are condemned to fail by the system. In other words, Diam's raps that this type of societal exclusion is contributing to a social separation in France, a country that is becoming sick. This deepening dichotomy is dividing French society in many ways, with both sides adopting increasingly hard attitudes when compared to the other. In recent years (and especially since 2015), that sort of divisiveness has been exploited as a recruiting tool by international organizations that promote terror against State institutions as a means to an end (as shown in the recent attacks on the periodical *Charlie Hebdo* and the terrorist attacks in Paris and Nice). Topical matter such as this appears throughout "*Lili*," as Diam's warned listeners about how the potential dangers of racism and exclusion can be divisive in more harmful ways.

As Diam's has evolved and matured as an artist, her commitment to making life better for women and others who face obstacles from French majority society has increased substantially. Unlike other performers in the music industry in France, Diam's has dedicated the majority of her royalties from the sale of the album "*S.O.S.*" to her foundation (entitled the "*Big Up Project*"), which provides support and funding for youth centers and non-governmental organizations that work with adolescents in sub-Saharan Africa. However, in the years following the success of "*S.O.S.*," Diam's once again withdrew from the spotlight. She resurfaced during an interview on a popular talk shown broadcast on the French television network TF-1 (in 2012) where she announced her indefinite sabbatical from hip-hop. It remains to be seen if she will stage a comeback in the future. Despite this new pause from recording, Diam's remains the most successful *rappeuse* in France, as well as being one of the most popular female artists of all time in French music. Despite the massive popularity that she has achieved as a *mégastar*, Diam's has made a career out of resisting being placed in any sort of set category concerning gender stereotypes, choosing instead to project a more positive outer image that contrasts her style from other female artists and musicians.

ANARCHIST EDUCATION AND *LE RAP RADICAL*

Despite the wide commercial success of Diam's, female hip-hop artists in France rarely choose to emulate the more radical side of the music put forth by their male counterparts, with Bams being a notable exception. That type of revolutionary rap, known in French as *le rap hardcore*, features songs with themes that center on discrimination, invisibility, and alienation with stated goals to encourage and teach listeners to resist and fight against the divisive system by any means necessary. Although we have shown that female rappers have not shied away from addressing subjects that discuss racism and despair among youth of color, they have typically avoided having a true "*pure et dure*" revolutionary pedagogical approach in their music. Aside from Bams, women in French hip-hop have preferred to employ a more delicate approach to their message; one to which all sectors of French society can relate. However, the arrival of a Marseille-based radical artist named Keny Arkana broke this pre-established schema. In fact, her entire musical repertoire tackles more controversial subjects in a revolutionary and political type of way, whereas previous artists resisted political labels and rapped about issues from a more humanistic perspective.

Keny Arkana's first forays into hip-hop music came via her participation in an underground group from Marseille named *État-Major*. This assemblage released several mix-tapes and vinyl tracks and went on to gain a small underground following that caught the attention of small record companies. However, none of these productions received much airplay. In the poor and working-class areas of Marseille, a small radical collective known as "*La rage du peuple*" ("People's Rage") was formed to protest a variety of global issues that affected youth negatively, with Keny Arkana being one of the founding members. In fact, it was her participation with this anarchist group that would eventually serve to motivate her music and career. Following her participation with "*la Rage*" and *État-Major*, Keny Arkana launched a solo career and the thematic narrative of her lyrics has been far more forceful than what has traditionally been the case amongst female rappers in France. For example, her songs focus on topics that relate to or juxtaposed with anti-globalism and anarchist movements, albeit as seen through a feminist lens.

Her first album, entitled *"Le missile est lancé"* ("The Missile is Launched") contains songs with themes that concentrate on a variety of left-of-center subjects dealing with globalism, capitalism, climate change, the Zapatista movement in Mexico, genetically modified foods (GMOs), and subjects as they relate to racism. In terms of stylistic delivery, Keny Arkana raps by employing direct language that is angry, forceful, violent, and more aggressive than any previous female artist. For example, she openly encourages revolt and protest by all available means and she refuses to be aligned with any larger political entity or ideology aside from those that are strategically allied with her own vision. Although women rappers in French have tackled so-called controversial themes and subjects in their lyrics, none have openly and repeatedly encouraged revolt and civil disobedience against the State by being aligned ideologically with political anarchist movements. Previous female artists such as Diam's and Bams focused on issues as they involved women of color living exclusively in France, whereas Keny Arkana concentrates on international protest movements and the juxtaposition of feminism and liberation in France with a global struggle for rights. This important distinction makes her stand out from other rappers. That said, despite this sort of revolutionary and aggressive approach, Keny Arkana's lyrics also express a positive effect since her messages are based in education and social activism, without concentrating on or glorifying petty street crime or social deviance that masquerades as resistance.

Perhaps, Keny Arkana's most well-known song echoes her social involvement. *"La rage du peuple"* ("People's Rage") is

a track that channels the anger of the anti-globalism movement, as it pays homage to the very anti-capitalist and openly
anarchist organization that she founded in Marseille. Lyrics
from "*La rage*" (along with its accompanying video, which
shows clips from anti-globalism protests from around the
world) outline the frustrations that anti-globalist groups have
vis-à-vis the current world order. The song's stated pedagogical goal is to educate uninformed listeners about how a variety of topics directly affect them in their day-to-day lives. In
"*La rage*," Keny Arkana makes a plea for her listeners to direct
their anger into a "*rage*" as they learn more about how they
can topple and demolish the current system, as shown here:

> Because we are enraged, we will stand up
> to everything,
>
> The rage to go through to the end to the
> place where we want to lead our lives (...)
>
> Anti-capitalist, anti-globalist, or wherever
> you're seeking the truth about the world,
>
> The resistance of tomorrow. Inshallah
> on the eve of a revolution. Globally and
> spiritually,
>
> The rage of the people, la rabbia del pueb-
> lo; because we're enraged,
>
> The type that will shake up your norms.
> Rage has taken over the people and the
> rage is huge.[12]

Later in the same track, she even goes as far to express her anger about genetically modified food (GMO) when she raps
"*La rage, car c'est la merde et ce que ce monde y adhère, et parce
que tous leurs champs OGM stérilisent la Terre*" ("Rage, it's
this shit this whole world adheres to, and because all of their

GMO fields sterilize the Earth"). Despite this sort of strong narrative, it is important to note that Keny Arkana does not endorse any sort of hate towards those in power. For example, in the same song she goes on to say: "*On a la rage, pas la haine. La haine est inerte et destructrice*" ("We have rage, not hate. Hate is inert and destructive").[13]

The type of forceful and confrontational thematic discourse shown in tracks like "*La rage*" separate Keny Arkana from other female rap artists in France since her message is not as much concerned with the unity of woman solely on gender lines alone as much as it focuses on unifying and educating the entire working class against the French government and its ties to corporate interests. Keny Arkana has not developed a massive following along the lines of Diam's since she is not very comfortable being labeled as a *rappeuse* in the commercial or artistic sense, though she is conscious of her place as an activist-teacher. For example, during an interview with the French radio network RFI, she once stated: "*Je dis que je ne suis pas une rappeuse contestataire, mais une contestataire qui fait du rap*" ("I am not a radical rapper, but rather a radical teacher who raps").[14] Even though this choice may limit Keny Arkana's overall popularity as it concerns album sales, it solidifies her reputation as a true radical-type educator in French hip-hop.

DISCUSSION AND CONCLUSION: THE FUTURE

It is unclear how women involved with hip-hop music in France will continue to evolve and develop as the music becomes more and more commercialized and commodified by industry marketers and advertisers. To use the United States as an example, aside from a few notable exceptions, women have been all but erased from mainstream rap music in recent years, and educational-style conscious hip-hop is not seen as commercially viable by Hollywood record executives. Contemporary male artists in the United States are presented to consumers via presentations that endorse concepts of the male gaze. Furthermore, the Grammy Awards mirrors this type of gender invisibility in American hip-hop as it eliminated the *Best Female in Rap* category in 2005. Whereas women were once extremely popular and were an integral part of hip-hop in the United States though the late 1990s, women are now once again hypersexualized and stereotyped in the industry. Moreover, in terms of American rap music, females in general continue to be the victims of misogynistic lyrical and visual presentations put forth by male rappers in their lyrics, songs, and videos. This sort of sexism even occurs among best-selling female hip-hop artists in the contemporary era. In 2015, Nicki Minaj's choice to self-promote her "brand" via the use of misogynist body imagery on her recent album differs starkly from the feminist and Afrocentric powerful presentation once employed by female rappers such as Queen Latifah. In France, this type of negative imagery is far less common. That said, blatant sexism is not invisible when best-selling contemporary French hip-hop artists (such as Booba) freely label women as "*putains*" (whores) in many songs and the use of misogyny to sell records is on the rise. Furthermore, despite good visibility in terms of album sales and airplay, women in French hip-hop remain marginalized by an industry that favors males. Although men continue to dominate rap music in France in terms of per capita release percentages, female rappers have shown that they can sell records and they are extremely popular when they are fully promoted by record companies. In other words, feminist messages resonate when they are heard and given full industry support and commercial airplay, and women rappers are able to be noticed because of the unique subject matter of their rap counteracts and confronts sexism in France. This sort of feminist lyrical protest follows a well-established tra-ditional French schema of resisting via poetry, stories, plays, and now hip-hop songs.

Our study is not exhaustive and it is our hope that this study stimulates researchers into examining similar topics for fur-ther academic investigations. As additional subject worth research would be to measure the effectiveness of feminist rapped messages in terms of how well they are being received and understood (or not) by consumers. Additional scholarly work is also needed in terms of measuring whether or not hip-hop consumers in France are listening to what is being rapped to them, or if they are merely hearing it. In short, fur-ther explorations could examine whether or not people are paying attention to the issues and subjects brought forth by these artists, and discern what the result of this "education" might be. Moreover, an analysis of other French music styles in terms of feminist-inspired songs or lyrics (perhaps juxta-posed against hip-hop) is also worthy of academic research.

The four artists briefly examined in this essay use the medium of French rap as a way in which to provide females agency in a socially expressive pedagogical space. This sort of "rapped classroom" is one where artists educate listeners whilst also denouncing patriarchal and misogynistic attitudes, whilst at the same time raising awareness as they concern issues that relate to the experience of women of color in France. In other words, the sense of "place" as defined in rap music is dissect-ed and discussed from a female perspective, just as it once was in American rap during its commercially conscious era. When evaluated under contemporary norms, female lyricists have played an important role in French rap as hip-hop phi-losophers by offering their students (consumers) a uniquely feminine view and perspective to a variety of issues affecting women of color in France that otherwise may not be heard, discussed, exposed, or understood in a country that still has a long way to go in terms of gender equity. Although this sort of pedagogical approach via music is not unique to hip-hop music, it is the most effective method in terms of reaching females from marginalized populations whose identity and sense of belonging are often put into question by majority society.

NOTES

1 All French to English translations that appear in this paper were done by the author, unless otherwise noted.

2 See: http://www.huffingtonpost.com/crystal-fleming/frances-approach-to-fight_b_7231610.html (retrieved Feb. 2018).

3 The cover photo of latest single by the American hip-hop artist Nicki Minaj (entitled "*Anaconda*") illustrates this afore-mentioned point, as the artist is featured in a misogynistic and suggestive pose that some may consider as sexist and/or degrading to women. The thematic idea of this photo was made by Nicki Minaj herself (*as she stated in radio/television interviews*). However, this decision may have also been endorsed by the advice from her producers and record company management.

4 All song lyrics that appear in this paper have been translated by the author and have not been published elsewhere in English. To reference the track's original words in French, see: http://www.hiphopfranco.com/lyrics/3630-lady_laistee__for_the_ladies.

5 Ibid. To reference the track's original words in French, see: http://www.hiphopfranco.com/lyrics/3625-lady_laistee__black_mama.

6 Ibid. To reference the track's original words in French, see: https://www.musixmatch.com/fr/paroles/Lady-Laistee/Un-peu-de-respect.

7 Ibid. To reference the track's original words in French, see: https://www.paroles.net/bams/paroles-douleur-de-femme.

8 The *Victoires de la Musique* are the French equivalent to the Grammy Awards in the United States.

9 All song lyrics that appear in this paper have been translated by the author and have not been published elsewhere in English. To reference the track's original words in French, see: http://www.rap2france.com/paroles-diam-s-jeune-demoiselle.php.

10 Ibid. To reference the track's original words in French, see: https://paroles2chansons.lemonde.fr/paroles-diam-s/paroles-la-boulette.html.

11 Ibid. To reference the track's original words in French, see: https://paroles2chansons.lemonde.fr/paroles-diam-s/paroles-la-boulette.html.

12 Ibid. To reference the track's original words in French, see: http://www.rap2france.com/paroles-keny-arkana-la-rage.php.

13 An interesting footnote to the above excerpt is Keny Arkana's linguistic insertion (*code-switching*) of Arabic and Spanish into her lyrical delivery. This is typical across French hip-hop and it is especially acute for rappers hailing from the very diverse city of Marseille.

14 See: http://www.rfimusique.com/musiquefr/articles/083/article_16663.asp (retrieved: 12 Feb. 2018).

REFERENCES

Adams, Terri, and Douglas Fuller. "The Words Have Changed but the Ideology Remains the Same: Misogynistic Lyrics in Rap." *Journal of Black Studies*, vol. 36, no. 6, 2005, pp. 938-957.

Bams. *Vivre ou mourir*. Trema, 1999.

Berry, Venise. "Feminine or Masculine: The Conflicting Nature of Female Images in Rap Music." *Cecilia Reclaimed: Feminist Perspectives on Gender and Music*, edited by Cook, Susan and Judy, Tsou, University of Illinois Press, 1994, pp. 183-201.

Bleich, Erik. "Anti-Racism without Races: Politics and Policy in a Color-Blind State." *Race in France: Multidisciplinary Perspectives on the Policy of Difference*, edited by Chapman, Herrick and Laura, Frader, Berghahn Books, 2004, pp. 48-74.

Blondeau, Thomas, and Hanak, Fred. *Combat Rap II: 20 ans de Rap français / Entretiens*. Le castor astral, 2008 .

Chang, Jeff. *Can't Stop, Won't Stop: A History of the Hip-Hop Generation*. St. Martin's Press, 2005.

Diam's. *Brut de femme*. EMI Music, 2003.

———. *Dans ma bulle*. EMI Music, 2006.

Duchen, Claire. *Feminism in France: From May '68 to Mitterrand*. Routledge, 1986 .

———. *French Connections: Voices from the Women's Movement in France*. University of Massachusetts Press, 1987.

Emerson, Rana. "Where my girls at? Negotiating Black Womanhood in Music Videos." *Gender and Society*, vol.

16, no. 1, 2002, pp. 115-135.

Faure, Sylvia, and Garcia, Marie-Carmen. *Culture hip-hop, jeunes des cités et politiques publiques*. La Dispute/SNÉDIT, 2005.

Fleming, Crystal. *Resurrecting Slavery: Racial Legacies and White Supremacy in France*. Temple University Press, 2017.

Forman, Murry. "Represent: Race, Space and Place in Rap Music." *Popular Music*, vol. 19, no. 1, 2000, pp. 65-90.

———. *The 'Hood Comes First: Race, Space and Place in Rap and Hip-Hop*. Wesleyan University Press, 2002.

Hebdige, Dick. *Cut 'n Mix*. Methuen, 1987.

Kokoreff, Michel. *Sociologie des émeutes*. Payot, 2008.

Lady Laistee. *Black Mama*. Barclay, 1999.

———. *Hip-hop Therapy*. Barclay, 2002.

Mallière, Éric. *La France nous a lâchés: Le sentiment d'injustice chez les jeunes des cités*. Fayard, 2008.

Layli, Phillips, Kerri Reddick-Morgan, and Dionne P. Stephens. "Oppositional Consciousness within an Oppositional Realm: The Case of Feminism and Womanism in Rap and Hip Hop 1976–2004." *Journal of African American History*, vol. 90, no. 3, 2005, pp. 253-277.

Prévos, André. "Two Decades of Rap in France: Emergence, Developments, Prospects." *Black, Blanc, Beur: Rap Music and Hip-Hop Culture in the Francophone World*, edited by A-P. Durand, Scarecrow Press, 2002, pp. 124-137.

Quinne, Ethne. "Who's the Mack? The Performativity and Politics of the Pimp Figure in Gangsta Rap." *Journal of American Studies*, vol. 34, no. 1, 2000, pp. 115-136.

Rose, Tricia. *Black Noise: Rap Music and Black Culture in Contemporary America*. Wesleyan University Press, 1994.

———. *The Hip-Hop Wars: What We Talk About When We talk About Hip-Hop, and Why it Matters*. Basic Books, 2008.

Strausz, Sté and Dole, Antoine. *Fly Girls: Histoire(s) du hip-hop féminin en France*. Au diablevauvert, 2010.

Tobias, Eva. "Flipping the Misogynist Script: Gender, Agency, Hip-Hop, and Music Education. Action, Criticism, and Theory for Music Education" vol. 13, no. 2, 2014, pp. 48-83 .

Troka, Donna. "You heard my gun cock: Female Agency and Aggression in Contemporary Rap Music." *African American Research Perspectives*, vol. 8, 2002, pp. 82-89.

Weekes, Debbie. "Where my girls at? Black Girls and the Construction of the Sexual." *All about the Girl: Culture, Power and Identity*, edited by Harris, Anita, and Fine, Michelle, Routledge, 2014, pp. 141-154.

World Economic Forum. 2016. Global Gender Gap Report 2016. http://reports.weforum.org/global-gender-gap-report-2016/economies/?doing_wp_cron=1520631060.5957889556884765625000#economy=FRA. Accessed: 9 Mar. 2018.

War, Patriotism, and Nationality in the Norwegian and Swedish Translations of *Cherry Ames*

by Marcus Axelsson

ABSTRACT

Helen Wells' novels of the nurse Cherry Ames follow the protagonist through student nursing to her life as a practicing registered nurse. The books, featuring her military service, were soon translated, reaching Iceland, Norway, and Sweden. This article focuses on how the themes of war, patriotism, and nationality are translated in the Norwegian and Swedish translations of Cherry Ames. When comparing these two countries, it is notable that the literature for young girls was somewhat scarcer in Norway in the middle of the twentieth century, where this kind of book had not been highly prioritized during the war. This article also focuses on how the representations of war, patriotism, and nationality are translated into Norwegian and Swedish and how the same themes are depicted on the respective book covers. Bearing in mind that Norway participated in the war, and Sweden did not, it is interesting to investigate whether war and patriotism are rendered differently in the Norwegian and the Swedish target texts and whether the American patriotism is preserved or in some way "domesticated" to make the novels more Scandinavian.

Keywords: Helen Wells, Cherry Ames, nursing, Scandinavia, translations, Norway, Sweden, patriotism, military service

Guerra, patriotismo y nacionalidad en las traducciones de *Cherry Ames* al noruego y sueco

RESUMEN

Las novelas de Helen Wells de la enfermera Cherry Ames siguen a la protagonista a través de su formación como enfermera y su vida cuando ya es enfermera registrada practicante. Los libros, que incluyen su servicio militar, pronto fueron traducidos y llegaron a Islandia, Noruega y Suecia. Este artículo se enfoca en cómo los temas de guerra, patriotismo y nacionalidad fueron traducidos en las traducciones de Cherry Ames al noruego y sueco. Al comparar estos dos países, es notable que la literatura para niñas jóvenes era algo más escasa en Noruega a mediados del siglo 20, donde no se le había dado una alta prioridad a este tipo de libros durante la guerra. Este artículo también se enfoca en cómo las representaciones de guerra, patriotismo y nacionalidad son traducidas al noruego y al sueco y cómo estos mismos temas son representados en sus respectivas carátulas. Teniendo en cuenta que Noruega participó en la guerra y Suecia no, es interesante investigar si la guerra y el patriotismo se cuentan de una forma diferente en los textos noruegos y los suecos, y si el patriotismo estadounidense fue de alguna forma "domesticado" para que las novelas fueran más escandinavas.

Palabras clave: Hellen Wells, Cherry Ames, enfermería, Escandinavia, traducciones, Noruega, Suecia, patriotismo, servicio militar

战争、爱国主义和民族性在小说《彻丽·埃姆斯》挪威语翻译和瑞典语翻译中的体现

摘要

海伦·韦尔斯的小说集《彻丽·埃姆斯》（Cherry Ames）讲述了主人公从学生护理期间到担任执业注册护士的生活经历。该系列小说以彻丽的兵役生活为主题，很快经过翻译流传到冰岛、挪威和瑞典。本文聚焦于战争、爱国主义和民族性这些主题如何通过挪威语版和瑞典语版的《彻丽·埃姆斯》得以表达。当比较这两个国家时，值得注意的是，20世纪中期的挪威相比瑞典拥有更为稀少的文学作品供年轻女孩阅读，在这一战争期间《彻丽·埃姆斯》这类著作并未获得高度重视。本文还聚焦于战争、爱国主义和民族性这三者如何在挪威语和瑞典语翻译中得以呈现，以及这些主题在系列小说封面的刻画方式。需要留意的是，挪威参与了战争，而瑞典没有，因此考察——描述战争和爱国主义的相关内容在挪威语和瑞典语翻译中是否会有差异，以及美国式爱国主义是否在书中有所体现，亦或是美国式爱国主义通过某种方式被"归化"而让小说变得更加斯堪的纳维亚——将变得十分有趣。

关键词：海伦·韦尔斯，《彻丽·埃姆斯》（Cherry Ames），护理，斯堪的纳维亚，翻译，挪威，瑞典，爱国主义，兵役

· · · · · · · · ·

Between 1943 and 1968, Grosset & Dunlap published 27 novels about the nurse Cherry Ames. Many of these American novels found their way to a number of European countries. Helen Wells (1910–1986) was the author of the majority of the books, and Julie Tatham (1908–1999) wrote some in the middle of the series. In the novels, the reader gets to know Cherry and follows her through her years as a student nurse and later as a practicing registered nurse. Over the years, she works as an army nurse, a chief nurse, flight nurse, veterans' nurse, visiting nurse, cruise nurse, and so on. There is little she does not do. The books about the impulsive and intrepid Cherry Ames were written for girls, and they could be described as career novels, i.e. novels about young protagonists, often girls, pursuing a career (cf. Finlay 1189). The focus on career and working life could be a reason why the novels became so popular in the United States and were exported to a number of countries in Western Europe.

Cherry arrived in Iceland first, then came to Norway, and some years later, to Sweden (see *The Cherry Ames Page*). In the Nordic countries, women have taken part in working life for quite some time; it is therefore not surprising that it was in these countries, the first translations of the novels about Cherry Ames emerged. Moreover, in Norway, the books arrived at a perfect time since there was an increasing need for nurses (Nygaard 50). If the novels, among other things, had the agenda of recruiting nurses for the Second World War, this did not stop them from also fulfilling a different purpose overseas in the postwar years. They filled both a practical purpose of recruiting nurses, and, most importantly, a purpose of educating and entertaining young female readers.

The Cherry Ames books fit into the category of popular literature. Previous research (see e.g. Sapiro, "Translation and the Field of Publishing," "Globalization and Cultural Diversity in the Book Market") has shown that products of popular culture easily spread from the United States to parts of the world that have a smaller domestic production of popular culture. Iceland, and especially Norway, was marked by the war in the period when the countries imported and translated Cherry

Ames, and their domestic literary production of popular culture for young girls was low. There were therefore good conditions for import at this time.

This article focuses on how the themes of war, patriotism, and nationality are translated in the Norwegian and Swedish translations of Cherry Ames. Including all the Nordic countries in this study would have been interesting, but too extensive. This article therefore only focuses on Norway and Sweden. When comparing these two countries, it is notable that the literature for young girls was somewhat scarcer in Norway in the middle of the twentieth century, where this kind of book had not been highly prioritized during the war. In the 1950s, there was hence a need for literature of this kind and it seems somewhat safe to conclude that this demand was a contributing factor as to why Cherry Ames, together with her peer Vicki Barr, and the somewhat younger Nancy Drew, were translated into the Scandinavian languages.

Although there was a need for this type of literature in postwar Scandinavia, and despite the fact that American popular culture products are easily imported into more peripheral European cultural systems, it took 8 years for the first book about Cherry Ames, *Cherry Ames, Student Nurse*, to be translated into Norwegian, and as much as 13 years for it to be translated into Swedish. One reason for the delay in this translation could be the literary status of the Cherry books. They were products of popular culture of low status (Nygaard 54). In addition, they were novels for girls, and girls were not the strongest buyers in the market in postwar Scandinavia.

Translation research shows that Sweden is the most central and the most closed literary system in Scandinavia (Lindqvist, "Det skandinaviska översättningsfältet—finns det" 77, 79). This means that it is harder for literature from abroad to be translated and enter the Swedish literary market. In general, it also takes longer for books to be translated and published there when compared with the rest of Scandinavia (Axelsson 67–72). This could be another reason why the Swedish translation of Cherry Ames came so much later. Previous research (see e.g. Lindqvist, *Översättning som social praktik* 217) shows that translations into Scandinavian languages are normally very faithful to the source text. Theories also suggest that literature translated into languages characterized as central, rather than peripheral is generally more adapted to the target culture (Even-Zohar 51; cf. Venuti 21). It is interesting to bear this in mind while carrying out the empirical analysis. A hypothesis would be that the Swedish translations, since Sweden is the most central literary system in Scandinavia, would be somewhat less source-text oriented than the Norwegian translations.

Of the 27 books about Cherry Ames, 21 were translated into Norwegian and 24 into Swedish. This signals that although the Swedes took some time to translate Cherry, they were more eager to hold onto her once they really got to know her. Norway stopped publishing the books after Cherry's Canadian experience in *Island Nurse* in 1960, whereas publication in Sweden ended after *Companion Nurse* in 1964.

Wells wrote the first novels in the series during the Second World War and shortly after it ended, and war and patriotism are recurring themes in the three wartime novels. These are *Army Nurse, Flight Nurse,* and *Chief Nurse,* written between 1944 and 1945. The topic of war in the Cherry Ames series has previously been addressed by Finlay (1190), who found that, in the first books, Cherry not only learns her profession, but also about war and sacrifice. Cherry sees the war as a noble cause, and in her role as a nurse, fulfils a "fictional function of being representative of the citizens of the United States [...]." The American participation in the war is never questioned. Instead, it seems that Cherry's decision to go to war is the only way to "preserve the simple, tranquil way of life in her all-American hometown" (Finlay 1194). The topics of war and patriotism have also been touched upon by Simon, who argues that Cherry's hopes, dreams, and personality always overshadow themes relating to war and her activities in the army (147).

As mentioned earlier, this article focuses on how the representations of war, patriotism, and nationality are translated into Norwegian and Swedish. It also focuses on how the same themes are depicted on the respective book covers. Bearing in mind that Norway participated in the war, and Sweden did not, it is interesting to investigate whether war and patriotism are rendered differently in the Norwegian and the Swedish target texts. It is also interesting to study whether the American patriotism is preserved or in some way "domesticated" (see Venuti 19–20) to make the novels more Scandinavian. For the analysis of the covers, theories from Kress and van Leeuwen's 2006 *Reading Images: The Grammar of Visual Design* are used. The material for the study consists of the wartime novels, namely *Army Nurse* (1944), *Chief Nurse* (1944), and *Flight Nurse* (1945), and their Norwegian translations *Cherrys hemmelige reise* from 1951, *Cherry Ames blir oversøster* from 1952, and *Cherry på vingene* from 1952. The Swedish counterparts are *Cherry Ames i fält* from 1956, *Cherry Ames—översköterska* from 1956, and *Cherry Ames vid flyget* from 1957. The main emphasis on the textual level is on *Flight Nurse*, since this novel takes place in Europe and, in a geographical context, is closer to Scandinavia than *Army Nurse* and *Chief Nurse*.

Firstly, it is appropriate to direct attention toward the translation of the titles. As previously mentioned, Scandinavian translations are usually close to their source text, and this is also the case in the Swedish translations of Cherry Ames, where the titles are close to literal translations of the American ones. The military theme is explicit in the title *Army Nurse* and this title has been almost literally translated in the Swedish version *Cherry Ames i fält* (literally "Cherry Ames in the Field"). The Norwegian titles, on the other hand, are somewhat surprisingly much freer and the war theme is less prominent or even omitted entirely. The title *Chief Nurse* (*Cherry blir oversøster*) is translated quite literally, but focuses more on Cherry's becoming a chief nurse, using the verb "blir" ("becomes"). *Flight Nurse* is translated using the fixed, metaphorical expression "på vingene" ("on the wings"), which could either refer to something having taken off and being airborne, or that something is going well. This title does little to indicate that Cherry is in the U.S. Air Force. Instead, it could be interpreted as Cherry's career taking off, or more literally, that she works as a pilot or a stewardess. In fact, the cover bears many resemblances to the cover of the Norwegian translation of another of Well's novels, namely *Silver Wings for Vicki* (*Vicki blir flyvertinne*). This novel was published in Norway in 1952, the same year as *Cherry på vingene*, by the same publishing house and using the same illustrator. There is a clear intertextuality between these two covers.

The Norwegian title that is most different from the American original is *Army Nurse*. This title has been changed entirely and translated as *Søster Cherrys hemmelige reise,* meaning "Sister (i.e. 'nurse') Cherry's secret journey." There is no trace of any war theme in this title, which seems to refer to the plot of the novel, where Cherry is sent abroad on a secret mission for the Army.

As regards the cover images, it could be noted that the Norwegian covers are less naturalistic than the Swedish and

American ones (cf. Kress and van Leeuwen 159; Björkvall 114). The Norwegian cover images could be described more as pop art à la Lichtenstein, whereas the American and Swedish ones are closer to real photography. It is interesting to note that the artist's name, Sten Nilsen, is actually mentioned on the cover that is the most pop artsy of them all, namely *Cherry på vingene* (see fig. 10). Nilsen created most of the Norwegian cover images for the Cherry books, and during the mid-twentieth century, he also produced a dozen other book cover illustrations.

Cherry is always the focal point of the cover illustrations. Her dark hair and brown eyes are mentioned early on in all of the novels and they are distinctly highlighted on all of the book covers. This is especially obvious in the illustrations that portray her using a medium close shot, i.e. at a distance where the onlooker can see Cherry from the waist and up (cf. Kress and van Leeuwen 124). Her different nurses' outfits are always highlighted and she is depicted in some kind of uniform on every cover. Most of the time, she is portrayed in her blue dress and white apron, but in some of the material used in this study, she also wears a military uniform, which adds extra symbolic value. The novels often mention how the uniforms lead to respect and admiration for Cherry and her fellow nurses, and this symbolism is carefully retained in the Scandinavian target texts.

In *Army Nurse*, Cherry has completed her education at Spencer hospital and has returned to her hometown of Hilton, Illinois. She receives a letter from the Army and joins its Nurse Corps. After a short stay at Spencer hospital for some training, she and her classmates are sent to Panama to work at an army base hospital. On the cover of the first American edition of *Army Nurse*, Cherry is portrayed standing on a boat, probably on her way to Panama, where she is to work as an army nurse (see fig. 1).

Figures 1–3. Cover Images of the American, Norwegian and Swedish Versions of *Cherry Ames, Army Nurse.* Images first published by Grosset & Dunlap (Ralph Crosby Smith), Forlagshuset (Sten Nilsen), and Bonniers (Martin Guhl).

Cherry is wearing a green army uniform in the illustration and is holding a pair of brown gloves in her right hand, while smiling and waving with her left hand. She looks straight at the reader and this eye contact has a communicative function where she asks for attention and that we, as onlookers, take part in her story and enter into an imaginary relation with her (cf. Kress and van Leeuwen 116–18). Another woman is standing next to her, also smiling, and other people can be seen in the background, notably a man in some kind of military uniform. The Swedish cover depicts Cherry standing outside a building, probably Spencer hospital, dressed in a graduation uniform. She is looking to the right with a determined gaze and does not establish any contact with the reader. We are invited to look at Cherry, but she does not necessarily demand anything from the reader (cf. Kress and van Leeuwen 119). Readers are put in a position where they wonder why Cherry looks so determined and what her mission in this book could be. This is a notable difference from the American source text, where it is clear that Cherry is going to the army and that she is clearly happy about this. The Swedish translation, *Cherry Ames i fält*, was published in 1956 and its cover image (see fig. 3) is very much based on the cover of the second American edition (see fig. 4).

Although there are no overt symbols showing the reader that Cherry goes to war in the novel, Cherry's posture and determined gaze indicate that she is looking toward a mission that she must accomplish and a duty that calls her. She is looking to the right, which according to Kress and van Leeuwen (64, 181) signals that she is looking toward the future. Cherry needs to go to war to help wounded American soldiers and she knows that this will lead to future peace for her country. Behind her, we see the school building, where she came from, where-

Figure 4. Cover Image of the Second American Edition of *Cherry Ames, Army Nurse*. Image first published by Grosset & Dunlap (Frank Vaughn).

as we can only hint the future through Cherry's determined gaze. Cherry's face is horizontal to the reader and she is thus depicted as equal to them, signalling to the readers that they can be a part of her world (cf. Björkvall 52), and even join her on her mission.

The Norwegian cover image of *Cherrys hemmelige reise* (see fig. 2) is entirely different from both the American and the Swedish versions. It portrays Cherry speaking on the phone. Her face bears an expression that could reveal feelings of consternation, worry, or even sadness, characteristics that are not typical of Cherry. She seems to be holding a handkerchief to her chin, which may suggest that she is crying, but this is difficult to grasp. She is depicted at a personal distance, i.e. a distance where the reader can identify with the character (cf. Kress and van Leeuwen 124). She is gazing slightly up and to the side. She does not look at the readers and does not demand anything from them. Instead, they are invited to look at her and wonder what may be troubling her, who she is talking to, what kind of conversation she is engaged in, and whether she is crying. Could the conversation have anything to do with the secret journey mentioned in the title? Although this cover is somewhat stripped of the details that we find on the American and Swedish covers, it may be the cover that engages readers the most since it challenges them to think about what might happen in the novel. Judging from the background, she appears to be in a hospital, probably at Spencer.

As stated above, the most obvious symbols of war and patriotism depicted on the cover of the first American edition of *Army Nurse* have been omitted from the Norwegian version. Here, there is nothing to signal that the novel is about Cherry going to war. As mentioned earlier, the title of the Norwegian target text is also rather different from the original, namely *Søster Cherrys hemmelige reise* ("Sister Cherry's secret journey"). However, the title is the only component of the book cover that could suggest a military theme—the journey is namely secret. It could be hypothesized that the war was still a painful memory in Norway in 1952 and that the publisher has tried to avoid this theme as much as possible on the book cover. In Sweden, the novel was not published until 1956 and its readers had not experienced the war. The war was not a theme that the publisher chose to highlight with any overt symbols, but Cherry's gaze and posture suggest that she has a mission to accomplish, be it in war or peace. Moreover, it is easy to understand that the Swedish publisher chose to base its cover on the second American edition, which is much less "war-like" than the first edition.

In the second wartime novel, *Chief Nurse*, Cherry is promoted to chief nurse and she receives an order to set up an evacuation hospital on a tropical Pacific island. She has many responsibilities and is in charge of some 60 nurses. She also faces great challenges under severe attacks from Japanese bombers. The title of the novel does not reveal that Cherry is going to war, but the cover image of the first American edition (see fig. 5) is probably the most war-like of the entire Cherry series, which somewhat compensates for the nonspecific title.

Figures 5–7. Cover Images of the American, Norwegian and Swedish Versions of *Cherry Ames, Chief Nurse.* Images first published by Grosset & Dunlap (Ralph Crosby Smith), Forlagshuset (Frank Vaughn), and Bonniers (Martin Guhl).

On the American cover, Cherry is depicted crouching beside a wounded soldier. She is using a pair of scissors to cut through his clothes while winding a bandage around his arm. Cherry is dressed in a green military uniform and is wearing a helmet. She is in the jungle, close to a Pacific beach, and another soldier can be seen in the background. In the second edition of *Chief Nurse* (see fig. 8), the military theme is absent from the cover and Cherry is instead engaged in conversation with a number of nursing colleagues.

Figure 8. Cover Image of the Second Edition of *Cherry Ames, Chief Nurse.* Image first published by Grosset & Dunlap (Frank Vaughn).

It could be argued that the latter illustration is erroneous since the narrator in the novel tells the readers that the nurses are always dressed in khaki uniforms. The nurses' white uniforms, their calm countenances, and the neat and tidy background indicate nothing of a temporary military hospital on a Pacific island. The cover image portrays Cherry smiling while engaging in conversation with three other nurses. They are all dressed in nurse uniforms and Cherry is, as always, the center of attention. She is positioned somewhat above the other nurses and is looking down on them, which may indicate her superior rank after being promoted to chief nurse. She is smiling complacently and there is no sign of the war to be seen anywhere in the image. The Scandinavian covers are very much based on this second edition, where the war is omitted. This is particularly true for the Norwegian cover (see fig. 6), which is very similar to the original. The only differences between the American and Norwegian cover images are the nurses' uniforms and the background. The Swedish illustration is somewhat different, however. On the cover of the Swedish edition (see fig. 7), Cherry and two other nurses are standing next to each other outdoors. Cherry is in the middle, and one of the nurses is looking at her, while the other is looking at a document in Cherry's hand. Cherry establishes contact with the reader with a determined gaze, but this gaze does not reflect her personality in the novel. Instead, she almost looks condescendingly at the reader from the corner of her eye with an undefinable smile on her lips. This could be a signal of Cherry's superior rank after her advance to the position as chief nurse (cf. Kress and van Leeuwen 118). There is a modern hospital building in the background, which is clearly not the evacuation hospital in the Pacific jungle. The cover of the book does not, therefore, reflect its story, since Cherry is in the Pacific jungle throughout the entire book and does not spend any time at such a modern hospital as depicted on the cover. This is clearly an example of all elements of the war being excluded from the covers of the translated books.

In *Flight Nurse*, Cherry and her friends complete their education to become flight nurses in Randolph Field, Texas. They are sent to England, where they encounter the harsh realities of the war. At one point, Cherry also experiences a German attack while flying wounded soldiers from the battlefront. The American, Norwegian, and Swedish covers of *Flight Nurse* are similar, and symbols of both war and patriotism are represented on all three covers (see figs. 9–11).

The Norwegian and Swedish covers are very much based on the American cover image. Cherry is portrayed at a personal distance. According to Kress and van Leeuwen's theories concerning the grammar of visual design, this distance allows the readers to identify with Cherry and her hopes and dreams (124). The most obvious symbol of patriotism represented on the cover is Cherry's clothing. She is wearing the U.S. Air Forces' uniform with the classic wings and the let-

Figures 9–11. Cover Images of the American, Norwegian and Swedish Versions of *Cherry Ames, Flight Nurse.* Images published by Grosset & Dunlap (Ralph Crosby Smith), Forlagshuset (Sten Nilsen), and Bonniers (Martin Guhl).

ters "US" on her chest. Cherry is wearing two U.S. broches on the Swedish cover and it is on this cover that the letters are easiest to decipher. On the American version, one U.S. broche is visible, but it is less prolific. On the Norwegian version, it is hard to make out the contours of the letters. It is noteworthy that this symbol of patriotism is actually more conspicuous on the Swedish cover than on the cover of the versions published in the United States and Norway—countries that participated in the war as allies. Cherry's posture and gaze are two other features in the illustration signalling patriotism. On the Swedish and American covers, Cherry is looking up to the side with a determined gaze. This could be seen as a symbol of determination and hope, where Cherry knows what she has to do in order to keep her country safe. In the American version, Cherry is looking somewhat to the right, which once again may mean that she is looking toward the future. Although Cherry is looking to the left on the Swedish cover, her determined gaze and posture have been retained. In fact, this posture and gaze remind us of political campaigns portraying candidates looking up to the side, as

if looking into a future where his or her political agenda has
been effectuated and led to a better world. Cherry's attire
and posture display an American patriotism that is retained
in the Swedish interpretation of the original cover image.

As regards the Norwegian cover illustration, Cherry's posture is much less patriotic and determined. In fact, the patriotic determination has been replaced by a romantic theme.
Cherry's head and gaze are still depicted in semi-profile and
she is still looking slightly upward, but she is looking into
the eyes of a man, most likely the pilot Captain Cooper, who
plays a major role in the novel. Her gaze can therefore be
more interpreted as one of admiration rather than determination and idealism. The patriotic theme has simply been
replaced by a romantic one, by introducing a man into the
original picture. This may have been a measure taken by the
publisher to make the book more appealing to young girls
in the 1950s, for whom the war theme was possibly not particularly enticing. However, romance is only an occasional
theme in the Cherry Ames series, and the Norwegian publisher has chosen to highlight a part of the plot that has a
rather peripheral position in the novel. It should be mentioned, though, that *Cherry Ames, Flight Nurse*, is one of
the earlier books in the series and the publisher could not
know that highlighting the romantic aspect of the Cherry
series would be misleading, since they did not know how
the complete Cherry series would turn out. It could also be
mentioned that a later book in the series, *Cherry Ames at
Spencer* (1949), was translated with the title *Cherry og drøm-
meprinsen*, literally "Cherry and the Dream Prince," also
foregrounding a romantic theme which actually has a rather
peripheral role in the plot. It is highly probable that also this
choice was a measure to make the novels more appealing to
young female readers.

In *Flight Nurse*, Cherry is portrayed very similarly on the Swedish and American covers and more of the patriotic features have been kept, or made even stronger, on the Swedish cover illustration. When studying the background of the images, however, the American and Norwegian images are more similar. The most conspicuous feature signalling American patriotism is actually on the Norwegian cover. Here, there is an airplane in the background, and two men and a woman are carrying a wounded soldier on a stretcher onto the plane. The plane on the Norwegian cover has the classic U.S. Armed Forces' roundel emblem with the white star in a blue circle painted on it—a symbol not present on the American edition. This could be a compensation for the omission of Cherry's own patriotism on the Norwegian cover image. The background of the Swedish illustration also has the airplane and people carrying a stretcher, but these elements are much more blurred and distant, and do not bear any major resemblance to the original. Compared to the American and Norwegian editions, a much wider background is depicted that includes an airport and an area of the sky with a plane. The most obvious symbol with an ideological value in the background is the Red Cross, which can be seen both on the tailfin of the plane and on a flag on the control tower. According to Björkvall's image analysis, it is often the case that the "real world" is situated at the bottom of an image, whereas dreams and ideals are presented at the top of the page, reflecting Western ideas about earth and heaven (90, 96). It is notable that the Red Cross flag is situated in the upper half of the image, symbolizing Cherry's ideals—helping and caring for the sick and the wounded. The Swedish background is somewhat less patriotic toward America, and instead, the publisher stresses Cherry's role as a helper by adding the Red Crosses. If we focus on the airport in the background, it seems to bear more resemblance to today's large international airports than to a wartime airbase, and this is interesting, bearing in mind that the Swedish translation was not published until 1957, compared to the American original, which was published in 1945 and the Norwegian, which was published in 1952. In 1957, the war, in which Sweden never participated, was already quite distant, and even more so for the book's intended readers.

Moving on from the book covers to the purely textual level, there are a number of passages about war, patriotism, and nationality that are interesting for further study. In the following episode, an omniscient narrator tells the reader of Cherry and her team's everyday routines:

> When Cherry's team flew to battle areas to pick up the wounded, they would never fly an empty plane but would haul troops or vital cargo. With such military cargo, they would have no right to the protection of a Red Cross painted on their aircraft. Instead, the white star of American combat forces was painted on its broad dark side. (Wells, *Flight Nurse* 11)

The star in the quotation is the star that we find on the cover of the Norwegian translation and it is obvious that this is where the artist has taken the idea from. The Swedish cover, on the other hand, seems erroneous since the airplane has a Red Cross painted on it. The narrator clearly states that there is no Red Cross on the airplane, but the publisher has still chosen to use it on the cover, and hence indirectly brand the more caring side of Cherry. In fact, the Swedish translations often tone down the war on the textual level. Passages where the war is spoken of in too easy-going terms are toned down or even omitted. At the beginning of *Flight Nurse*, there is a passage where the pilot Wade Cooper is talking about how he once, against orders, had carried out a one-man attack on a Japanese target. This attack is described as a heroic accomplishment in all of the three translations, but the heroic part is somewhat toned down in the Swedish translation, whereas the fact that it was carried out against orders is emphasized. After having told Cherry about this heroic accomplishment, Cooper then brags about it. This passage is omitted from the Swedish translation: "I guess I was something of a smart aleck. Jeepers, what a time I had for myself! When you fly one of those high-powered bombers, why, you're just sitting there with a thousand horses in your lap and a feather in your tail" (8). In fact, Cooper's easy-going way of describing this accomplishment is almost stronger in the Norwegian target text. In the source text, Cooper speaks of the attack in an easy-going manner and that he had a good time bombing Japanese targets alone in his airplane, but he admits that he was a smart aleck then, implying to the reader that things might be different now. In the Norwegian translation, "smart aleck" is translated to "fin fyr" (10), indicating that he was a "good man" in doing this.

There are also other passages in the novel where people nonchalantly talk about the war that have been omitted from the Swedish target text. When Cherry and her friends arrive in England in *Flight Nurse*, they are ordered to work in a military hospital rather than flying to the front and hauling wounded soldiers as they had hoped. They make moping comments about having "crossed an ocean merely to help out on a ward" (40). These comments have been omitted from the Swedish target text, resulting in a translation that makes Cherry and her friends appear more serious and less "belligerent" than in the source text and the Norwegian target text. As compensation for not being allowed to fly, Cherry and her friends are al-

lowed to take some time off and visit the nearby village. They
catch a ride with the postman and are fascinated by the quaint
landscape and the English architecture, at the same time as
they are depressed by the ravages of the war, and, most of all,
thankful for the fact that they live far away from the war in
America. On their excursion, they experience cultural differences between the United States and England. They can see
the country's poverty reflected in a window shop where there
are "no eggs, no red meat, no oranges" (43). They even see
the ravages of war in a house, where one of the walls is missing and they can see straight into a kitchen where a woman
stands by the stove. They also wonder if they are allowed to
visit a café and eat some of the food that was so hard to come
by in England. They are surprised by the waitress' dialect in
the café and can barely understand her. The passage where
Cherry and her friends go to this village stretches over almost
five pages, all of which are omitted from the Swedish target
text, resulting in a translation where the overall American
perspective in the novel is significantly toned down. In this
passage, Cherry utters a sentence that sums up her thoughts
about the war and her feelings of patriotism: "Not very gay,
this business of having war in your own front yard," Cherry
summed up. She thought gratefully how lucky she was to be
an American" (45), which is a sentence that has been kept
and translated quite literally in the Norwegian target text.

Another part of the book where the geographical context,
and hence also nationality, has been altered is a passage
where Wade tells Cherry and the wounded soldiers where he
has flown before. He tells them that he has flown "[i]n China
and over the Hump" (13), translated as "[i] Kina eller over
dammen" (14) in the Norwegian target text, meaning over
"China and the Atlantic Ocean." As regards "over dammen,"
we are no longer in Asia, but still in an area well trafficked by

the American army during the war. In the Swedish version, Cooper has flown "I Kina och över Kalotten" (13), where the latter geographical region denotes the northernmost part of arctic Scandinavia. The action has thus been drastically moved away from the Hump and everything linked to the geographical areas where the U.S. Air Force was active during the Second World War. This could be an act of domestication, where the action is set closer to home for the Swedish readers. Geographical names in general seem to have been made less American in the Swedish target texts than in the Norwegian ones. Even the geographical term "New England" is translated literally into "Nya England," which is not considered correct in Swedish. Geographical names have been made less specific and less American, also making Cherry appear less American. For example, when boarding the vessel to England, Cherry and a couple of her friends are divided into different groups. Cherry and her friends are placed together with three other nurses forming a group of six. They tell each other where they come from (Illinois, Pennsylvania, New England, and Minnesota) and this passage, where metalinguistic comments on the girls' dialects are made, has been left out in the Swedish translation.

In another passage, Cherry, Cooper, and a couple of fighter pilots drink Coca-Cola and meet some soldiers who express their admiration for the flight nurses. They say, "You flight nurses are our real pin-up girls" (39), which has been translated to "Dere flysøstre er virkelige pin-up girls" (30) in Norwegian, which has almost the exact same meaning as in the source text. Despite today's negative connotations, this is meant as a compliment. The pilot who utters these words argues that the nurses, who do so many good deeds, are genuine, admirable, and good-looking. He says that when the pilots salute the girls, they do so because they mean it and not only because they follow Army customs. Another fighter pilot joins the conversation and tells Cherry that the nurses can mean the difference between life and death for many soldiers. This passage has been omitted from the Swedish translation, resulting in a censorship of the pin-up section, and an omission of the part where the nurses' role in the war is mentioned.

When comparing the Norwegian and Swedish translations with the source text, it is clearly the case that the Swedish translations are the least source-text oriented on a purely textual level. This is in line with earlier research showing that translations into languages of central literary systems are freer. It appears as if the publisher wants to protect the reader from the war and to make the geographical contexts less specific. At the same time, it is necessary to mention that the case seems to be the opposite concerning the portrayal of Cherry on the cover image of *Army Nurse* and, to some extent, *Flight Nurse*.

In the wartime novels, it is inevitable that the enemies are mentioned. In *Flight Nurse*, a mother comes with her child to Cherry's hospital after a bombing. She says: "This time, I thought, the Jerries will have had enough of bombing the Drews. But it seems I was wrong" (58). The slang is toned down in the Norwegian version, rendering the text even more explicit as to whom the enemy is, namely *tyskerne* ("the Germans"): "Denne gangen tenkte jeg nok tyskerne ville hatt nok av å bombe oss, men jeg hadde nok tatt feil" (43). This sentence is omitted from the Swedish version. In another episode, Cherry's friend Dr. Joe tells Cherry in a letter what has happened to some people he knows in England. One line of the letter is: "Then the Germans bombed London" (21). This is translated quite literally in the Norwegian target text as "[s]å bombet tyskerne London" (18), whereas the sentence is set in a passive voice in the Swedish translation, probably to avoid mentioning the Germans: "[s]edan bombarderades London" (17). Another, very tart, remark about the Germans is also toned down in the Swedish target text. A character tells Cherry: "[...] I have no daughter—thanks to the Germans" (84), which is quite literally translated into Norwegian as "[...] jeg har ingen datter ... takket være tyskerne" (64), whereas the Swedish translator has chosen to phrase it more neutrally: "[...] jag har ingen dotter, för krigets skull" (57) ("I have no daughter, because of the war"). Once again, the Swedish target text provides a more neutral description of events.

In *Flight Nurse*, the enemy is Germany, whereas in *Army Nurse* and *Chief Nurse*, it is Japan. Passages where the Japanese are named as the enemies have not been omitted or made less explicit in either target text. A very clear example of this appears in *Chief Nurse*, where Japanese bombers attack the island where Cherry's temporary hospital is located. This attack makes Cherry furious. She thinks of the attackers: "The beasts, inhuman killers" (152), which is literally translated as "Disse umenneskelige morderne" (132) in Norwegian, and "Odjur, omänskliga mördare" (118) in Swedish. However, the parts where the Germans are referred to in negative terms are sometimes omitted or rendered less explicit in the Swedish translations, as shown above. It is possible that this strategy is used in order to avoid perpetuating a grudge against the Germans after the war or transferring any lingering animosity to coming generations, who had not experienced the war. This would not benefit European peace. It is as if the translator has adopted Cherry's own creed of forgiving and seeing the best in people as guidelines for how to translate the text. The Japanese participation in the war, however, was quite distant for the Scandinavians, and naming Japan as the enemy would not be so great a risk as naming the Germans.

When considering all of the novels in the Cherry series, the Swedish target texts are always shorter than both the American source text and the Norwegian target text. This is the case even when taking spacing and font size into account. *Cherry på vingene* contains 161 pages, whereas *Cherry Ames vid flyget* is only 139 pages long. Previous research has shown that literature of low prestige is translated less literally than literature of high prestige (Lindqvist). Lindqvist has studied the translation of Harlequin novels and found that Swedish publishers ask their translators to cut 10–15 percent of the book (78). The Cherry series could be categorized within the segment of low prestige literature, and it is therefore possible that the publisher has asked the translator to make the target text shorter than the source text. If this was the case, then the sections referring to the war would be the easiest to cut down on, since the topic was unlikely to appeal to potential readers. Results suggest that this is what has happened in *Cherry Ames vid flyget*.

At the textual level, this study has shown that the themes of war, patriotism, and nationality are less pronounced in the Swedish translations of Cherry Ames. There is a tendency that nationalities and geographical names are rendered less specific or omitted entirely. The omission of nationalities is especially clear concerning the German enemy. The fact that there are more changes in the Swedish target text could be linked to the fact that Sweden never participated in the war, and that it is a country that has remained neutral for a long time. It could also be linked to the fact that Cherry was introduced in Sweden quite a long time after the war. Another reason why the Swedish translations seems to be less faithful to the American originals could be that Sweden, with a more central literary system, uses less source-text oriented translations than Norway. As regards the book covers, however, results are inconclusive as to whether the Swedish or Norwegian covers are farthest from the originals. The war seems to be less salient on the book covers of the Norwegian target texts, especially concerning the titles, which are much freer in relation to the American source text. It could be argued that the war was still a painful memory in Norway at the time, and that the publisher has tried to brand the novels differently in order to attract more readers. It is clear that certain elements appear to have been omitted, highlighted, changed, or even added to the cover images by the Norwegian and Swedish publishers in order to make the books more appealing to their readers.

Bearing these results in mind, one must still note that although Cherry is in the army and the war is a major theme in some of the books, Cherry is first and foremost a nurse. In fact, she has to remind herself on several occasions that she is also a soldier. There is never any sign of the war being portrayed as something good. Cherry goes to war because she has to. In the military, Cherry often finds it hard to adapt to the strict rules and to make her superiors listen when she has something important to say. She is always guided by her sense of right and wrong and, ultimately, she always makes the right decisions—decisions that her superiors also approve of. These aspects of the Cherry books, namely her desire to care for the sick and wounded, and her sense of right and wrong, are always translated in full in both the Norwegian and Swedish target texts. It is clear that Cherry's own identity and aspirations always transcend the topics of war and patriotism.

WORKS CITED

Axelsson, Marcus. *"Kalla mig inte mamsell!" En jämförelse av
tre skandinaviska översättares behandling av kulturspecifika
element i fransk- och engelskspråkig skönlitteratur.* Department of Scandinavian Languages, 2016. Print.

Björkvall, Anders. *Den visuella texten: multimodal textanalys i
praktiken.* Hallgren & Fallgren, 2009. Print.

"Cherry Ames around the World." *The Cherry Ames Page.*
Web. http://web.archive.org/web/20040804102436/.
http://www.netwrx1.com/CherryAmes/foreign.html.

Even-Zohar, Itamar. "The Position of Translated Literature
within the Literary Polysystem." *Poetics Today*, vol. 11, no.
1, 1990, pp. 45–51. Print.

Finlay, Adrianne, 2010. "Cherry Ames, Disembodied Nurse:
War, Sexuality and Sacrifice in the Novels of Helen Wells."
Journal of Popular Culture, vol. 43, no. 6, 1900, pp. 1189–
206. Print.

Kress, Günther, and Theo van Leeuwen. *Reading Images: The
Grammar of Visual Design.* Routledge, 2006. Print.

Lindqvist, Yvonne. "Det skandinaviska översättningsfältet—
finns det?" *Språk och Stil*, vol. 25, 2015, pp. 69–87. Print.

———. *Översättning som social praktik: Toni Morrison och
Harlequinserien Passion på svenska.* Stockholm Studies in
Scandinavian Philology, 2002. Print.

Nygaard, Karl-Henrik. "Cherry og kallet." *Sykepleien*, vol. 99,
no. 6, 1990, pp. 50–54. Print.

Sapiro, Gisèle. "Globalization and Cultural Diversity in the
Book Market: The Case of Literary Translations in the US

and in France." *Poetics*, vol. 38, 2016, pp. 419–39. Print.

———. "Translation and the Field of Publishing: A Commentary on Pierre Bourdieu's 'A Conservative Revolution in Publishing.'" *Translation Studies*, vol. 1, no. 2, 2008, pp. 154–66. Print.

Simon, Linda. "Cherry Ames—A New Woman for the 1940's." *Girls' Series Fiction and American Popular Culture*, edited by LuElla D'Amico, Lexington Books, 2016, pp. 147–65. Print.

Venuti, Lawrence. *The Translator's Invisibility: A History of Translation*. Routledge, 1995. Print.

Wells, Helen. *Cherry Ames, Army Nurse*. Grosset & Dunlap, 1943. Print.

———. *Cherry Ames, Chief Nurse*. Grosset & Dunlap, 1944. Print.

———. *Cherry Ames, Flight Nurse*. Grosset & Dunlap, 1945, Print.

———. *Cherry Ames i fält*. Albert Bonniers förlag, 1956. Print.

———. *Cherry Ames—översköterska*. Albert Bonniers förlag, 1956. Print.

———. *Cherry Ames vid flyget*. Albert Bonniers förlag, 1957. Print.

———. *Cherry blir oversøster*. Forlagshuset, 1952. Print.

———. *Cherry på vingene*. Forlagshuset, 1952. Print.

———. *Søster Cherrys hemmelige reise*. Forlagshuset, 1952. Print.

A Conversation with *Nanette*: A Not-So-New Proposal for an Invitational Rhetoric

by Nanette Rasband Hilton

ABSTRACT

Hannah Gadsby's 2018 comedic routine, *Nanette*, is a global live stage, *Netflix*, and viral sensation. However, Gadsby's success comes at the expense of an Other from whom she derived the title of her show and casts as a scapegoat for societal sins. Invitational Rhetoric, as modeled by five female writers from nineteenth century Margaret Fuller to twenty-first century Rita Felski, teaches a better way for resolving ideological conflict, working toward understanding, and promoting peaceful communities.

Keywords: Invitational Rhetoric, Othering, *Nanette*, Margaret Fuller, Phenomenological Alterity, Virginia Woolf

Una conversación con *Nanette*: una propuesta no tan nueva para una retórica de invitación

RESUMEN

La rutina cómica de Hannah Gadsby en 2018, Nanette, es un escenario global en vivo en Netflix y una sensación viral. Sin embargo, el éxito de Gadsby viene a costa de un Otro del que ella deriva el título de su programa y coloca como un chivo expiatorio para los pecados de la sociedad. La retórica por invitación, según el modelo de cinco escritoras, desde Margaret Fuller en el siglo XIX, hasta Rita Felski del siglo XXI, enseña una mejor manera de resolver conflictos ideológicos, trabajar hacia la comprensión y promover comunidades pacíficas.

Palabras clave: retórica invitacional, otredad, Nanette, Margaret Fuller, alteridad fenomenológica, Virginia Woolf

与Nanette的对话：一项针对邀请式修辞学的并不全新的提议

摘要

2018年汉纳·加斯比的单口喜剧表演"Nanette"在Netflix播出后引起了极大的轰动。然而，加斯比所获的成功以他者为代价，即其表演的标题Nanette；同时将她刻画为社会罪恶的替罪羊。邀请式修辞学（Invitational Rhetoric）由5位女性作家建构，包括19世纪的马哈雷特·福勒和21世纪的丽塔·费尔斯基。该修辞学就解决意识冲突、努力达成理解、推动和平社区提出了更好办法。

关键词：邀请式修辞学，他者化，Nanette，马哈雷特·福勒，现象学的变化，弗吉尼亚·伍尔夫

· · · · · · · · ·

"No, No, Nanette regales my ears" nearly a century since its 1919 Broadway debut, this time it's not Doris Day on Broadway,[1] but rather Hannah Gadsby on Netflix. I can't resist responding, that's *my* name. I share it with only one other person on the planet—whom I've met—in junior high school over three decades ago. It was startling to hear another person called by my name then; we became friends. Recently, I was surprised to be called out by name again, but this time, as a mean pejorative when Gadsby's comic routine hit the fan. While discussing feminist rhetoric in a university seminar focusing on female writers, I unknowingly followed the advice of *Wired* Senior Editor Alexis Sobel Fitts as I examined Gadsby's rhetorical moves, the way she "quietly built and broke different interlocking threads" in her sensationalized staged exposé of the homophobia she feels. She names this phenomenon *Nanette*.

"Nanette ranked among the Top 1000 [names] until '77, peaking in 1956" (Rosenkrantz and Satran) and made it to the endangered list by being "given to only five babies each in 2013, the lowest number counted by the U.S. Social Security Administration. Once usage dips below that, they become the dodo birds of baby names." Nanettes are rare and, apparently, need protection.

I investigated Gadsby's motivation to appropriate my name— the name that has become an international phenomenon in the world of stand-up? comedy?. Watching the Netflix hour-long version provides no explanation for the title since that part of her live routine was clipped. Could there be a *Moby Dick* without the whale? A *Jane Eyre* without Jane? Maybe it's unimportant, just a matter of semantics ... Semitics ... sematic ... any Tom, Dick, or Harry would have sufficed? Why is *Nanette* minus Nanette? Why did Gadsby name her show in such a personalized manner giving a face-slap to every Nanette everywhere? Maybe she knew there weren't many of us. We pose no threat—easy pickin's. Apparently, Gadsby was in a bar where she sighted Nanette working. How did Gadsby know the barista's name if they never spoke? Perhaps Nanette wore a uniform with a nametag as she silently served Gadsby. Maybe a *regular* shouted, "Hey, Nanette, get me a drink!"

Asked this question in an interview by *Variety* entertainment and business magazine Features Editor Jenelle Riley, Gadsby admits that she never spoke with Nanette, that they never had any direct contact, and that she has not followed-up with her further (par. 14–15).

But, thanks to Gadsby, now we're "The 'Nanette' problem," observes Peter Moskowitz. "One of the problems with 'Nanette,'" Moskowitz recognizes, is Gadsby's location of "the problem not in exploitative structures that might implicate Gadsby's audience [and herself], but within ourselves." He laments that "If only we could respect each other, then things would change. If only we could be more civil in our public debates." Calling defenseless Nanette out in a public forum for something she didn't do—most likely a miscommunication between strangers—is neither respectful nor civil. Stranger danger is a reality: the stranger we remain, the more danger we face.

Gadsby claims no foul, excusing herself and Nanette saying, "No offence to Nanette, she might have just had a tough day. I was purely projecting. I feel pretty bad because she was just getting on with her life. It's one thing for me to open up this viral sensation upon myself but she's just doing her thing" (Riley, par. 15). Yet Gadsby's shot is fired and all Nanette's— all five of us—fall victim. We're the minority bullied by a Netflix star who uses our name to signify hate.

In defense of endangered species, the barista Nanette "Gadsby encountered at a café" accused of making her "feel uncomfortable," I have to ask, really? You "two never spoke" yet your interaction "was enough to leave its mark" (Aubrey, par. 4)? Gadsby admits "in the live show I talk about her but in the film version it was cut for time. I've never seen her since, I assume she's still kicking about somewhere. She was just an older lady who I would normally love to talk to, but because of what I represented, we didn't" (Riley, par. 14). *We* didn't? Or *you* didn't? Who deterred the conversation? Is ageism at play? In her routine, Gadsby's narrow-minded mother evolves, even becomes the heroine of diversity. Gadsby also anticipates giving Grandma a second chance. But Nanette is cast in concrete, stereotyped to her doom. I cringe anticipating my name becoming an adjective like "Pollyannaish."[2]

The negative stereotype affixed to both *Nanette* and *Pollyanna* is an injurious act of phenomenological abjectivity by either the rhetor or the reader, whether done intentionally or ignorantly. Gadsby concedes that she "projected" her own abjectification, that Nanette did nothing of note. Similarly, Porter's young heroine, Pollyanna, was the model of optimism for the cynical adults and despondent children with whom she came in contact yet is today unfairly remembered. In the face of severe trial, Pollyanna chose to find hope instead of despair. She was the "tonic" for those suffering emotional misery (Porter 137). Instead of remaining this symbol of hope for us today, her name connotes naïveté, gullibility, and childishness. We're a poorer society in choosing this association over the loadstar Porter actually provides in her classic story. And in so choosing, *Pollyanna* risks being relegated to the dusty margins of outdated, sentimental novels not hip enough for today's readers. Again, we impoverish ourselves and the next generation by our oversight when *Pollyanna* could be just the medicine our discordant society needs—especially people like Gadsby who perceive offense where none is given.

Nanette is Gadsby's scapegoat—the person on whom she heaps society's sins and expects to silently carry them away. The term *scapegoat* is just as culturally ubiquitous, yet often used in ignorance, as is *Pollyannaish*. An etymological study of *scapegoat* may illustrate Gadsby's irresponsibility in sacrificing Nanette.

The first 15 chapters of the Bible's *Leviticus* teach how individuals can become reconciled to God through sacrifice or how they can "wash away their sins" through ceremony and obedience to His laws. The Day of Atonement described in *Leviticus 16*, celebrated in modern day as Jewish Yom Kippur, symbolized atonement for the entire Israelite nation as a priest officiated the personification of a goat as savior of the community by shouldering their collective sins and releasing it into the wilderness never to be seen again.

The English word for this symbolic goat was fashioned by William Tyndale in his 1530 translation of the English Bible. He translated the Hebrew word *azazel*, found only in connection with this Levitical ceremony, as *ez azel* or the *goat (ez)* which *escapes (azel)*. The concept of this is that the goat represents "*one that bears the blame for others*" whether guilty or innocent (*Merriam-Webster*). Thus, we see the origins of the scapegoat archetype employed by Gadsby.

These origins surpass language and religion as seen in text archives of Jungian writings, the *Torah* and *Qumran* and in the twenty-fourth century BC Syria (Zatelli). The ancient Greeks had a scapegoating ritual, much like Gadsby's burdening of Nanette with all society's bigotry in which they cast out of the community a mendicant, cripple, or criminal, either in response to a natural disaster or calendrical crisis; regardless of one's language or religion, today this is recognized in America as abhorrent societal practice.

Why didn't Gadsby converse with Nanette when she had the opportunity? Was she too shy? Her stage performance and celebrity shed doubt on this possibility. Who judged? Condemned? Sentenced? It wasn't Nanette. Instead, Nanette is the marginalized silenced soul on display, commodified for the benefit of Gadsby's capitalistic and rhetorical goals. In effect, Gadsby cast Nanette from the community, burdened with blame.

Gadsby's show "became an instant viral sensation, prompting praise on social media from everyone from Jon Favreau to Kathy Griffin to Roxanne Gay" (Riley, par. 3). It's reported as being "[s]tartlingly frank and personal" and a moment in which Gadsby boldly declares she's "quitting comedy," an issue "her legions of new fans are sure to take issue with." I can hear them chanting, standing, demanding an encore, "No, No, Hannah!" as they plead with her to continue. They may get their wish as Gadsby's celebrity star rises higher with every Netflix viewing "in people's private spaces and homes .... breaking the contract essentially of what stand-up comedy should be—light entertainment" (Riley, par. 7). Gadsby revels in her new limelight while on tour, reporting that "To get recognized in New York is weird because that's definitely a place you shouldn't be recognized...I don't quite know what to make of it" (Riley, par. 4). Money is what Gadsby will make of it—money and fame, at Nanette's expense. It is in Gadsby's best interest not to confront Nanette, not to get a different perspective than that on which she built her box-office hit, not to relinquish her power. Gadsby's power is directly related to the subjective position in which she placed Nanette.

Historically, it is recounted that in ancient Israel, the scapegoat once returned from whence it "escaped" after which great pains were taken to ensure it never happened again:

> ... the man in whose charge the goat was
> sent out, while setting him free, was in-

structed to push the unhappy beast down
the slope of the mountain side, which was
so steep as to insure the death of the goat,
whose bones were broken by the fall. The
reason for this barbarous custom was that
on one occasion the scapegoat returned to
Jerusalem after being set free, which was
considered such an evil omen that its recur-
rence was prevented for the future by the
death of the goat. (*Baker's*)

But every societal scapegoat, every *Nanette*, must take a
stand, declaring herself or himself the inclusive, nurturing,
nonjudgmental person she or he is—or at least come to the
discussion table to offer their point of view. For the sake of us
all, *Nanette* can't simply disappear. Silenced voices are characterized by Others. Isn't that Gadsby's message? None of us
can afford to be silent lest a comedian abuse us on stage. Si-
lence is suicide—another of Gadsby's messages. Gadsby has
the power in this contrived relationship and chose to smear
all five Nanettes in a campaign of prejudice and hate. (OK,
maybe there're a few more of us left—I'm only guessing since
I've yet to meet another one since junior high.)

Following Derrida's definition of the Other as a subject of
phenomenological alterity, Gadsby begrudgingly claims
Other status for herself and thereby the privilege of slander-
ing Nanette. Yet, simultaneously she turns this objectionable
lens on Nanette, making her the Other. This two-pronged,
oscillating approach is the shaky framework upon which
Gadsby's show is built and causes viewers difficulty in re-
ceiving and believing her message. The instinctive practice
of Othering, with often negative consequences, is a common
core of contemporary social discourse, whether addressing
gender, race, religion, or any variant stratification influencing

intersubjectivity. This conceptual schema of Othering is integral to Gadsby's argument, yet ironic in its application.

Language is a key to identifying the Other as Toni Morrison points out in her book *The Origin of Othering* , writing that "The resources available to us for benign access to each other, for vaulting the mere blue air that separates us, are few but powerful: language, image, and experience, which may involve both, one or neither of the first two" (35). Gadsby intently appropriates and peddles these keys to identifying an Other by naming her show an unpopular, out-of-fashion name: *Nanette*. I doubt she would have titled her show *Ema, Olivia,* or *Ava* as, according to a U.S. baby-naming website, these are the most popular baby names for girls in 2018 (*Mom365*). Gadsby was instead reaching to the margins of society when she named her show—a place from which she (and most institutions of power) didn't anticipate any resistance.

Morison points out that mankind abjectifies the stranger out of self-preservation, as does Gadsby by her own admission. Though Morison's is primarily a study of color, it can be applied to any situation where people are marginalized and objectified. Morison's examination of Othering motives may explain Gadsby's hypocritical attack on Nanette as she writes, "The necessity of rendering the [Other] a foreign species appears to be a desperate attempt to confirm one's own self as normal ... The danger of sympathizing with the stranger is the possibility of becoming a stranger. To lose one's rank is to lose one's own valued and enshrined difference" (29-30). Whatever transpired between Gadsby and her Nanette was interpreted by Gadsby as a call to arms. She chose to attack Nanette, crossing the lines of human decency by disparaging her name and character, portraying Nanette as a stereotypical bigot. Morrison further explains Gadsby's bad behavior by noting that what we often abjectify in others is a quality we see in ourselves, writing that "there are no strangers. There are only versions of ourselves, many of which we have not embraced, most of which we wish to protect ourselves from" (38).

My name is now an offensive slur like homo, fag, dyke....Parents are unlikely to name their newborns *Nanette* and when I introduce myself to a stranger, they may give me that look, you know the one, Hannah, "when someone looks at you like you're scum of the earth" (qtd. Aubrey, par. 6). In the 1950 film adaptation of the Broadway musical "No, No, Nanette," Doris Day sings "No, No, Nanette regales my ears ... Sometime, perhaps, I'll have my way, when I am old and turning grey, but just as yet it's always no, no, no, no ... Nanette!" Wherever Gadsby's Nanette is, she's still that "older woman," getting older every day, singled out as the sacrificial scapegoat for Gadsby's rhetorical and financial purposes. It is as if Gadsby says, "No, No, Nanette, you shall not speak!" Nanette represents every subjugated person condemned to a life of silent anonymity, excluded from the grand social conversation.

Rather than perpetuating the Aristotelian pattern of patriarchal rhetoric wherein the rhetor (Gadsby) works to persuade his audience to his way of thinking and dominate them in the process, I suggest Gadsby and all of us take a different rhetorical tact as we interact with one another: experiment upon the Invitation Rhetoric feminist theorists Sonja K. Foss and Cindy L. Griffin propose. Foss and Griffin espouse a "new rhetoric ... united by a set of basic principles" including "equality, immanent value, and self-determination" (4). Aren't these the privileges Gadsby claims and accuses Nanette of withholding? This isn't really *new rhetoric* but rather the same claim humans have made since time immemorial. The *old rhetoric* employed by Gadsby at Nanette's expense thrives on the "rush of power" (qtd. Foss 3) with "[t]he value of the self deriv[ed] not from a recognition of the uniqueness and inherent value of each living being but from gaining control over others." Foss and Griffin instead propose "an environment that facilitates understanding, accords value and respect to others' perspectives, and contributes to the development of relationships of equality" (17).

This new rhetoric was actually practiced and promoted by nineteenth-century American writer and social reformer Margaret Fuller who cultivated a multi-ethnic, transclass, transgender, transnational sensibility through her heterogeneous texts—bestsellers like *Summer on the Lakes* which painted a sympathetic portrait of Native Americans' plight under white colonization and *Women in the Nineteenth Century* which was the first American feminist manifesto. These books were loaded with what Jeffrey Bilbro calls "rich cultural diversity" inviting readers to "engage in a dialectic, communal hermeneutic, one that might act as a check on self-serving, individualist interpretations and thereby contribute to a harmonious culture" (64). Evidence of Fuller's commitment to inclusivity includes her famous monthly subscription "Conversations" fostering dialogic interchange among women who were normally excluded from intellectual inquiry and discussion. Fuller's texts are models of dialectical conversation between disparate groups, "one Fuller curates in order to educate readers to be loving interpreters" of one another. Fuller's writing, only recovered and added to the canon in the last 30 years, models Foss and Griffin's Invitational Rhetoric and champions inclusivity long before it was politically correct. Like Nanette, Fuller was silenced from the intellectual conversation because she didn't have the power to speak for herself—she drown in a tragic shipwreck after which her bestsellers were heavily edited in reprinting to the point that Fuller disappeared from the intellectual conversation. Today, scholars spanning the Atlantic are working to resurrect Fuller's authentic voice.

Had Gadsby engaged Nanette, perhaps simply with, "Wazup?" she would have something authentic to say in her routine. Perhaps Nanette would have corroborated Gadsby's suspicions, giving her the stink-eye and spitting in her general direction. However, invoking social norms and striking the middle ground of possibilities, I expect they would have had a civil interchange, no matter how brief or superficial. Gadsby could have accomplished what Fuller believed to be the aim of conversation: to educate the participants and bring them to greater understanding. Fuller defended her frequent "inclusion of various excerpts from other books" to create a heterogeneous amalgamation of voices by claiming "one must look 'at both sides to find the truth'" (qtd. Bilbro 67), a belief Gadsby and all of us would do well to adopt.

Following in the rhetorical tradition of twentieth-century writer, Virginia Woolf, who contrived an epistemological dialog between herself and those by whom she felt marginalized in her *Three Guineas*—an exploration on how war might be prevented—I imagine yet another alternate reality wherein Gadsby and Nanette have a conversation.

Again, envision Gadsby saying to Nanette, "Wazup?"

But this time, Nanette drearily replies, "Arrrg, what a day. I had to put my dog down. By the time I left the vet I'd missed my bus. Got in late cuz of the five mile walk. Boss been on my case all day. So, here I am, still. Missed my bus home, too."

Gadsby's eyes open wide as she realizes what's really on Nanette's mind—a mind she misread.

"Damn, Girl!" Gadsby exclaims, "Hug!" as she stands and reaches over the bar to embrace Nanette.

And, striking a Pollyannaish tone, Gadsby continues, "That must have been so haaarrrd," pulling the word in empathetic emphasis. "But, look on the bright side," Gadsby cheers, "if you hadn't gotten here late, we'd never've met. And *you* are exactly the woman I intend to celebrate in my next gig—that female model of fortitude who gives us all courage to go on. I'm gonna name it after you, Girlfriend!"

Another hug.

Here I stop imagining because, had this exchange actually occurred, Gadsby's show wouldn't have fed the clamoring crowd of accusers ready to critique every *Nanette*/Other they see through their lens of hermeneutical suspicion; the show wouldn't be the popular sensation it is.

Is my imagined version of the two women's exchange sappy like *Pollyanna* is purported to be? Perhaps. But isn't it a better model of human interaction than Gadsby's version?

Everyone is quick to engage in what literary critic Rita Felski calls "a spirit of skeptical questioning or outright condemnation" (2). It's the *low fruit*—just check the daily news. "Why is it," asks Felski "that critics are so quick off the mark to interrogate, unmask, expose, subvert, unravel, demystify, destabilize, take issue, and take umbrage?" (5). Gadbsy is Nanette's self-appointed critic who fails to follow through with the requisite conversation to confirm her suspicion. The harder task for Gadsby and every accuser is to converse with their subject before marking them a suspect while reaching beyond the zone of comfort with the hope of exonerating and understanding an Other. Felski and her allies preach a "hermeneutics of restoration" wherein the critic approaches her subject "in the hope of revelation" (32). To reap this *superior fruit* requires real effort, actual interaction, discourse, and collaboration. These are the moves that would have saved Nanette and every other Other, along with Gadsby's feelings and integrity. These moves involve what Felski calls "shrugg[ing] off the mantle of knowing skepticism by embracing a renewed sense of idealism, purpose, and utopian possibility" (188).

Just as Woolf's interlocutor claimed to want a war-free utopia, Gadsby claims to want social acceptance, harmony, and peace for herself and others like her—those victimized and marginalized. To usher in this utopian society, people must hear and heed Woolf's mandate that portends Foss and Griffin's "new rhetoric" wherein she instructs,

> ... we can best ... prevent war not by repeating your words and following your methods [, Hannah Gadsby and institutions of power,] but by finding new words and creating new methods. We can best help you to prevent war not by joining your society but by remaining outside your society but in cooperation with its aim. That aim is the same for us both. It is to assert "the rights of all—all men and women—to the respect in their persons of the great principles of Justice and Equality and Liberty." (170)

Just as the Broadway musical "No, No, Nanette," experienced an ebb and flow in popularity over time, so do ideologies. Fuller's 1840 commitment to dialogic inclusivity was taken up by Woolf's 1938 directive to practice a new rhetoric, something other than the past patriarchal rhetoric which proved tired and unsuccessful in promoting peace. In 1927, Porter believed that even a child can persuade society toward utopia as her Pollyanna planted hope and positivity instead of pessimism and suspicion. Foss and Griffin issued a 1995 "Proposal for an Invitational Rhetoric" intended to make every voice heard, foster community collaboration and harmony, echoing their foremothers' century-old appeal for peace. And in 2015, Felski continues the attack on critical suspicion which leaves everyone wounded and poor. Together, this genealogy of women writers call for a not-so-new way of seeing and making meaning. What would be new is for society to regard their message, to accept the invitation to talk to one another. Gadsby's 2018 message is a step backwards.

As for Nanette, I counter Gadsby's memorialization of her. I add her name to the record of the fallen and forgotten. Nanette is M.I.A. (missing in action), possibly "still kicking about somewhere" (Aubrey, par. 5). She represents all the Others who suffer silently and are never heard, known, or understood because they are powerless. I commemorate her as someone who, in the end, was sacrificed for the cause of Justice, Equality, and Liberty—may her name be so remembered.

WORKS CITED

Aubrey, Sophie. *MamaMia*, 20 Jul. 2018, http://www.mamamia.com.au/why-is-nanette-called-nanette/. Accessed 12 Sept. 2018.

Baker's Evangelical Dictionary of Biblical Theology. "Scapegoat." http://www.biblestudytools.com/dictionary/scapegoat/. Accessed 14 Nov. 2018.

The Bible. "Leviticus." New International Version, Zonder-van, 2002, pp. 167–169.

Bilbro, Jeffrey. "Learning to Woo Meaning from Apparent Chaos: The Wild Form of Summer on the Lakes." *Writing the Environment in Nineteenth-Century American Literature: The Ecological Awareness of Early Scribes of Nature,* edited by Steven Petersheim and Madison P. Jones IV. Lexington Books, 2016 .

Felski, Rita. *The Limits of Critique.* The University of Chicago Press, 2015.

Foss, Sonja K., and Cindy L. Griffin. "Beyond Persuasion: A Proposal for an Invitational Rhetoric." *Communications Monographs,* vol. 62, Mar. 1995.

Gadsby, Hannah. *Nanette.* Netflix Studios, LLC., 19 Jun. 2018. http://www.netflix.com/watch/80233611 (Links to an external site.). Accessed 12 Sept. 2018.

Merriam-Webster Dictionary. http://www.merriam-webster.com/dictionary/scapegoat. Accessed 14 Nov. 2018.

Mom365.com. "Top 100 Girl's Names for 2018." http://www.mom365.com/baby-names/top-girl-names. Accessed 13 Nov. 2018.

Morrison, Toni. *The Origin of Others.* Harvard University Press, 2017.

Moskowitz, Peter. *The Outline.* 20 Aug. 2018. http://www.theoutline.com/post/5962/the-nanette-problem-hannah-gadsby-netflix-review?zd=1&zi=ly24lrn7. Accessed 12 September 2018.

Porter, Eleanor H. *Pollyanna.* 1927. Puffin Books, 1994.

Riley, Jenelle. *Variety.* 6 Jul. 2018. http://www.variety. com/2018/tv/features/hannah-gadsby-nanette-quitting-comedy-1202867395/. Accessed 14 Nov. 2018.

Rosenkrantz, Linda, and Pamela Redmond Satran. "15 Once-Popular Baby Names on the Verge of Extinction." *Parenting,* 17 Mar. 2015, updated 6 Dec. 2017. http://www.huffingtonpost.com/2015/03/17/ unpopular-baby-names-going-extinct_n_6859318.html. Accessed 12 Sept. 2018.

Wired. "Seriously, We Really Need to Talk About *Nanette*." 31 Jul. 2018, http://www.wired.com/story/hannah-gadsby-nanette-discussion/. Accessed 14 Nov. 2018.

Woolf, Virginia. *Three Guineas.* 1938. Harcourt, Inc., 2006.

Zatelli, Ida. "The Origin of the Biblical Scapegoat Ritual: The Evidence of Two Eblaite Text." *Vetus Testamentum,* vol. 48, Fasc. 2, Apr. 1998, pp. 254–63.

NOTES

1   In the remake of the Broadway musical "No, No, Nanette" titled "Tea for Two," Doris Day sings "No, No, Nanette regales my ears ..." "Sometime, perhaps, I'll have my way, when I am old and turning grey, but just as yet it's always no, no, no, no ... Nanette!"

2   Eleanor H. Porter's 1913 best-selling novel Pollyanna is responsible for the positive and negative associations of blind optimism and inaugurated terms such as the adjective "Pollyannaish" and noun "Pollyannaism."

Crime and Sexuality in the 1955 and 1981 Adaptations of John Steinbeck's *East of Eden*

by Daryl Malarry Davidson

ABSTRACT

This article analyzes the two adaptations of John Steinbeck's crime- and sexuality-laden novel *East of Eden*, which had to undergo transformation of both narrative and style to accommodate translation to Elia Kazan's 1955 feature film and then to Harvey Hart's 1981 television miniseries. The paper uses a critical approach within the contexts of Dudley Andrew's three modes of adaptation—*borrowing, intersecting,* and *transforming*—as well as within contexts that are conventional, historical, cultural, and limitary in relation to the different eras of Kazan's and Hart's productions. The analysis indicates that through omissions of characters and scenes, the creation of composite characters, truncation, allusion, dramatic license, and other elements, Kazan, Hart, and, respectively, screenwriters Paul Osborn and Richard Shapiro, render tried-and-true visual forms as well as indications of their own creativity. This paper concludes that censorship affected the evolution of Steinbeck's sprawling tale—from the Production Code Administration's reconsideration of the word *madam* and its struggle with the onscreen depiction of a brothel in the mid-1950s, to television sponsor Procter & Gamble's objection to the portrayal of adultery in 1981.

Keywords: adaptation, borrowing, censorship, intersecting, miniseries, transforming

La sexualidad y el crimen en las adaptaciones de 1955 y 1981 de *Al este del edén* de John Steinbeck

RESUMEN

Este artículo analiza las dos adaptaciones de la novela *Al este del edén*, de John Steinbeck, que está cargada de crimen y sexualidad y que tuvo que sufrir una transformación de narrativa y estilo para adaptarse a la traducción a la película de 1955 de Elia Kazan y luego a la miniserie de televisión de 1981 de Harvey Hart. El documento utiliza un enfoque crítico dentro de los contextos de los tres modos de adaptación de Dudley Andrew: *adopción, intersección y transformación,* así como en contextos convencionales, históricos, culturales y limitativos en relación con las diferentes épocas de las producciones de Kazan y Hart. El análisis indica que, a través de omisiones de personajes y escenas, de la creación de personajes compuestos, del truncamiento, de la alusión, de la licencia dramática y otros elementos, Kazan, Hart y, respectivamente, los guionistas Paul Osborn y Richard Shapiro presentan formas visuales probadas y verdaderas. así como indicaciones de su propia creatividad. Este documento concluye que la censura afectó la evolución del extenso relato de Steinbeck, desde la reconsideración de la Administración de Código de Producción de la palabra *madam* y su lucha con la representación en pantalla de un burdel a mediados de la década de 1950, hasta la objeción del patrocinador televisivo Procter & Gamble a representar el adulterio en 1981.

Palabras clave: adaptación, adopción, censura, intersectar, miniseries, transformación

1955年和1981年关于约翰·史坦贝克作品《伊甸之东》的改编：犯罪和性

摘要

本文分析了对约翰·史坦贝克所著小说《伊甸之东》（此书内容充满犯罪和性）进行改编的两部作品。《伊甸之东》的叙述方式和风格在改编过程中都经历了转变，从而产生了1955年伊利亚·卡赞的剧情片、以及1981年哈维·哈特的电视迷你剧。在达德利·安德鲁所提出的三种改编模式——借用、交会、转变——这一背景，以及有关卡赞和哈特各自作品所属时代的传统、历史和文化背景下，本文采用了批判性方法。分析显示，通过省略某些角色和情节，卡赞、哈特，和各自的电影电视作家——保罗·奥斯本和理查德·夏皮罗，他们对复合角色、删节、隐喻、艺术许可、以及其他元素的塑造催生了行之有效的视觉表现，同时展现了创造力。本文结论认为，审查制度影响了对史坦贝克作品的改编，包括电影制作法典委员会（Production Code Administration）对"夫人"这一词的反复考量、和其在20世纪60年代中期就银幕对妓院的描绘表示反对，以及电视赞助商宝洁公司在1981年拒绝电视剧对通奸的刻画。

关键词：改编，借用，审查制度，交会，迷你剧，转变

· · · · · · · · ·

INTRODUCTION

Screenwriter Paul Osborn, who wrote Elia Kazan's 1955 feature adaptation of John Steinbeck's 55-chapter novel *East of Eden*, "had tried six times without success to compress ... [it] into a two-hour film" (Massey 375). He eventually decided to eliminate roughly the first two-thirds of the novel. The film was more critically acclaimed than its source material (Railsback and Michael 94), despite extreme alterations. Lee, the Trask family's trustworthy, Chinese servant in the novel, may have been effaced because racism towards people from East Asia still existed, as Kazan's film was released within a decade after the end of WWII. This omission makes *East of Eden* go south somewhat since Lee is the character who makes some of the others realize that mankind has the freedom to choose good over evil. It is Lee who introduces the Hebrew word which means "thou mayest," *timshel*; the word is completely absent in Kazan's film. Even though Osborn removed all traces of Lee, Kazan's 117-minute film still stands on its own despite missing other characters and plot points that feature prominently in the novel. With its disturbing issues of crime and sexuality, John Steinbeck's novel *East of Eden* had to undergo transformation of both narrative and style in order to accommodate translation to director Elia Kazan's vision as a feature film and then to director Harvey Hart's conception as a soapy miniseries; both adaptations move between Dudley Andrew's three modes of adaptation—*borrowing, intersecting*, and *transforming*—and these adaptations also exemplify conventions, historical and cultural contexts, and limitations of their respective eras.

The literary limitations of soliloquies, memories, and stream of consciousness must be externalized for the two-dimensional media of film and television. For instance, Steinbeck chose to have Cathy/Kate think about her son Cal Trask's introduction of his twin, Aron, to her after the fact. Steinbeck places Aron's induction into the army between Cal's taking him to see "something interesting" and Kate's recollection of their surprise visit. Both Kazan and Harvey Hart in his 1981 miniseries dramatize the boys' visit, for it is the climax of the narrative.

Adaptation "involves complex transitions, both cultural and ideological, in response to changing modes of storytelling and adaptive intent" (Neipris 256). The process involves cutting entire scenes and characters without ruining the narrative. Andrew posits three modes of film adaptation. Through the most frequent mode, *borrowing*, "the artist employs, more or less extensively, the material, idea, or form of an earlier, generally successful text" (98). For example, Steinbeck borrows the story of Cain and Abel from the Old Testament. Secondly, *intersecting* preserves "the uniqueness of the original text ... to such an extent that it is intentionally left unassimilated in adaptation. The cinema, as a separate mechanism, records its confrontation with an ultimately intransigent text" (99). Thirdly, "*[t]ransforming* is adaptation that seeks to deploy the full power of cinematic techniques and material both to remain faithful to the original and at the same time to make a full transformation of it in the new medium" (Abbott 113).

Sometimes characters are not eliminated but instead merged, resulting in a *composite* character. Steinbeck has Deputy Horace Quinn question Adam Trask about how he was shot; Adam lies by claiming he accidentally shot himself. Then, the disbelieving deputy says to Julius Euskadi, a curious citizen, "I'm going to run to papa. I need the sheriff." Deputy Quinn deputizes Julius to ensure that Adam does not flee or try to hurt himself. The deputy reports to the Monterey County sheriff. The sheriff finds out that Adam's wife, Cathy, who shot him within two weeks after delivering their twins and then disappeared, now works for the madam Faye as a prostitute. After interrogating "Kate," the sheriff does not arrest her but warns her to keep pretending that she is somebody else and not hurt her husband or their two sons. He also orders Kate to dye her hair so that she will not be recognized. Richard Shapiro, the writer of the miniseries, not only eliminates

Julius but he makes Deputy Quinn and the sheriff one and the same: *Sheriff* Horace Quinn. On the other hand, Osborn assigns the composite character Sam, the Sheriff, some characteristics of both the philosophizing Lee and another character he eliminated—the Trask family's wise friend, Samuel Hamilton.

An instance of Andrew's concept of *borrowing* occurs when Sheriff Quinn does something that does not happen in the novel; in fact, Steinbeck never places the sheriff and the madam Faye in the same scene. The miniseries presents the viewer with a nostalgic visual: the sheriff tenderly touches Faye's face before departing after they briefly discuss the newly arrived Kate—the same way the departing Clark Gable, as Rhett Butler, tenderly touches the face of Ona Munson, who plays Belle Watling, the madam with a heart of gold, in *Gone with the Wind*.

The critical acceptance of any film or television production relies on a director's decision on visuals, be they nostalgic or innovative. Film and television both rely on editing, i.e. simultaneous action, which is difficult to replicate in media and in other art forms. Characters can be portrayed in a variety of situations, for example, those that involve crime and sex. Audiences come to know characters through what they say and what they do, while at the same time get to know them even better by what other characters say about them and what other characters do for or against them. Representing crime onscreen these days is not difficult, but making audiences aware of the motivations for the crime can sometimes be likened to an uphill battle. Steinbeck's character Cathy, later known as "Kate," is too bad to be true because "she is unmotivated: she does not know what she wants, the novelist does not know, and the reader can hardly find her relentless villainy plausible" (Schwartz 22). In Kazan's film, she is not actually evil but instead morally ambiguous because, due to the limitations of censorship, the viewer does not observe the sexual manipulation, the drug use, and the other awful things she does in the novel. However, there is nothing ambiguous about Harvey Hart's Cathy Ames. Hart introduces Cathy when she is a child; her mother discovers her engaging in sex-play with two boys in the barn. Mrs. Ames is on the verge of notifying the constable about "those two little criminals" having "forced" her daughter. "And I will see those two little criminals in the Massachusetts State Prison," she warns their fathers. The aim of Mrs. Ames is that the boys "must be made to pay .... To *pay* .... Bare!"

The viewer of the miniseries at first probably considers Cathy to just be sexually curious. However, in the three paragraphs immediately before Steinbeck introduces Cathy, he talks about humans who are physically monstrous as well as those who are mentally or psychically so. He elaborates on the "inner monster" who has no conscience. Steinbeck also speaks to Cathy's strange appeal in that "[e]ven as a child she had some quality that made people look at her, then look away, then look back at her, troubled at something foreign. Something looked out of her eyes, and was never there when one looked again" (72; ch. 8).

As Hart's Cathy smiles while her mother makes her watch the two boys being whipped by their fathers, the viewers for the first time hear Cathy's music box-chimed leitmotif, the children's ditty "Put Your Little Foot (Right There)." Whether intended to exemplify Andrew's concept of *borrowing* or not, what comes to mind for some viewers is the Academy Award-nominated performance of Patty McCormack, who, at age 10 in 1956, chilled audiences in the eponymous role of *The Bad Seed*; the leitmotif for McCormack's character is the traditional French children's song "Au Clair de la Lune."

Steinbeck seems to consider a tendency to commit sin as something inherent in a character. Ditsky asserts that sexuality in fiction is a warning to the reader and that Steinbeck thinks a person who can choose to be good or evil because he or she *may* (11). According to Shapiro, "Steinbeck didn't really address the sexuality ... that kind of sexual tension that goes on between men and women" (*Archive of American Television*). As far as the miniseries character of Cathy is concerned, the earliest correlation between sexuality and crime *per se* is pedophilia: fifteen-year-old Cathy's Latin teacher, Mr. Grew, has had sex with her. Hart cast a middle-aged actor, Nicholas Pryor, for the part of Mr. Grew, whom Steinbeck describes as "a pale intense young man" (78; ch. 8). Hart's casting decision here makes the crime of pedophilia even more disgusting. In the novel, when Cathy is 14, her sexually obsessed teacher kills himself. At 16, she runs away to Boston, her father brings her back, and he whips her. On the other hand, Hart's 15-year-old Cathy, referencing Lewis Carroll's *Alice in Wonderland*, tells Mr. Ames she can become so small that he will not be able to see her. She does not run away until *after* the death of her parents, *neither of whom has ever whipped her.* Cathy has removed them from her life by setting their house ablaze, faking her own death in the process. In the novel, Cathy commits a fourth crime by robbing her father of all his savings. As Steinbeck so succinctly puts it, "Cathy left a scent of sweetness behind her" (88; ch. 8).

To significantly contribute to the audience's perception of and emotional response to the introduction of Cathy and to her triad of crimes—arson, a double murder, and pseudocide—Hart demonstrates quite an artistic arsenal. He effec-

tively utilizes lens choices; camera angles and movement;
the match dissolve of Cathy that shows the transition of plot
points from her childhood to her adolescence; non-diegetic music, including the aforementioned leitmotif of Cathy;
and the *mise-en-scène* elements of set design, décor, lighting
setup, and prop selection (such as the ironic cross around
Cathy's neck at different times throughout the miniseries).
Hart makes a special effort to render superimposition. The
nearly still shots of each of Cathy's parents are blended with
their house fire to illustrate the immediate fate of this evil
character's first murder victims. Hart repeats this effective
editing technique: a shot of Cathy's cross in the palm of a
neighbor is overlapped with a shot of her smiling as she escapes on a train. These kinds of superimpositions are stylistically superior and contribute an uncomfortable degree of
coolness to the narrative. Furthermore, Cathy's girlish pink-
and white-colored costumes, modest makeup, and looped
braids help actress Jane Seymour portray the 15-year-old
villainess so effectively when she is actually twice Cathy's
age (Calio 109).

Writers appreciate that there are more expansive challenges
and possibilities for variations of extended character depth,
ongoing plotting, and other modes of creativity in long-form
series than in feature films (Mittell "Narrative Complexity"
30). An occurrence of Andrew's mode of *transforming* is ex-
emplified in the miniseries when the neighbors of the Ames',
outraged at their murders that evening, form a vigilante mob
and assault and disturb the peace of hobos at their riverside
camp. In a twist that is not part of the novel, Adam happens
to be one of the few hobos to escape and, demonstrative of
his strong moral character, he helps an old man flee the wrath
of the townspeople. The following morning, a conversation
between Adam and the old hobo inspires Adam to return

home. This dramatic license of Hart creates a better storyline because in the novel Adam returns home to Charles before the Ames family is even introduced.

Hart makes another *transforming* improvement on Steinbeck's work by establishing another effective connection between characters. The respected Bostonian businessman who is secretly a whoremaster, Mr. Edwards, takes his wife and their two young sons to the same revival that Charles and Adam have come to after the former is unable to cure his brother's "knocker fever" due to so many ladies of the evening in the area suddenly "getting religion." There, Edwards comes across two from his "stock," Jane and Molly; they also happen to be the particular prostitutes that the Trask brothers have come to town to hire. Edwards frog-marches the women away to a room at a nearby inn, where he commits assault and battery upon them (most of which appears offscreen) after they refuse to return to work. Edwards later commits assault and battery upon Cathy, who surprises him—as well as the viewer—by fighting back. Fascinated by both these despicable characters, the viewer does not know whom to root for but watches intently, caught up in the suspense.

Having emerged in the 1970s and being "[s]imilar to soap operas, miniseries were serial in form, and focused on intrapersonal and familial relationships, often presented as melodrama. However, while the soap opera continues to be denigrated as low culture, the miniseries, because of its historic content, was seen as upscale television" (Rymsza-Pawlowska 86). Rymsza-Pawlowska finds the miniseries to share historical gravitas with the novel, tracing major events in the lives of the main characters (85).

CULTURAL AND HISTORICAL CONTEXTS

Kazan's feature film adaptation of *East of Eden* as well as Harvey Hart's television miniseries adaptation are shaped by the historical and cultural contexts of, respectively, the first half of the 1950s and the early 1980s in America. Both eras share certain characteristics, including melodrama, one kind of which Frye describes as "comedy without humor" (167).

In the relationship between Cal and his father, Adam, there is much conflict. Cal hates that Adam favors his twin brother, Aron. In order to please his father after Adam's disastrous business venture of trying to transport ice-packed lettuce by train, Cal commits what seems to be a crime in Adam's eyes but really is not: war profiteering during WWI, as Cal has decided to buy beans from poor farmers in the Salinas Valley at a very low price and then resell the beans to the British. Adam's rejection of Cal's gift of thousands of dollars and his suggestion that Cal pay it back to the farmers he "robbed" leads Cal to commit another crime that really is not: he emotionally "kills" Aron by taking him to meet their notorious mother, Kate, whom Aron believes to be dead.

In the early 1980s, melodrama swept television in the form of "nighttime soaps." Regarding Hart's *East of Eden* miniseries, *Time* magazine reported, "While this eight-hour TV movie has clear cultural pretensions, it is really 99-and-44/100% pure soap" (Corliss 68). Hart's version bears "a form ... dominating the television ratings in series such as *Dallas, Dynasty,* and *Falcon's* [*sic, Falcon*] *Crest* .... [T]he longer format was more capable of realizing Steinbeck's epic sweep by including the first two-thirds of the plot excised in the earlier film" (Railsback and Michael, 94). Railsback and Michael also noted that the miniseries abandoned Steinbeck's development of archetypes for prurient pursuits. By the time *East of*

Eden aired, *Dynasty* had just been created by Richard Shapiro and his wife, Esther Shapiro. The storylines of episodes that were to air during that season were similar to those of *East of Eden*. The character Walter Lankershim, a feisty, hard worker, persuades the sensitive Steven Carrington to visit a bordello with him. The promiscuous Fallon Carrington marries the enamored Jeff Colby, but not out of love. Another bride, Krystle Carrington, does not get along with the servant Joseph Anders, and later she takes steps not to have children. Claudia Blaisdel, a mother and unfaithful wife, packs her things and runs away. Future seasons of *Dynasty* featured additional dark plot elements that no doubt brought *East of Eden* to viewers' minds: arson, battery, blackmail, murder, and suicide.

Most importantly, there is a single element of melodrama which is ubiquitous through all temporal and formal modes of melodramatic entertainment: the attachment genre, which runs the cinema's gamut from the various versions of the tearjerker chestnut *Madame X* to the heartwarming dramedy *Forrest Gump*, to the pornography-plotted *Boogie Nights*, and to the science-fiction classic *Star Wars*. Kate's reunion with her sons is typical of the attachment genre, according to Hogan's definition:

> The main story typically involves a lengthy separation caused by one of the parents or by some outside force. This is commonly followed by one party seeking the other and finding him or her after some errors or misrecognitions. The reunion, however, is often not fully successful and the parents and children may end up separated again. One main difference in subtypes concerns

> whether or not the parent abandoned the
> child and, if so, whether it was for selfish or
> selfless reasons. (234)

Almost everyone becomes separated from his or her parents,
and so the viewer can relate to the parent–child plot (Hogan 203). Hogan points out that the resolution often is tragic, and he also notes that the separation can last a long time
(200). Thus, when Kate asks Cal, "Who are you? What do
you want?" the viewer accepts that she has not seen him for
nearly two decades.

East of Eden has other significant cultural and historical
contexts. "Where Steinbeck's novel champions individual responsibility, Kazan's film attacks the hypocrisy of narrowly individualistic morality. While both the film and the
book celebrate the individual's freedom to choose good over
evil—leaving little to subtle suggestion—Kazan's film more
thoroughly expresses the moral temper of midcentury America" (Dill 167). Kazan's Cal rejects the authority of his father;
according to Springer, teenagers of the 1950s started to reject
parental authority (17).

During the midpoint of the Eisenhower Era, there existed an
antipathy for communism, almost as if it were a public health
problem. The Cold War had begun seven years before Kazan's *East of Eden* was filmed. Kazan "drew criticism for being
among the first Hollywood insiders to cooperate with the investigation held by the House Un-American Activities Com-
mittee during the Red Scare in 1952 .... [His] testimony cost
him dearly among Hollywood's elite" (Railsback and Michael 196). He and Osborn built up Steinbeck's minor, four-
page storyline about the German tailor, Mr. Fenchel, who
finds himself in financial arrears from purchasing too many
war bonds and whom the citizens of Salinas harass after the

United States and Germany become opposing forces during World War I. Steinbeck's depiction of anti-German hysteria seems engendered by World War II (Millichap 150). Kazan and Osborn turn Fenchel into "Mr. Albrecht," the Trasks' elderly shoe-repairman friend and neighbor, who experiences the crimes of vandalism and arson when "strong men—about thirty of them ... tore down Mr. Fenchel's white picket fence and burned the front of his house. No Kaiser-loving son of a bitch was going to get away with it with us" (Steinbeck 515–6; ch. 46). This German character is eliminated altogether in Harvey Hart's miniseries.

The 1950s were not only affected by the Red Scare; the decade also marked the beginning of the end of the Production Code Administration (PCA), "Hollywood's self-censorship agency, which was phased out in the 1960s and replaced by the current ratings system administered by the Motion Picture Association of America" (Schatz 47). The United States had endured the brutality and horror of WWII, coming through less innocent but more mature. Suddenly, the hand holding of the PCA and the church at the movie theater seemed less important.

CENSORSHIP

Between the performances of James Dean in the feature film and Sam Bottoms in the miniseries, the viewer observes the character of Cal Trask committing various crimes, including automobile theft, breaking curfew, destruction of property, illegal boarding of a train, illegally setting off a fire alarm, theft, trespassing, money burning, and voyeurism. He steals a coal chute and even something as simple as salt water taffy. Underage, Steinbeck's Cal never drinks alcohol until after he introduces Aron to their mother. On the other hand, Hart's

Cal drinks a little before that plot point, and Kazan's Cal hits the bottle throughout the film.

Cal also commits the crimes of destruction of property, disturbs the peace, and assault and battery. At one point, James Dean's character even admits to Abra, Aron's girlfriend, after he beats Aron up, "I was trying to help him .... Who am I kidding? I—I tried to kill him." Another of Cal Trask's crimes is stalking, and the object of his obsessive pursuit is his mysterious mother. Kazan's film opens as teenaged Cal, accompanied by foreboding, non-diegetic music, is following Kate while she goes to make her weekly bank deposit. Steinbeck explains that Cal has arranged his school schedule to be able to trail Kate on Monday afternoons.

Prostitution is the main correlation between crime and sexuality in the novel, the feature film, and the miniseries. However, prostitution is most implicit in Kazan's adaptation, during whose first 10 minutes it is established that Kate practices the world's oldest profession through camera shots and dialogue. The teller compliments a plumpish, African-American woman on making a "nice, fat deposit. You sure are in the right business, Sally." Then, he tells Kate, "Another nice deposit. You and Sally are sure in the right business." Behind a window, a couple of respectable-looking women whisper about Kate as she passes outside. When he is asked by her bouncer, Joe, why he has been following Kate around, Cal replies, "Any law against following around the t-town ... 'm-m-madam'—whatever you call her?" During preproduction, there were objections to James Dean's line because, according to Simmons, "'madam' was on the Code office list of forbidden words. However, Kazan was successful in justifying that, at that stage, it was not feasible for Shurlock to impose new limitations in order to strike that word.

Nineteen-fifties Hollywood had deemed the novel too difficult to adapt because Kate had to operate a brothel instead of just, for example, a saloon for it to emotionally kill her wholesome other son, Aron, and cause him to enlist in the army, which leads to another tragedy of his father's suffering a stroke and becoming incapacitated. However, according to Simmons, Kazan rose to the challenge and eventually worked around three options given to him by executives at the Breen Office, at the Production Code Administration, and at Warner Brothers. Kazan also refused to portray the suggestion of Kate being arrested along with Cal when he disturbs the peace at her establishment.

> Ultimately, a relatively simple compromise was arranged whereby the original whorehouse scenes were set in "Kate's Place," a rough saloon and gambling house that served as a front for Kate's more lucrative operations in another building down the street. Kazan would be allowed to show the exterior of her brothel, but all interior scenes were to be located in either the saloon or Kate's attached office and living quarters. In this way, the letter of the Code was observed but Kazan could clearly identify Kate's evil profession. (Simmons)

Thanks to some changes that Kazan made in the shooting script and that the PCA approved, viewers mistook the saloon that was among some other deteriorated places for a brothel anyhow. Perhaps, the Production Code's allowance of this slip contributed to its revision in 1956 to permit references to prostitution and drugs (Maltby 568), the latter of which are used in the novel by Kate, by other prostitutes, and by the bordello pianist, Cotton Eye.

Censorship probably did not come into play as much with Hart's television production, because the constraints of television had evolved over time. For example, during the 1970s, there was partial nudity in the landmark miniseries *Roots*, and the situation comedy *Maude* tackled abortion during a two-part episode that aired even before the *Roe v. Wade* decision (Sarafino par. 37). However, in one scene of Hart's miniseries, Jane Seymour, during her Golden Globe-winning performance as Cathy/Kate, "gives birth to unwanted twins with such savagery that her screams had to be toned down for the network censors" (Calio 109). Sometimes advertisers object to television material. Concerned about gratuitous sex, violence, and profanity, Procter & Gamble, then television's biggest sponsor, withdrew advertisements from more than fifty programs during the 1980–81 season, including *East of Eden* because they objected to the inclusion of the scene in which Cathy sleeps with her brother-in-law, Charles (Gitlin 258–259).

In 2014, it was announced that actress Jennifer Lawrence was going to star in not just one, but two movies adapted from Steinbeck's novel, with writer-director Gary Ross at the helm (Appelo par. 1). Lawrence had been nominated twice for an Academy Award, winning once, and was nominated for two other Oscars since then. Her 2018 film *Red Sparrow* marks the actress's first onscreen nudity (Fisher par. 2). Should these two productions of *East of Eden* come to fruition with Lawrence appearing as licentious Cathy/Kate, it will be interesting to see how the sexuality of the character is taken to another level.

CONCLUSION

Both Elia Kazan's and Harvey Hart's adaptations of John Steinbeck's crime- and sexuality-ridden *East of Eden* move between Dudley Andrew's three modes of adaptation—*borrowing, intersecting,* and *transforming.* Through omissions of characters and scenes; through the creation of composite characters; and through truncation, allusions, dramatic license, editing techniques, and *mise-en-scène* elements, Kazan and Hart render both conventions and creativity in their respective productions. Distinctions between these adaptations are apparent due to the cultural and historical influences of the periods during which they were produced: aspects of melodrama, societal issues, and the politics of the mid-1950s and the early 1980s. And finally, censorship affected the tale's evolution—from the Production Code Administration's reconsideration of both the word "madam" and its struggle with the onscreen depiction of a brothel in the mid-1950s, to the objection of sponsor Procter & Gamble to the portrayal of wedding-night adultery during the 1980–81 television season.

ACKNOWLEDGMENTS

The author expresses special thanks to Dr. Brian McAllister, Dr. Michael Porte, Cobi Wilfred Simpson Powell, Chris Hite, and Garrett J. Cummins for their invaluable feedback and constructive comments. Material from this study was presented at the Ohio Communication Association conference, Orrville, Ohio, in 2018.

WORKS CITED

Primary sources

East of Eden. Director Elia Kazan, performances by James Dean, Raymond Massey, and Jo Van Fleet. Warner Home Video, 1955.

East of Eden. Director Harvey Hart, performances by Timo-
thy Bottoms, Jane Seymour, and Bruce Boxleitner. Acorn
Media Group, 1981.

Steinbeck, John. *East of Eden*. Penguin Books, 2002.

Secondary sources

Abbott, H. Porter. *The Cambridge Introduction to Narrative*.
Cambridge UP, 2008.

Andrew, Dudley. *Concepts in Film Theory*. Oxford UP, 1984.

Appelo, Tim. "Jennifer Lawrence's 'East of Eden' May Be
Two Movies, Says Director." *Hollywood Reporter*, 12
Apr. 2014, https://www.hollywoodreporter.com/news/
jennifer-lawrences-east-eden-may-695666. Accessed 24
Apr. 2018.

The Bad Seed. Directed by Mervyn LeRoy, performances by
Nancy Kelly, Patty McCormack, and Henry Jones. Warner Home Video. 1956.

Calio, Jim. "Jane Seymour Finds Her Big Breakthrough West
of the Atlantic in TV's *East of Eden*." *People*, 16 Feb. 1981,
pp. 108-09 .

Corliss, Richard. "Season of the Nightsoaps: Beyond *Dallas*: Sexy New Series Populate Prime Time." *Time*, 9 Feb.
1981, pp. 68-69.

Dill, Scott. "An Image of Social Character: Elia Kazan's *East
of Eden*." *East of Eden: New and Recent Essays*, edited by
Michael J. Meyer and Rodopi, Henry Veggian, , 2013, pp.
167-81.

Ditsky, John. *Essays on East of Eden*. John Steinbeck Society
of America/Ball State University, 1977.

Fisher, Luchina. "Jennifer Lawrence on Going Nude for the First Time in 'Red Sparrow': 'I Got Something Back that Was Taken from Me.'" *ABC News.* 27 Feb. 2018, http://abcnews.go.com/GMA/Culture/jennifer-lawrence-nude-role-time-red-sparrow/story?id=53387955. Accessed 25 Apr. 2018.

Frye, Northrop. *Anatomy of Criticism: Four Essays.* Princeton UP, 1957.

Gitlin, Todd. *Inside Prime Time.* Pantheon Books, 1983.

Gone with the Wind. Directed by Victor Fleming, performances by Clark Gable, Vivien Leigh, and Ona Munson. Warner Home Video, 1939.

Hogan, Patrick Colm. *Affective Narratology: The Emotional Structure of Stories.* U of Nebraska P, 2011. Massey, Raymond. *A Hundred Different Lives.* Little, Brown and Company, 1979.

Maltby, Richard. *Hollywood Cinema.* 2nd ed., Blackwell Publishing, 2003.

Millichap, Joseph R. *Steinbeck and Film.* Frederick Ungar Publishing Co., 1983.

Mittell, Jason. "Narrative Complexity in Contemporary American Television." *Velvet Light Trap,* no. 58, Fall 2006, pp. 29-40 .

Neipris, Janet. *A Masterclass in Dramatic Writing: Theater, Film, and Television.* 2nd ed., Routledge, 2017.

Railsback, Brian and J. Michael *A John Steinbeck Encyclopedia.* Greenwood P, 2006.

Richard Shapiro: Show Creator/Producer/Writer—Interview, Part 3. *Archive of American Television*, http://emmytvlegends.org/interviews/people/richard-shapiro#. Accessed 22 Mar. 2018.

Rymsza-Pawlowska, Malgorzata J. "Broadcasting the Past: History Television, 'Nostalgia Culture,' and the Emergence of the Miniseries in the 1970s United States." *Journal of Popular Film and Television*, vol. 42, no. 2, Jun. 2014, pp. 81-90.

Sarafino, Jason. "The 15 Most Controversial TV Show Episodes of All Time." Complex, 17 Sept. 2013, http://www.complex.com/pop-culture/2013/09/most-controversial-tv-show-episodes/. Accessed 24 Apr. 2018.

Schatz, Thomas. "Film Industry Studies and Hollywood History." *Media Industries: History, Theory, and Method*, edited by Jennifer Holt and Perren Alisa, Wiley-Blackwell, 2009, pp. 45-56.

Schwartz, Delmore. "Films." Review of *East of Eden*, directed by Elia Kazan. *New Republic*, 24 Apr. 1955, p. 22.

Simmons, Jerold L. "The Production Code & Precedent: How Hollywood's Censors Sought to Eliminate Brothels & Prostitution in *From Here to Eternity* & *East of Eden*." *Journal of Popular Film and Television*, vol. 20, no. 3, Fall 1992, pp. 70-80.

Springer, Claudia. *James Dean Transfigured*. U of Texas P, 2007.

The Perils of Algorithmic Hiring and Title VII

by Brian Mosich

ABSTRACT

Algorithmic hiring works at all levels of employment, from entry level to CEO. When applicants submit a resume, an algorithm will mine all available data about them and then compare it to information provided by the company's top performs to determine whether to offer an interview. Where one lives, what type of websites one visits, and whether one has been purchasing unscented lotion could have more of an impact than where one went to school or one's work history. Using algorithmic hiring provides a way for companies to inadvertently exclude applicants based on protected Title VII classes. This paper discusses how the protections offered by Title VII as written are unprepared for the realities of Big Data, and how these protections may be completely circumvented if the EEOC does not act soon.

Keywords: Title VII, Algorithmic Hiring, Big Data

Los peligros de la contratación algorítmica y el Título VII

RESUMEN

La contratación algorítmica funciona en todos los niveles laborales, desde el nivel de entrada hasta el CEO. Cuando los solicitantes entregan un CV, un algoritmo minará todos los datos disponibles acerca de ellos, y después los comparará a la información proporcionada de los trabajadores de más alto rendimiento en la empresa para determinar si se ofrece una entrevista. Dónde vive, qué tipo de páginas web visita y si ha comprado crema sin aroma podrían tener más impacto que el haber asistido a una universidad específica o la historia laboral. El utilizar la contratación algorítmica les proporciona a las empresas una manera de excluir inconscientemente solicitantes basándose en clases protegidas por el Título VII. Este documento analiza cómo las protecciones ofrecidas por el Título VII tal como están escritas no están preparadas para las realidades de Big Data, y cómo estas protecciones pueden ser completamente eludidas si la EEOC no actúa pronto.

Palabras clave: Título VII, contratación algorítmica, Big Data

算法招聘和《民权法案》第七条的风险

摘要

基于算法的招聘模式存在于所有招聘等级（从最基本的员工到CEO）。当应聘者提交简历后，一项算法便会提取一切可用数据，之后将其与公司最佳表现所提供的信息进行比较，进而确定是否安排面试。一个人所居住的地方、所浏览的网站类型、是否已购买过无味护肤乳，这些都可能比其所就读过的学校或工作经历更具影响力。通过使用算法招聘，能让公司在无意间将基于受《民权法案》第七条保护的阶层人群排除在应聘者之外。本文探讨了由《民权法案》第七条所提供的保护如何在大数据这一现实前一筹莫展，以及这些保护措施如何能被完全规避——如果公平就业机会委员会不迅速采取手段。

关键词：《民权法案》第七条；算法招聘；大数据

INTRODUCTION

Without Swift Action from the EEOC, Algorithmic Hiring is Poised to Undermine 50 Years of Title VII Protections

In the first episode of the series Futurama, Phillip J. Fry awakens in the future. After being subjected to a series of tests, a computer mechanically displays his permanent career assignment of delivery boy. This humorous moment may also prove to have been very prophetic in how technology may impact our daily lives. Hiring quality new employees is historically one of the most difficult problems in maintaining a business. Even if an employer only spends a couple seconds reviewing each resume, the labor quickly adds up. Employers do not want to spend months training new employees only for them to take positions with other companies. Often applicants look perfect on paper, but are not a great fit for the employer's corporate culture. Modern technology has created a solution with algorithmic hiring. Harvest data from your top performing employees, and use it to hire more people like them.

Title VII of the Civil Rights Act of 1964 makes it an unlawful employment practice for an employer to fail or refuse to hire because of such individual's race, color, religion, sex, or national origin.[1] These legal protections are grounded in a foundation of if an employer is going to exclude an applicant due to one of these criteria, it must show it is due to a business necessity.[2] Aside from these codified categories, the layman might assume everything else is fair game. That everything else is where the dangers of algorithmic hiring begin to grow. Can an employer use distance from the workplace to disqualify workers?[3] How about favoring applicants who visit websites that provide Japanese Manga?[4] Facially these qualities may seem safe. The Supreme Court has held that not only is overt discrimination proscribed by the Civil Rights Act of 1964, but practices that are fair in form but discriminatory in operation[5] are also proscribed by statute. The problem is algorithmic hiring practices demonstratively work, and if a practice produces proven business results, it may be impossible for a court challenge against it to succeed.

Algorithmic hiring starts when an employer decides to collect information from their most successful employees and use that to find similar applicants. However, if they failed to select a diverse pool of employees to emulate, employers run the very real risk of opening their business to a disparate impact claim.[6] Vague qualities can open a business to a potential lawsuit. For instance, employers may fear local traffic conditions may frequently cause employees to be late for work, and respond by excluding applicants who live more than a certain distance from the workplace.[7] In one case, this variable was responsible for the removal of almost all African-American applicants. The African-American applicants lived in a nearby suburb and were completely excluded from the final applicant pool. This problem was only noticed when the algorithm programmers themselves were testing to data to find out how the final results were created. This one variable alone completely culled African Americans from the applicant pool. Had an applicant had access to this data, whether or not a potential employer would be liable for failing to notice would ultimately depend on the courts.[8]

When a hiring algorithm can take into account hundreds if not thousands of seemingly unrelated variables, the employer or employment bears the ultimate responsibility for ensuring a nondiscriminatory outcome. If an unscrupulous employer is actively seeking a discriminatory outcome, it can easily can they hide behind these same variables. The benefits of hiring algorithms can be massive, both in reducing hiring costs and minimizing turnover costs. Algorithmic hiring programs offer targeted searches, but do not make employees aware of the perils in relying on time-saving methods. However, a potential employer may be left with questions about real-world long-term legal risks, and companies who offer these services are quick to dismiss the legal liability.

Currently, algorithmic hiring remains a legal grey area. It can be impossible for a potential employee to know why their resume was excluded from an interview. Even if they can determine they were excluded due to algorithmic hiring, and had access to the exact algorithm, the legal requirements necessary to win such a case would be almost impossible. Victims of discrimination simply do not have access to know if their resume was excluded by a live person, or by a computer. Even if it was excluded by a computer, there is often no means short of a lawsuit to force companies to reveal the criteria used. Worse even with the data, and the criteria used, the data analysis necessary to prove discriminatory hiring practices is often out of reach.

Ultimately, the Equal Employment Opportunity Commission (EEOC) should be our best resource by giving guidance to employers on how to properly utilize these tools, as well as the best source of hope for victims of discrimination due to systematic disparate impact caused by improperly designed and tested algorithms. By forcing companies who provide or use algorithmic hiring to publicly disclose their criteria and perform rigorous checks on how each data point impacts the makeup of the applicant pool, they may be able to ensure the decades of progress made possible by Title VII of the Civil Rights Act of 1964 are not lost.

HISTORY OF THE PROBLEM

"Knowledge is power," wrote Sir Francis Bacon.[9] It was true in 1597, and it is true now.

In 2013, it was estimated that worldwide we had produced over 4 zettabytes of data.[10] A zettabyte is the equivalent of a trillion gigabytes. This is expected to rise to over 44 zettabytes by the year 2020.[11] People produce a large amount of information every day. From snapping photos on their phones to something sending Tweets or browsing the Internet, little pieces of information add up to create a large amount of information about individuals. Internet marketers have been tapping into this for years. When a person searches for a product on Amazon, they'll later see advertisements for that product show up on other websites they visit.[12] A person's shopping preferences and browsing habits are remembered, and used to directly market to them electronically. These criteria are also available for harvesting and use by companies offering algorithmic hiring services.

The digital age and the breadth of information it has made available are both creating new problems and eroding the protections enacted to combat old problems. Former President Obama requested a study on how "Big Data" will transform the lives of Americans.[13] Exploring the dangers and the impacts in the public sector, this study represented President Obama's forward-thinking nature in understanding a problem that would transcend his presidency. Key areas under government control, such as healthcare, education, homeland security, law enforcement, and privacy law,[14] are all expected to undergo rapid changes due to these tools in the coming years. In the private sector, the benefits and risks of Big Data warned about in the study are quickly coming to pass. The complete secrecy that algorithms operate under has left almost no meaningful ways to identify harm, or allow for way to hold a discriminating decision maker responsible.[15] Moreover, individuals impacted by algorithms are unable to understand, or contest either the information that has been gathered, or what the algorithm suggests about the potential applicant.[16]

One of the key limiting factors to sorting information had been computational power. Data scientists would need a large amount of data and were limited to very specific questions. Now, however, computational capabilities have expanded to the point where "finding a needle in a haystack" is not only possible, but practical.[17] Now that computational power is no longer an issue, the value of large data pools is becoming more prevalent. A researcher at the Broad Institute discovered that a genetic variant linked to schizophrenia was invisible when analyzing 3,500 cases, weakly identifiable when using 10,000 cases, but statistically significant with 35,000 cases.[18]

This information explosion is quickly reinventing a large number of industries, especially in employment. Kelly Trindel, Chief Analyst for the Office of Research, Information and Planning at the EEOC, cautioned big data in regard to employment has different meanings to different people, noting that big data are more than simply very large data sets with a significant amount of rows and columns.[19] The size of the datasets is not what defines big data, but the nature, source, how it is collected, merged, transformed, and utilized. In her testimony, Ms. Trindel suggested that "[i]n the employment context, I would define big data as follows: big data is the combination of nontraditional and traditional employment data with technology-enabled analytics to create processes for identifying, recruiting, segmenting and scoring job candidates and employees."[20]

Employers have long been used to using traditional employee data to make hiring decisions. Applications and resumes that lead to interviews can only tell an employer so much about a potentially employee. Employers browsing candidate's social media has been an accepted reality, and now the further rise of nontraditional employee data is raising concerns. Nontraditional employment data are a collection of information "maintained by the employer, public records, social media activity logs, sensors, geographic systems, internet browsing history, consumer data-tracking systems, mobile devices, and communications metadata systems."[21] Other sources of data, such as combinations of words on resumes, personality test results, facial recognition software, and individual performance ratings on tests can also be considered.[22] Companies may also choose to include "internal company information such as frequency of meetings, locations of meetings, recipients and content of employee emails, and records of employee participation in wellness programs."[23]

This list of data sources continues to expand with information such as a person's face and voice being reduced to a string of code.[24] All of this information is gathered, quantified, and combined with other sources for use by employers. Potential employers may gather the data themselves or purchase it from information brokers. From there, the data can be used to uncover underlying patterns for use in predicting outcomes for similarly profiled groups of employees or applicants.[25]

Facial recognition and voice analysis data are likely to prove especially problematic because it may allow companies to potentially sidestep Title VII racial protections by favoring datasets that match certain ethnicities and exclude others. Distilling down a person's facial features into data points would allow for potential comparison to an "ideal." A potential employer could ask an algorithm to produce candidates with facial features indicating only those of Asian-American descent, with a voice or speech pattern. These data points would be innocuous amongst a large number of other criteria. Similarly, facial features could also be used to potentially spot genetic disorders in potential applicants and exclude them.[26] While this possibility may potentially run directly into the protections offered under the Genetic Information Nondiscrimination Act into Title VII, no courts have yet faced this issue.[27] While the true extent of the possibilities in terms of facial recognition programs on hiring have yet to fully be explored, it is data in use today and the dangers are real.[28]

Employers collect applicant data and compare it against data gathered from existing or former employees looking for factors that emerge as strong predictors of future success. One algorithm might have over 100,000 individual possible data points that are potentially scorable.[29] However, for many candidates, there will be missing data. An algorithm may score results for each candidate based on only 500 data points; however, those data points may not be the same from candidate to candidate.[30] Once the traditional and nontraditional data are combined, employers can begin to screen passive or active job applicants, or even target how employee training resources are allocated. Once employers develop a profile of an ideal candidate, they can begin to search for either current or potential applicants who will fit into that mold such as the prior example of one company favoring applicants for a programming position who visited websites that provide Japanese Manga.[31] This also allows employers to exclude applicants due to potential for absenteeism, safety incidents, or probability of turnover.[32] Applicants may be excluded not because they might actually have a high rate of absenteeism, but because they fit the company's profile of someone who might. As an example, the distance an applicant lives from the workplace has been used to disqualify applicants.[33] Losing out on an employment opportunity because a person's social media posts included a large number of posts about caring for sick relatives during work days is becoming a reality.

The initial push for use of big data analytics in employment has been spearheaded largely by departments comfortable with work with data analysis such as marketing and operations.[34] Marketing departments have long been familiar with segmenting the population and identifying groups of people for targeted advertisements. An employer wants to know its target audience and find effective ways of reaching them.[35] The most famous example is Target's "Pregnancy Prediction Score," which Target used to predict if a customer was pregnant, and successfully estimate the due date within a small window.[36] This allowed Target to send coupons to customers at specific stages of pregnancy using nothing more than the shopping habits for items like lotion and cotton balls.[37] Applied to a potential applicant pool, these same innocuous criteria, easily buried in the noise of 100,000 or more possible factors, could be used to completely exclude potentially pregnant women from consideration were a company worried about an applicant taking maternity leave shortly after being hired. In terms of bringing a claim, it would be difficult for an applicant to prove they were discriminated against based on pregnancy at the time the applied, especially if they did not themselves even know they were pregnant at time of application.

Employers will want to use this algorithm power to improve their resources in regards to hiring, retention, and promotion. However, employers must be mindful not to discriminate against employees, or potentially employees based on protected characteristics. Discrimination based on race, color, religion, sex, national origin,[38] disability,[39] genetic information,[40] or pregnancy[41] is forbidden by law. How each criteria applied by the algorithm affects each of these protected classes cannot be ignored, and those coming from a marketing background may not understand the legal ramifications for certain criteria. Imagine a potential employer is heading into a very busy year and does not want to risk losing any of its new hires to maternity leave. Adding a variable to exclude any applicants who have used pregnancy in their social media posts, or who have searched for fertility treatments, could quickly lead to a Title VII violation if discovered. What if the criteria, similar to those used in the Target Pregnancy Prediction Score, were used to exclude applicants? Employees could be excluded from consideration due to pregnancy who either had no idea they were pregnant, or had no intention of becoming pregnant but had preferences that corresponding to the algorithms expectations.

People living with disabilities are especially at risk. Many innocuous behaviors can show a correlation with mental illness. For instance, academic research has shown that certain patterns of usage of social media platforms can be related to mood disorders.[42] In 2014, The Samaritans, a British Suicide-Prevention group, developed an application that would notify users when someone they followed on Twitter posted certain phrases that indicated they might be at risk of killing themselves.[43] While the application was later disabled over privacy and stalking concerns, it highlighted the ability for a potentially employer to review a person's entire social media history and develop a profile of an employee's potential mental illness. If a machine can determine, or think it can determine if certain social media posting patterns correlate with heightened absenteeism or desire to change jobs,[44] an employee could experience a loss of promotion or preemptive disciplinary behavior without any understanding of why. For existing employees, the EEOC has offered guidance on

Employer Wellness Programs,[45] but these same criteria could be applied against potential applicants.

In her testimony, Kelly Trindel addressed these risks. She noted: "As an example of the type of EEO problems that could arise with the use of these algorithms, imagine that a Silicon Valley tech company wished to utilize an algorithm to assist in hiring new employees who 'fit the culture' of the firm. The culture of the organization is likely to be defined based on the behavior of the employees that already work there, and the reactions and responses of their supervisors and managers. If the organization is staffed primarily by young, single, white or Asian-American male employees, then a particular type of profile, friendly to that demographic, will emerge as 'successful.' Perhaps the successful culture-fit profile is one of a person who is willing to stay at the job very late at night, maybe all night, to complete the task at hand. Perhaps this profile is one of a person that finds certain perks in the workplace, such as free dry cleaning, snacks, and a happy hour on Fridays preferable to others like increased child-care, medical and life insurance benefits. Finally, perhaps the successful profile is one of a person who does not own a home or a car and rather appears to bike or walk to work. If the decision-makers at this hypothetical firm look to these and other similar results to assist in the recruiting of passive candidates, or to develop a type of screen, giving preference to those future job-seekers who appear to 'fit the culture,' the employer is likely to screen out candidates of other races, women, and older workers. In this situation, not only would the algorithm cause adverse impact, but it would likely limit the growth of the firm."[46]

Ultimately, the relationships among the variables are exclusively correlational in nature. There is no certainty that an individual employee's distance from work will increase their absenteeism, or that a love of Manga will make an employee a better coder.[47] There is no guarantee that the ideal employee is not amongst the large percentage of resumes discarded by the system. Algorithms are, at their basic level, opinions, biases, and prejudices embedded in code.[48] While they can mimic human decision making if the decision making criteria are fundamentally flaws, those flaws will be present in the final output. The old programmer truism remains as true today as ever. Computers make very fast, very accurate mistakes.

While algorithmic hiring can be a powerful tool for employers, it contains the very real risks of inadvertently or intentionally discriminating against those protected by Title VII. Data analysis can also reveal existing bias inside the company's hiring practices. Companies have used machine learning and language analysis to analyze job postings. In doing so, have identified phrases that indicate existing gender bias.[49] Language-like "'top-tier,' 'aggressive,' and sports or military analogies like 'mission critical' decrease the proportion of women who apply for a job. Language-like 'partnerships' and 'passion for learning' attract more women."[50]

By hiring employees with similar qualities and skillsets to existing employees, employers enjoy a better chance of hiring the right person for the role. On the surface, algorithmic hiring can assist companies with translating stacks of resumes into hiring qualified applicants. This can significantly reduce both the time and costs of identifying which employees to hire. A poor hiring decision can result in the sunk costs of hiring and training an employee who may later be fired due to being unable to perform their duties. Companies that have used algorithmic hiring have reported positive results such as a 38 percent reduction in employee turnover.[51]

Studies have shown that a properly designed analysis of potential employee metadata outperforms human decisions by at least 25%.[52] This effect holds with any situation provided a large number of candidates and across all levels of hiring, including front line, middle management, and upper management.[53]

Unfortunately, there are some downsides to algorithmic hiring practices that carry serious legal complications. In order to create the hiring algorithms, companies rely on their existing worker pool as well as qualities of the 'ideal worker' provided by management.[54] If an employer's worker pool has already been tainted by previously discriminatory hiring practices, they are likely to inadvertently continue to engage in discriminatory hiring practices.[55] A workplace composed of a significant number of a single sex, or a significant number of a single race, may skew their results toward those groups.[56] Algorithms may end up targeting minorities due to facially neutral parameters that can lead to disparate impacts. These disparate impacts may take significant time to be revealed, meaning that either accidental or intentional racism in the programming can have wide ranging and far reaching consequences.

Reputable companies that provide the services of designing the algorithms for algorithmic hiring are aware of the potential legal consequences of violating the law and do take steps to locate and correct any unintentional side effects of their data points. If a particular variable is found to be excluding an abnormally large amount of a single group, it can be refined or discarded. However, even the most innocuous of variables can end up having a disparate impact. For instance, one company noticed that by excluding potentially employees who lived more than a certain distance from the workplace resulted in the loss of a disproportionate amount of African-American candidates. This leads the company to discover that most of the African-American candidates lived in the outlying suburbs of the area. By trying to exclude employees most likely to be late, or miss work due to traffic or transportation problems, this variable had, in effect, excluded a large amount of African-American applicants.

Algorithmic hiring practices, while continuing to prove their time and cost savings to human resource managers across the country, carry with them an ever increasing legal risk. In the past, the benefits of "Big Data" have proved invaluable, but potential legal challenges and regulatory changes may be forthcoming. As technology advances, the disparate impact of current algorithmic hiring based on the past discriminatory hiring practices is going to be easier to prove at times when companies may be under greater scrutiny from the EEOC. The real-world risk of disparate impact have been called into scrutiny by the Equal Employment Opportunity Commission (EEOC) and, in a recent open meeting, were discussed at length. Finally, the EEOC stands ready to step into the issue. On October 13, the EEOC held a meeting titled "Big Data in the Workplace: Examining Implications for Equal Employment Opportunity Law." The insights from the speakers, experts in their field, as they present their view on this topic to the EEOC allows us a glimpse of the direct information presented to the Commission. The EEOC's examination of the problems of algorithmic hiring indicates that guidance on these issues might be coming.

If a disparate impact claim based around algorithmic hiring to reach the Supreme Court, it is difficult to predict how such a claim would be resolved. Traditionally, the Court has offered "Chevron Deference" to the interpretations of regulatory agencies. In terms of judicial review, if Congress has not directly addressed the precise question at issue, the court will consider the issue only if the agency's answer is based on a permissible construction of the statute.[57] Chevron deference has been a powerful tool of regulatory agencies, as it has allowed for the enforcement of the spirit of the law in the face of emerging technological and social changes. However, Chevron is not above criticism, and current Supreme Court Justice Neil Gorsuch has expressed serious doubts about the legality of the legislative branch's power to delegate power to the executive branch.[58] In terms of the disparate impact of algorithmic hiring, whether the final answer on how to handle these cases comes from the EEOC or the Courts, it is an issue that will someday have to be addressed.

Unfortunately, the EEOC guidelines on hiring practices can be rather nebulous in terms of algorithmic hiring. Hiring procedures that have an adverse impact constitute discrimination unless they are justified.[59] However, when two or more selection procedures are available that serve the user's legitimate interest, and are substantially equally valid for a given purpose, the user should use the procedure demonstrated to have a lesser adverse impact.[60] In terms of algorithmic hiring practices, a company could run millions of permutations on the data leading very different results in whom to interview. The algorithms are also constantly evolving, and at each stage could prove to be more or less discriminatory to some combination of protected applicants.

The EEOC does mandate that records be kept, especially in regard to potentially impact. Employers should maintain and have available for inspection records or other information which will disclose the impact tests, and other selection procedures have upon employment opportunities by race, sex, or ethnic groups.[61] However, in terms of algorithmic hiring, there are very likely to be a large number of applicants, and the procedures are likely to be administered frequently.[62] Running hundreds or thousands of permutations on data based on various variables in an attempt to cull an employer's applicant pool to a manageable number means that an employer would only need to retain such information on a sample basis.[63] An employer would not need to maintain the exact algorithm, or the exact dataset used for comparison. This would further limit discovery options, as a plaintiff may have no means of examining the exact qualifications used to disqualify them from employment.

Employers should be running tests on the results to ensure the selection methods themselves are not producing a disparate impact and performing other validation studies.[64] Even if the selection criteria does produce a disparate impact on an individual, the EEOC views this information as showing that "the total selection process does not have an adverse impact, the Federal enforcement agencies, in the exercise of their administrative and prosecutorial discretion, in usual circumstances, will not expect a user to evaluate the individual components for adverse impact, or to validate such individual components, and will not take enforcement action based upon adverse impact of any component of that process, including the separate parts of a multipart selection procedure or any separate procedure that is used as an alternative method of selection."[65] Effectively negating the holding in Teal that rejected a "bottom line" defense and disregarding the Title VII protections are supposed to allow the individual to compete.[66]

Validating algorithmic hiring practices using validity studies will prove deeply problematic. Validity studies should be based on review of information about the job.[67] The study must be technically feasible,[68] which, with the modern computer power-backing algorithmic hiring, a large number of test become feasible. However, the criteria used should be relevant to the job, or group of jobs in question.[69] They must represent critical or important job duties and work behaviors developed from a review of job information.[70] Bias must also be considered in all areas of criteria selection, application, and subjective evaluation.[71] For companies used to working with marketing data, the legal requirements for using similar tools for employment contexts can be full of potential pitfalls. Attempting to ensure the testing procedure is in full compliance with the requirements of all technical standards for validity studies[72] is daunting. Even if fully successful a selection procedure, even if fully validated against job performance, cannot be imposed upon members of a race, sex, or ethnic group where other applicants have not been subjected to that standard or one that denies the same employment, promotion, membership, or other employment opportunities as have been available to other employees or applicants.[73]

Distilled down to its essence, algorithmic hiring problems are very similar to the issues the Supreme Court faced in Griggs versus Duke Power Co. In Griggs, African-American workers fought against the discriminatory effect of requiring a high school education, as well as satisfactory scores on two professionally prepared aptitude tests. Existing employees could seek promotion into certain departments only after passing these aptitude tests. In the opinion, Chief Justice Burger famously said "The objective of Congress in the enactment of Title VII is plain from the language of the statute. It was to achieve equality of employment opportunities and remove barriers that have operated in the past to favor an identifiable group of white employees over other employees. Under the

Act, practices, procedures, or tests neutral on their face, and even neutral in terms of intent, cannot be maintained if they operate to 'freeze' the status quo of prior discriminatory employment practices." Despite this ruling, the reality is modern algorithms that are designed around data points cultivated by existing star employees do freeze the status quo, while simultaneously making legal challenges to their use almost impossible for a potential employee to successfully challenge.

CONCLUSION

Addressing the legal concerns of algorithmic hiring practices in terms of disparate impacts can theoretically come from several sources. It is possible for the legislature to pass law offering individuals more protections in the modern digital world. However, a bill was recently passed in the Senate allowing Internet Service Providers to sell browsing data, indicating in the short term it is unlikely much help will be forthcoming from the legislature. As expected, the President signed this bill, indicating, in terms of digital privacy and information misuse, the new administration is unlikely to offer the same protections and priorities as the prior administration.

In 2016, the UN passed a nonbinding resolution that internet access is a basic human right. President Obama attempted to increase available of internet access to the poor, minorities, and rural areas. Sadly, the FCC disagreed in 2015, arguing that Internet access is not a basic human right. This makes all uses of the internet subject to the whims of the Internet Service Providers, and the private companies managing the websites themselves. How this information is ultimately collected and used is going to be a complicated battle in the years to come.

Employers are already mining all public information about potential applicants. While the EEOC has held a meeting in 2014 to discuss future guidance,[74] checking an applicant's social media continues to be acceptable practice. Traditionally, a potential employer just usually has a live person review the material. All public information being downloaded into companies' robust algorithmic hiring divisions servers and resold to other employment agencies looking to perform searches. Algorithms are complicated beasts manufactured out of hopes, dreams, and past results. They are as unreliable as economic models, throwing correlations at the wall to see what sticks. They work, so employers are going to use them. Google already has the capability to sell all of an individual's search information. Amazon and other sites use an individual's searching data to feed customer ads. Facial recognition systems and voice analysis can already turn a person's look and sound into datapoints to be fed into a system. A phone using Google MAP data is already tracking its location, making a person's driving habits potentially public information.

The best source of change is going to be the EEOC itself. While the EEOC was looking into the issue as of October of 2016, it remains to be seen if the priorities of this regulatory agency survive the change in administration. Under the new administration, regulations promulgated requiring more transparency in employer hiring practices that allow for disparate impact lawsuits will probably be rolled back. The EEOC would need to promulgate new guidelines forcing employers and employment agencies to ensure transparency with their algorithms. Even with completely transparency, there is little use in finding out a potential employee lost a job because they did not read certain websites, or eat at certain restaurants.

The EEOC needs to act, and quickly, to establish clear rules on how algorithmic hiring can and cannot be used to comply with Title VII. A hands-off or half-hearted approach could serve only to eviscerate the 50 years of progress. Employers and employment agencies need to be required to run, document, and maintain data analysis at every stage of the algorithmic hiring process. Variables that are found to exclude a large number of a protected class must be documented and either discarded, or individually justified as directly related to performance of the job. Attempts to conceal the true impact of certain variables should be harshly discouraged. The onus is already on both employers and employment agencies to comply with Title VII, guidance that codifies how that is to be properly done in the age of big data is vital, with delays only making the problem worse. Requiring companies to maintain specific data sets and document how their algorithms impacted the applicant pool in terms of protected classes will be vital in allowing companies to identify disparate impacts before the hiring process proceeds, and allow potential plaintiffs the evidence they need to bring forth lawsuits if companies fail to act upon this data.

NOTES

1   42 U.S.C. § 2000e-2 (2012).

2   *El v. Se. Pennsylvania Transp. Auth.* (SEPTA), 479 F.3d 232, 245 (3d Cir. 2007).

3   *Written Testimony of Kelly Trindel, PhD, Chief Analyst Office of Research, Information and Planning, EEOC,* Equal Employment Opportunity Commission (13 Oct. 2016), https://www.eeoc.gov/eeoc/meetings/10-13-16/trindel.cfm.

4 Don Peck, *They're Watching You at Work*, ATLANTIC (Dec. 2013), http://www.theatlantic.com/magazine/archive/2013/12/theyre-watching-you-at-work/354681/.

5 *Griggs v. Duke Power Co.*, 91 S. Ct. 849, 853 (U.S. 1971).

6 42 U.S.C. *Supra* note 1.

7 Trindel, *Supra* note 3.

8 42 U.S.C. *Supra* note 1.

9 Sir Francis Bacon, *Meditationes Sacrae and Human Philosophy.* 1597.

10 Mary Meeker and Liang Yu, *Internet Trends*, Kleiner Perkins Caulfield Byers (29 May 2013), http://www.slideshare.net/kleinerperkins/kpcb-internet-trends-2013/.

11 Mikal Khoso, *How Much Data Is Produced Every Day?* (13 May 2016), http://www.northeastern.edu/levelblog/2016/05/13/how-much-data-produced-every-day/.

12 Drew Barton, *How Do Some Banner Ads Follow Me from Site to Site* (29 Mar. 2013), https://southernweb.com/2013/03/how-do-some-banner-ads-follow-me/.

13 *Executive Office of The President, Big Data: Seizing Opportunities, Preserving Values* (May 2014), https://obamawhitehouse.archives.gov/sites/default/files/docs/big_data_privacy_report_may_1_2014.pdf [hereinafter *Executive Office*].

14 *Executive Office, Supra* note 13, at 22–32.

15 *Executive Office, Supra* note 13, at 46.

16 GAO, *Information Resellers: Consumer Privacy Framework Needs to Reflect Changes in Technology and the Marketplace*, GAO-13-663, 2013, http://www.gao.gov/assets/660/658151.pdf.

17 *Executive Office, Supra* note 13, at 6.

18 Manolis Kellis, *Importance of Access to Large Populations, Big Data Privacy Workshop: Advancing the State of the Art in Technology and Practice,* Cambridge, 3 Mar. 2014, http://web.mit.edu/bigdatapriv/ppt/ManolisKellis_PrivacyBigData_CSAIL-WH.pptx.

19 Trindel, *Supra* note 3.

20 *Id.*

21 *Id.*

22 *Written Testimony of Kathleen K. Lundquist, PhD, Organizational Psychologist, President and CEO, APTMetrics, Inc.* Equal Employment Opportunity Commission (13 Oct. 2016), https://www.eeoc.gov/eeoc/meetings/10-13-16/lundquist.cfm.

23 Lundquist, *Supra* note 22.

24 Trindel, *Supra* note 3.

25 *Id.*

26 Kate Sheridan, *Facial-recognition software finds a new use: Diagnosing genetic disorders* Statnews (10 Apr. 2017), https://www.statnews.com/2017/04/10/facial-recognition-genetic-disorders/.

27 42 U.S.C. § 2000ff-1 (2008).

28 Lundquist, *Supra* note 22.

29 *Id.*

30 *Id.*

31 Don Peck, *Supra* note 4.

32 Trindel, *Supra* note 3.

33 *Id.*

34 Trindel, *Supra* note 3.

35 *Id.*

36 Kashmir Hill, *How Target Figured Out A Teen Girl Was Pregnant Before Her Father Did,* Forbes, 16 Feb. 2012, https://www.forbes.com/sites/kashmirhill/2012/02/16/how-target-figured-out-a-teen-girl-was-pregnant-before-her-father-did.

37 *Id.*

38 42 U.S.C. *Supra* note 1.

39 42 U.S.C. § 12112 (2012).

40 42 U.S.C. § 2000ff (2012).

41 42 U.S.C. § 2000e (k) (2012).

42 Lin, L. y., Sidani, J. E., Shensa, A., Radovic, A., Miller, E., Colditz, J. B., Hoffman, B. L., Giles, L. M. and Primack, B. A., "Association between social media use and depression among U.S. young adults." *Depress Anxiety*, vol. 33, 2016, pp. 323–331. http://onlinelibrary.wiley.com/doi/10.1002/da.22466/.

43 Natasha Singer, "Risks in using social media to spot signs of mental distress." *New York Times*, 26 Dec. 2014, https://www.nytimes.com/2014/12/27/technology/risks-in-using-social-posts-to-spot-signs-of-distress.html.

44 Trindel, *Supra* note 3.

45 *EEOC Issues Final Rules on Employer Wellness Programs* Equal Opportunity Employment Commission (16 May 2016), https://www.eeoc.gov/eeoc/newsroom/release/5-16-16.cfm.

46 Trindel, *Supra* note 3.

47 Don Peck, Supra note 4.

48 Gideon Mann and Cathy O'Neil, "Hiring algorithms are not

neutral." *Harvard Business Review*, 9 Dec. 2016, https://hbr. org/2016/12/hiring-algorithms-are-not-neutral.

49 Claire Cain Miller, "Can an algorithm hire better than a human." *New York Times*, 25 Jun. 2015, https://www.nytimes. com/2015/06/26/upshot/can-an-algorithm-hire-better-than-a-human.html.

50 *Id.*

51 John Rossheim, *Algorithmic Hiring: Why Hire By Numbers?*, https://hiring.monster.com/hr/hr-best-practices/recruiting-hiring-advice/strategic-workforce-planning/hiring-algorithms.aspx.

52 Nathan R. Kuncel, Deniz S. Ones, and David M. Klieger, "In hiring, algorithms beat instinct." *Harvard Business Review*, May 2014, https://hbr.org/2014/05/in-hiring-algorithms-beat-instinct.

53 *Id.*

54 Lauren A. Rivera, "Guess who doesn't fit in at work." *New York Times*, 30 May 2015, https://www.nytimes. com/2015/05/31/opinion/sunday/guess-who-doesnt-fit-in-at-work.html.

55 Trindel, *Supra* note 3.

56 *Written Testimony of Michael Housman Workforce Scientist, hiQ Labs,* Equal Employment Opportunity Commission (13 Oct. 2016), https://www.eeoc.gov/eeoc/meetings/10-13-16/housman.cfm.

57 *Chevron, U.S.A., Inc. v. Nat. Resources Def. Council, Inc.,* 467 U.S. 837, 842 (1984).

58 *Gutierrez-Brizuela v. Lynch,* 834 F.3d 1142, 1148 (10th Cir. 2016).

59 29 CFR § 1607.3 A (2017).

60 29 CFR § 1607.3 B (2017).

61 29 CFR § 1607.4 A (2017).

62 *Id.*

63 *Id.*

64 29 CFR § 1607.5 (2017).

65 29 CFR § 1607.4 C (2017).

66 *Connecticut v. Teal,* 457 U.S. 440, 451 (1982).

67 29 CFR § 1607.14 A (2017).

68 29 CFR § 1607.14 B (2017).

69 29 CFR § 1607.14 B (2) (2017).

70 *Id.*

71 *Id.*

72 29 CFR § 1607.14 (2017).

73 29 CFR § 1607.11 (2017).

74 *Social Media Is Part of Today's Workplace but its Use May Raise Employment Discrimination Concerns,* Equal Employment Opportunity Commission (12 Mar. 2014), https://www.eeoc.gov/eeoc/newsroom/release/3-12-14.cfm.

"None of You Cared Enough": The Problematic Moralizing of *13 Reasons Why*

by Graeme John Wilson

ABSTRACT

13 Reasons Why, a television series adapted from the 2007 novel *Thirteen Reasons Why* by Jay Asher, quickly evolved into a cultural phenomenon following its premiere in 2017. The plot of *13 Reasons Why* concerns the aftermath and fallout of a high school girl's suicide, and was intended by producers to deconstruct social stigmas attached to the act and examine motivations for suicide. While the series has initiated an ongoing dialogue about suicide, *13 Reasons Why* has also generated significant controversy regarding its portrayal, and the ultimate influence of the series has been called into question by professional organizations, who argue that *13 Reasons Why* could possibly inspire copycat suicides. Suicide prevention advocacy groups have similar concerns that at-risk youth who view the series may instead be motivated, instead of deterred, to commit suicide. By applying rhetorical criticism to select episodes of *13 Reasons Why* and employing audience reception and social learning theory for its framework, this research essay utilizes *13 Reasons Why* as a vessel to examine the greater influence of media texts on audiences and whether they can be held wholly accountable for provoking subsequent audience behaviors.

Keywords: *13 Reasons Why*, suicide, audience reception theory, social learning theory, rhetorical criticism

"A ninguno de ustedes le importó": La moralización problemática de *Por trece razones*

RESUMEN

Por trece razones, una serie televisiva adaptada de la novela *Por trece razones* de Jay Asher, evolucionó rápidamente a fenómeno cultural después de la premier en 2017. La trama de *Por trece razones* se refiere a lo que sucedió después y a las consecuencias del suicidio de una niña de escuela secundaria, y fue concebida por los productores para deconstruir los estigmas sociales vinculados al acto y examinar las motivaciones del suicidio. Si bien la serie ha iniciado un diálogo continuo sobre el suicidio, *Por trece razones* también ha generado una gran controversia con respecto a su interpretación, y la influencia final de la serie ha sido cuestionada por organizaciones profesionales, que argumentan que *Por trece razones* podría inspirar suicidios. Los grupos que apoyan la prevención del suicidio tienen preocupaciones similares de que los jóvenes en riesgo que ven la serie pueden estar motivados a suicidarse, en lugar disuadirse. Al aplicar la crítica retórica para seleccionar los episodios de *Por trece razones* y al utilizar la recepción de la audiencia y la teoría del aprendizaje social para su marco teórico, este ensayo de investigación utiliza *Por trece razones* para examinar la influencia general de los textos de los medios de comunicación en las audiencias y para examinar si se les puede responsabilizar por completo de provocar comportamientos posteriores a la audiencia.

Palabras clave: Por trece razones, suicidio, teoría de la recepción de audiencia, teoría del aprendizaje social, crítica retórica

"汝等关心不足"：难以对《十三个原因》道德化

摘要

由2007年 Jay Asher所著同名小说改编而来的电视剧《十三个原因》，在2017年上映后便快速发展为一种文化现象。该剧情节有关于一名中学女生自杀所引起的后果。该剧制片人希望以此解构与自杀相关的社会耻辱，同时检验自杀的动机。在该剧揭开越来越多有关自杀的对话时，它同时还引起了关于该剧内容的大量争议，且专业机构也对该剧产生的最终影响提出质疑，前者认为该剧有可能为那些想要模仿自杀的群体带来灵感。自杀预防倡导团体也有相似的担忧，他们认为那些处于危险边缘的青年在观看该剧时并不会受到阻碍，而是被激励自杀。通过将修辞批评用于选取该剧的部分情节，并使用观众接收理论和社会学习理论搭建框架，本文将该剧作为导体，检验社媒内容对观众产生的更大的影响，以及这些内容能否对"引发观众行为"负全责。

关键词：《十三个原因》，自杀，观众接收理论，社会学习理论，修辞批评

· · · · · · · · ·

In the early twentieth century, as film gradually emerged as the preeminent form of entertainment media, there was frequent debate about the possibility of visual texts encouraging amoral behavior among younger audiences. In response, media producers advocated utilizing the platform to inform and educate audiences regarding contemporary social concerns, an early example being *Traffic in Souls*. Released in 1913, *Traffic in Souls* was advertised as a necessary text for audienc-

es, discussing taboo topics such as sexuality and prostitution within a moralizing framework (Stamp 44). Nevertheless, such fears did not subside and finally culminated in the
Payne Fund Studies, "a series of sociological and psycholog-
ical inquiries into the effects of motion pictures on youth"
(Vasey 127) conducted in the late 1920s and early 1930s.
First published in 1933, these studies mark the first serious
attempt to analyze media influence. Following the Payne
studies, there have been continuous inquiries into how violence in media such as film, television, and videogames can
influence viewers to exhibit more aggressive, violent behaviors because they are idealized in entertainment (Signorelli
18). Contrastingly, much less attention had been paid to the
possible influence popular media can exert toward suicidal
behavior. Scientific studies regarding this particular subject
were not conducted until the 1960s (Blood and Perkis 155).
However, with the 2017 release of the web television series
13 Reasons Why, this topic was launched into the forefront
of public debate.

13 Reasons Why, adapted by Brian Yorkey from the 2007
novel *Thirteen Reasons Why*, premiered on streaming service
Netflix on March 31, 2017, immediately accruing commercial success. As with its source material, the plot of *13 Reasons
Why* concerns the aftermath and fallout of a high school girl's
suicide. The student, Hannah Baker, dies from overdosing on
pills in the novel; in the television adaptation, she cuts her
wrists in her bathtub, the act of which is portrayed on-screen
in a flashback during the first season finale, "Tape 7, Side A."
In both versions, her classmate and friend Clay Jensen subsequently receives a package containing 13 tapes Hannah
recorded before her suicide. Each tape identifies a specific
person that Hannah, a victim of bullying and sexual assault,
blames for her suicide. Clay, who had secretly been in love

with Hannah, begins a crusade against the individuals on the tapes, wanting them to pay for their actions. Throughout the series, Clay, who is overcome with guilt at failing to prevent Hannah's death, repeatedly states that "we let her down" and "we all killed her."

In an interview with *Teen Vogue*, Jay Asher, the author of the novel and a consultant for the television series, described the franchise as a "cautionary tale," with the overarching narrative in both mediums designed to increase awareness regarding at-risk youth (Elizabeth, "'13 Reasons Why' Author Jay Asher on Working with Selena Gomez and the Netflix Adaptation"), as suicide is currently the second leading cause of death among teenagers (Curran 14); Asher himself was initially motivated to write the book after a teenage relative attempted suicide. However, while Asher's intentions are admirable, the ultimate influence of the series has been called into question. Notably, the National Association Psychologists (NASP) released a statement regarding *13 Reasons Why*, the first time the organization had ever done so for a television series, stating that it could possibly inspire copycat suicides:

> Research shows that exposure to another person's suicide, or to graphic or sensationalized accounts of death, can be one of the many risk factors that youth struggling with mental health conditions cite as a reason they contemplate or attempt suicide. (Howard, "Why Teen Mental Health Experts Are Focused on '13 Reasons Why'")

Suicide prevention advocacy groups have similarly expressed concerns that at-risk youth who view the series may instead be motivated, instead of deterred, to commit suicide, arguing that "the show actually doesn't present a viable alternative to suicide" (Thorbecke, "'13 Reasons Why' Faces Backlash from Suicide Prevention Advocacy Group"). Besides navigating the social relevance and impact of *13 Reasons Why*, the debate surrounding the perceived influence of the series, both positive and negative, continues historical debates regarding the greater influence of media texts on audiences, and whether they can be held wholly accountable for provoking subsequent audience behaviors.

FRAMEWORK AND METHODOLOGY

For its theoretical framework, this research essay employs audience reception and social learning theory. Audience reception is a qualitative theory used to deconstruct audience interpretation of media texts. Development of the theory is popularly attributed to sociologist Stuart Hall, who argued that audiences could develop varied interpretations of the same media content, some resistant to the dominant ideology, or "preferred reading" (9), of their peer groups. Hall used several contemporary television series for his research, such as the 1960s western series *The Virginian* (7). Thus, audience reception is an appropriate framework through which to navigate the varied interpretations of *13 Reasons Why*, particularly that rebuke the "preferred reading" of the series as communicating deterrent to self-harm. Additionally, social learning theory, developed by psychologists Albert Bandura and Richard Walters in the 1960s, suggests that individuals can adopt new behaviors through observing and subsequently imitating others (Signorelli 16). The prominence of television in contemporary American culture suggests that the medium can provide models for younger, more impressionable viewers to base personal behavior on (Duvall et al. 101), even potentially fatal behavior.

For its methodological approach, this critical essay utilizes textual analysis, a prominent research method used to analyze the content of media texts. Although textual analysis has been extensively applied to cinematic texts, scholars only began applying the method to television series during the 1970s. Since then, textual analysis has developed into one of the foremost methods within the field of television studies (Gray and Lotz 28). Textual analysis includes several varying approaches, one being rhetorical criticism. Rhetorical criticism is a form of textual analysis through which scholars can both identify the messages of a media text and evaluate their persuasive ability; such messages can be intentionally incorporated by the authors or otherwise. Rhetorical criticism is employed by media scholars to analyze how these messages can influence their audiences' perception of reality (Frey et al. 2; 235). Resultantly, rhetorical criticism was the best suited method for this research essay, to contrast the intentional commentary producers incorporated into *13 Reasons Why* with audience interpretation of these messages.

ANALYSIS

The debate regarding a possible relationship between suicide in fiction and contagion suicide can be traced as far back to the 1770s, when German writer Johann Wolfgang van Goethe published the novel *The Sorrows of Young Werther*, whose eponymous protagonist fatally shoots himself following a failed relationship. The novel generated high sales and influenced contemporary European culture, with many readers emulating the doomed Werther in appearance and manner. Following its publication, a notable increase in suicides across Europe was attributed to *The Sorrows of Young Werther*, and the novel was subsequently banned (Gould et al. 1270). However, television, which has since succeeded literature in eminence in contemporary entertainment, can prompt much stronger visceral reactions from audiences, due to its inherently visual nature.

In 1999, the Surgeon General of the United States acknowledged, based on extensive study, the possibility that viewing suicide in fictional media texts could influence vulnerable youth into mimicking the act (Hecht 164). Suicide contagion can be attributed to social learning theory, where audiences mimic behaviors glorified in media (Gould et al. 1269); *The Sorrows of Young Werther* represents an early historical example of such a phenomenon. Today, television is one of the primary mediums, along with film and music, which have been researched relating to media influence on suicide, with social learning theory frequently being utilized for the framework. However, such studies are recognized to be laborious, as "determining whether those who completed suicide after the presentation of a given television program ... were influenced by it is clearly difficult to establish in the case of completed suicides" (Blood and Perkis 157). Additionally, while different studies have indicated causal causation between viewings of suicide in media and the subsequent attempting of suicide, "these studies are small or have methodological problems" (158), thus failing to demonstrate consistency when replicated. Research indicates that viewing suicide in media alone is unlikely to act as a trigger, and instead must work in tandem with other factors such as location, seasonal trends, and, most frequently, mental illness. However, it is important to note that this research also suggests the possibility for media portrayals of suicide to function as deterrents for viewers:

> Not all studies have hypothesized that fictional portrayals of suicide on television have a negative effect. Some have suggest-

ed that appropriate portrayals, for example,
those that emphasize negative consequences or alternative courses of action, could actually have a positive, educative effect, and
have found this to be the case. (157)

This has been the producers' acknowledged goal for *13
Reasons Why*: to "have a positive, educative effect" on its
audience regarding contemporary issues facing high school
youth, such as bullying, sexual assault, and suicidal ideation.
However, despite the suggested moralizing framework of the
series, *13 Reasons Why* still presents a revenge fantasy. This
is a common and universal suicide fantasy, emphasizing the
effect that the suicide will have on the individual's peers:

This suicide fantasy has a markedly sadis-
tic orientation, with [the individual] often
enjoying the role of the invisible observer
of others' suffering, especially due to their
feelings of guilt and remorse because of the
suicide. There is a sense of retaliation, revenge and irrevocable, everlasting triumph.
(Campbell 175)

13 Reasons Why neatly fits this criteria, as Hannah's motivations behind manufacturing the tapes were to ultimately
obtain retaliation and revenge. In "Tape 7, Side A," Hannah
states on her final tape that, "Some of you cared. None of you
cared enough," thus negating her own agency regarding her
suicide and instead firmly redirecting responsibility for the
action toward her peers. Each tape identifies a specific person who pushed Hannah to commit suicide, through actions
such as spreading rumors regarding her sexual history and
even sexually assaulting her. Hannah herself acknowledges
in an earlier tape that she hopes "these tapes will start a new

butterfly effect," resulting in retribution against those whom she perceived wronged her. Researchers have noted that any potential influence of media texts on suicidal viewers largely depends on "the nature of the fictional portrayal, suggesting that the likelihood of an imitation effect may be dependent on .... the depiction of the consequences of the suicide" (Blood and Perkis 157). While Hannah's suicide is presented as a tragedy, her posthumous plan does ultimately bear fruit. Once their roles in Hannah's suicide become known, the individuals involved are either overcome with guilt or faced with consequences, thus justifying Hannah's decision to commit suicide. In an interview with *Slate*, Alex Moen, a licensed school counselor, criticized this aspect of *13 Reasons Why*'s narrative:

> [It's] essentially a fantasy of what someone who is considering suicide might have— that once you commit suicide, you can still communicate with your loved ones, and people will suddenly realize everything that you were going through and the depth of your pain ... the cute, sensitive boy will fall in love with you and seek justice for you, and you'll be able to orchestrate it, and in so doing kind of still be able to live. Especially when you're a teenager, your brain doesn't do a very good job of reminding you of the truth that, in fact, you will be dead, and that's really the only outcome that's important. (Martinelli, "13 Reasons Why's Controversial Depiction of Teen Suicide Has School Counselors Picking Up the Pieces")

Roen and many other school counselors were also critical of how *13 Reasons Why* portrayed their profession. The

only individual Hannah ever actually confides in during the
series is the school counselor, Kevin Porter, who, she visits
during a flashback in "Tape 7, Side A." Hannah indicates she
is struggling with depression and admits she was raped. Her
assault is detailed in the preceding episode, "Tape 6, Side B,"
where it is revealed that Bryce Walker, a popular athlete from
a wealthy family, raped Hannah during a party at his house.
However, Hannah is reluctant to name Bryce as her rapist:

> Porter: "If you don't want to give me a
> name, if you don't want to press charges
> against this boy—if you're not even sure
> you can press charges, then there really is
> only one option."
>
> Hannah: "What is it?"
>
> Porter: "I'm not trying to be blunt here,
> Hannah, but you can move on."
>
> Hannah: "You mean, do nothing?"
>
> Porter: "Is he in your class?"
>
> Hannah: "He's a senior."
>
> Porter: "That means he'll be gone in a few
> months."

Moen explained that the scene was wholly unrealistic, as
school counselors "are mandated reporters, meaning that if
we learn that someone has been harmed or may be harmed,
we have a duty by law to report it ... We don't have to launch an
investigation. We bring whatever information we do have to
the police or to parents or Child Protective Services" (Martinelli, "13 Reasons Why's Controversial Depiction of Teen
Suicide Has School Counselors Picking Up the Pieces").

Porter is subsequently identified on Hannah's 13th tape as the final reason in her decision to commit suicide. Hannah explains that after recording the previous 12 tapes, "I decided to give life one more chance. But this time, I was asking for help because I know I can't do it alone." However, Hannah resigns to kill herself after her failed talk with Porter. Because Porter is portrayed as inept by failing to recognize Hannah's obvious suicidal ideation or aid her recovery from sexual trauma, school counselors, and psychologists argue that at-risk youth could interpret these scenes as representing the futility in seeking help from school faculty or other adults (Balingit, "Educators and School Psychologists Raise Alarms about '13 Reasons Why'").

In addition to the narrative framework and portrayal of school counselors, the depiction of Hannah's suicide in "Tape 7, Side A" also generated significant criticism. Hannah's suicide is presented in graphic detail, with writers for the series detailing their goal to portray the act as painfully and realistically as possible to deter audiences from considering suicide as an option (Sheff, "*13 Reasons Why* Writer: Why We Didn't Shy Away from Hannah's Suicide"). However, this decision was criticized as misguided by mental health professionals for breaking promulgated guidance on depicting suicide in visual media, with the visceral nature of the scene backfiring by potentially serving as a trigger for suicidal youth (Butler, "'13 Reasons Why' Depicts a Graphic Suicide. Experts Say There's a Problem with That").

Despite such prominent criticisms, *13 Reasons Why* quickly became a popular success. Jumpshot, a marketing analytics firm, determined that *13 Reasons Why* was Netflix's second-most streamed television series in the 30 days following its premiere (Spangler, "Netflix's 'Marvel's the Defenders' Poised for Binge-Viewing Pop, Data Indicates") and the

year's most discussed program on social media (Martinelli,
"13 Reasons Why's Controversial Depiction of Teen Suicide Has School Counselors Picking Up the Pieces"). Netflix
subsequently renewed 13 Reasons Why for a second season,
which premiered on May 18, 2018. Because the entirety of
the novel was adapted for the program's first season, 13 Reasons Why's second season consists of original content. This
season of the series reveals that Bryce has raped numerous
students besides Hannah and functions as a commentary on
high school rape culture; the process in which rape is nor-
malized in a community (Boswell and Spade 133) through
"fundamental attitudes and values [that] are supportive of
gender stereotypes and violence against women" (McMahon
357). Suicide still remains a prominent topic in the season,
with Clay hallucinating the deceased Hannah and pursuing
evidence against Bryce, blaming him especially for Hannah's
decision to kill herself—Bryce is ultimately arrested for fel-
ony sexual assault and sentenced to probation. However,
seemingly in response to the criticisms of the first season,
the second season opener, "The First Polaroid," opens with
a short video warning. This warning will also play before the
opening episodes of future seasons:

> 13 Reasons Why is a fictional series that
> tackles tough, real-world issues, taking a
> look at sexual assault, substance abuse, sui-
> cide, and more. By shedding a light on these
> difficult topics, we hope our show can help
> viewers start a conversation. But if you are
> struggling with these issues yourself, this
> series may not be right for you, or you may
> want to watch it with a trusted adult. And
> if you ever feel you need someone to talk
> with, reach out to a parent, a friend, a school

counselor, or an adult you trust, call a local
helpline, or go to 13ReasonsWhy.info.

Such course correction is also integrated into the season's actual narrative. Porter is consumed with guilt at his failure to
help Hannah and retroactively portrayed as poor in his job,
thus acknowledging criticism toward the character, and fired
from the school in the penultimate episode of the season for
his poor performance. In "The Missing Page," the school's
principal—portrayed as an antagonistic figure in his drive to
protect the school's reputation, regardless of the well-being
of its actual students—wonders aloud if Hannah wanted to
glorify her death and "live on after," a position also implied by
the defense during the trial. This directly alludes to the criticisms of 13 Reasons Why's preceding season being a "revenge
fantasy." However, Clay disagrees with the principal, explaining to him that the tapes have "start[ed] a conversation. I
mean, we weren't talking about these things before Hannah."
Hannah herself directly challenges such accusations in "The
Third Polaroid," when Clay hallucinates Hannah explaining
that "it wasn't revenge! I had to tell my own story. I wanted
people to know what happened so maybe it wouldn't happen
again." Therefore, 13 Reasons Why and its creative personnel
maintain both the beneficent intent of the series and its ability to "start a conversation" regarding delicate issues such as
suicide and sexual assault. 13 Reasons Why has certainly accomplished its goal to provoke conversation, as more than
600,000 news reports have been published about the series
and its themes (Althouse et al. 1527). Upon release, both
seasons also contributed to an increase in Internet searches
regarding suicide-related topics, although it is important to
note that it is unclear if such searches are representative of
self-education regarding suicide or are indicative of suicidal
thoughts (Ethgen and Bruyère 99).

The reason the program has provoked such extensive debate regarding its portrayal of suicide is because the relative risk of copycat suicide is higher among younger viewers, particularly 15–19 year olds; the typical age group of high school students (Gould et al. 1270). It is also worth noting that social learning theory "purports that similarity between the viewer and role model will influence whether or not televised behaviors are modeled" (Duvall et al. 112). Because the vast majority of *13 Reasons Why*'s extensive ensemble are teenagers, the series has the potential to exert significant influence among younger audiences. This was demonstrated when a school superintendent in Florida reported an increase in suicidal behavior among students following the premiere of the program's first season, with several students specifically identifying *13 Reasons Why* as a trigger and motivator for their behavior (Balingit, "Educators and School Psychologists Raise Alarms about '13 Reasons Why'"). However, this is not to say that suicide should not be discussed in *13 Reasons Why* or other popular media, or that the program itself is without any merit. The program depicts a considerable number of interracial relationships, which remain underrepresented in popular television (Craig-Henderson 71), and actively rebukes the practice of victim blaming, in which survivors of violent crimes such as sexual assault are blamed by authorities and peers for their trauma (George and Martínez 110). However, while it is observed that "teenagers will be able to connect with the show's portrayals of peer pressure, toxic masculinity, and slut-shaming," *13 Reasons Why*'s placing "responsibility for a person's suicide on the survivors of suicide loss, creat[ing] a false illusion that a suicidal person can be in control after her death, and offer[ing] no alternatives" (Martinelli, "13 Reasons Why's Controversial Depiction of Teen Suicide Has School Counselors Picking Up the Pieces") is undeniably dangerous and, despite the best intentions of *13 Reasons*

Why's creative team, communicates a message entirely anti-thetical to the intended commentary of the program.

CONCLUSION

As evidenced through *The Sorrows of Young Werther*, "the magnitude of the increase in suicides ... is proportional" to its prominence in cultural dialogue (Gould et al. 1271). Although no actual completed suicides have been attributed to *13 Reasons Why*, its cultural prominence does imbue the series with considerable influence. While the purpose of *13 Reasons Why*—to raise awareness regarding suicide—is commendable, the program's social commentary is diluted due to its presentation as a revenge fantasy, wherein Hannah's suicide ultimately results in legal and moral consequences against those who wrong her in life. This betrays the intended message of *13 Reasons Why* by glamorizing suicide as a method of attack against those who persecute you. Numerous mental health experts have expressed concern about the series for this reason, arguing that *13 Reasons Why* may actually help influence members of its audience towards committing suicide. This scenario is unfortunately not one outside the realm of possibility, after acknowledging the recognized influence of fictional portrayals of suicide in popular media.

Although positioned as a breakthrough text, *13 Reasons Why* ultimately continues the flawed portrayal of suicide in popular media by failing to actually articulate any alternative to suicide, or promote resources available for at-risk youth. Notably, "guidelines for the treatment of fictional portrayals of suicide in film and television have not been developed" (Gould et al. 1275). Mass media has the potential to be a powerful tool in educating audiences about suicide prevention, informing viewers of causes and warning signs of suicide. Although *13 Reasons Why* has generated significant controversy regarding its content, it has also initiated an on-going dialogue about suicide, itself a praiseworthy achievement when considered the continued social stigma attached to the subject. However, it is acknowledged that, "focusing public attention on suicide without taking recommended efforts to minimize harm can be counterproductive, and even dangerous" (Gilbert, "Did *13 Reasons Why* Spark a Suicide Contagion Effect?"). Therefore, one can only hope that future seasons of *13 Reasons Why* exhibit a more nuanced portrayal of such delicate issues and succeed in educating its audiences safely, as intended by Asher, without unintentionally portraying the act of suicide as glamorous or romantic.

WORKS CITED

Althouse, Benjamin M., et al. "Internet Searches for Suicide Following the Release of 13

Reasons Why." *JAMA Internal Medicine*, vol. 177, no. 10, 2017, pp. 1527–1529.

Balingit, Moriah. "Educators and School Psychologists Raise Alarms about '13 Reasons Why'." *The Washington Post*, 2017, https://www.washingtonpost.com/local/education/educators-and-school-psychologists-raise-alarms-about-13-reasons-why/2017/05/01/bb534ec6-2c2b-11e7-a616-d7c8a68c1a66_story.html?nid&utm_term=.53dce563a07e

Blood, R.W., and Jane Pirkis. "Suicide and the Media Part II: Portrayal in Fictional Media." *Crisis*, vol. 22, no. 4, 2001, pp. 155–162.

Boswell, A. Ayres, and Joan Z. Spade. "Fraternities and Collegiate Rape Culture: Why Are Some Fraternities More Dangerous Places for Women?" *Gender & Society*, vol. 10, no. 2, 1996, pp. 133–147.

Butler, Bethonie. "'13 Reasons Why' Depicts a Graphic Suicide. Experts Say There's a Problem with That." *The Washington Post*, 2017, https://www.washingtonpost.com/news/arts-and-entertainment/wp/2017/04/14/the-problem-with-how-13-reasons-why-treats-suicide/?tid=hybrid_collaborative_3_na&utm_term=.ececeae24fb7

Campbell, Donald. "Pre-suicide States of Mind." *The Psychoanalytic Therapy of Severe Disturbance: Psychoanalytic Ideas*, edited by Paul Williams, Karnac, 2010, pp. 171–184.

Craig-Henderson, Kellina M. *Black Men in Interracial Relationships: What's Love Got to Do with It?* Transaction Publishers, 2006.

Curran, David K. *Adolescent Suicidal Behavior*. Routledge, 2010.

Duvall, Amy C., et al. "Family Communication and Television: Viewing, Identification, and Evaluation of Televised Family Communication Models." *Television and the Self: Knowledge, Identity, and Media Representation*, edited by Kathleen M. Ryan and Deborah A. Macey, Lexington Books, 2013, pp. 99–118.

Elizabeth, De. "'13 Reasons Why' Author Jay Asher on Working with Selena Gomez and the Netflix Adaptation." *Teen Vogue*, 2017, http://www.teenvogue.com/story/13-reasons-why-author-jay-asher-selena-gomez-netflix-adaptation

Ethgen, Olivier, and Olivier Bruyère. "Epidemiological Product Assessment." *Consumer Perception of Product Risks and Benefits*, edited by Gerard Emilien et al., Springer, 2017, pp. 85–104.

Frey, Lawrence R., et al. *Investigating Communication: An Introduction to Research Methods.* 2nd ed. Allyn & Bacon, 1999.

George, William H., and Lorraine J. Martínez. "Victim Blaming in Rape: Effects of Victim and Perpetrator Race, Type of Rape, and Participant Racism." *Psychology of Women Quarterly*, vol. 26, no. 2, 2002, pp. 110–119.

Gilbert, Sophie. "Did *13 Reasons Why* Spark a Suicide Contagion Effect?" *The Atlantic*, 2017, https://www.theatlantic.com/entertainment/archive/2017/08/13-reasons-why-demonstrates-cultures-power/535518/?utm_source=atlfb

Gould, Madelyn, et al. "Media Contagion and Suicide among the Young." *Behavioral Scientist*, vol. 46, no. 9, 2003, pp. 1269–1284.

Gray, Jonathan, and Amanda D. Lotz. *Television Studies.* Policy Press, 2012.

Hall, Stuart. "Encoding and Decoding in the Television Discourse." *Council of Europe Colloquy on "Training in the Critical Heading of Televisual Language."* Council & the Centre for Mass Communication Research, University of Leicester, 1973.

Hecht, Jennifer M. *Stay: A History of Suicide and the Philosophies Against It.* Yale University Press, 2013.

Howard, Jacqueline. "Why Teen Mental Health Experts Are Focused on '13 Reasons Why.'" *CNN*, 2017, http://www.cnn.com/2017/04/25/health/13-reasons-why-teen-suicide-debate-explainer/

Martinelli, Marissa. "13 Reasons Why's Controversial Depiction of Teen Suicide Has School Counselors Picking Up the Pieces." *Slate*, 2017, http://www.slate.com/blogs/browbeat/2017/05/01/school_counselors_talk_netflix_s_controversial_teen_suicide_drama_13_reasons.html

McMahon, Sarah. "Understanding Community-Specific Rape Myths: Exploring Student Athlete Culture." *Journal of Women and Social Work*, vol. 22, no. 4, 2007, pp. 357–370.

Sheff, Nic. "*13 Reasons Why* Writer: Why We Didn't Shy Away from Hannah's Suicide." *Vanity Fair*, 2017, http://www.vanityfair.com/hollywood/2017/04/13-reasons-why-suicide-controversy-nic-sheff-writer

Signorielli, Nancy. *Violence in the Media: A Reference Handbook*. ABC-CLIO, Inc., 2005.

Spangler, Todd. "Netflix's 'Marvel's The Defenders' Poised for Binge-Viewing Pop, Data Indicates." *Variety*, 2017, https://variety.com/2017/digital/news/netflix-marvel-the-defenders-binge-viewing-data-ratings-1202532453/

Stamp, Shelley. "Moral Coercion, or the National Board of Censorship Ponders the Vice Films." *Controlling Hollywood: Censorship and Regulation in the Studio Era*, edited by Matthew Bernstein, Rutgers University Press, 1999, pp. 41–59.

"Tape 2, Side A." *13 Reasons Why*, created by Brian Yorkey, season 1, episode 3, Netflix, 2017.

"Tape 6, Side B." *13 Reasons Why*, created by Brian Yorkey, season 1, episode 12, Netflix, 2017.

"Tape 7, Side A." *13 Reasons Why*, created by Brian Yorkey, season 1, episode 13, Netflix, 2017.

"The Box of Polaroids." *13 Reasons Why*, created by Brian Yorkey, season 2, episode 12, Netflix, 2017.

"The First Polaroid." *13 Reasons Why*, created by Brian Yorkey, season 2, episode 1, Netflix, 2017.

"The Missing Page." *13 Reasons Why*, created by Brian Yorkey, season 2, episode 9, Netflix, 2017.

"The Third Polaroid." *13 Reasons Why*, created by Brian Yorkey, season 2, episode 7, Netflix, 2017.

Thorbecke, Catherine. "'13 Reasons Why' Faces Backlash from Suicide Prevention Advocacy Group." *ABC News*, 2017, http://abcnews.go.com/Entertainment/13-reasons-faces-backlash-suicide-prevention-advocacy-groups/story?id=46851551

Vasey, Ruth. "Beyond Sex and Violence: 'Industry Policy' and the Regulation of Hollywood Movies, 1922–1939." *Controlling Hollywood: Censorship and Regulation in the Studio Era*, edited by Matthew Bernstein, Rutgers University Press, 1999, pp. 102–129.

Staging Vaudeville for a Twenty-First-Century Audience

by David Monod and Lyndsay Rosenthal

ABSTRACT

From the 1890s to the second decade of the twentieth century, vaudeville was the most popular and trend-setting entertainment in the United States. This article describes a new database on vaudeville that contains tens of thousands of reviews of performances. It also provides examples of some of the new insights researchers can gain into popular entertainment by employing the database, particularly referencing performance style.

Keywords: Vaudeville, Keith-Albee, digital humanities, popular music, Tin Pan Alley, performance, progressive era, mass entertainment

Puesta en escena de vodevil para una audiencia del siglo XXI

RESUMEN

Desde la década de 1890 hasta la segunda década del siglo XX, el vodevil fue la forma de entretenimiento más popular y vanguardista de los Estados Unidos. Este artículo describe una nueva base de datos sobre el vodevil que contiene decenas de miles de reseñas de actuaciones. También proporciona ejemplos de algunos de los nuevos conocimientos que los investigadores pueden obtener acerca del entretenimiento popular mediante el empleo de la base de datos, en particular, haciendo referencia al estilo de actuación.

Palabras clave: vodevil, Keith-Albee, humanidades digitales, música popular, Tin Pan Alley, actuación, era progresiva, entretenimiento masivo

为二十一世纪观众举行杂耍表演

摘要

自19世纪90年代到20世纪20年代，杂耍表演是美国最为流行、最引领潮流的娱乐方式。本文描述了一项包含数以万计的杂耍表演评论的新数据库。本文还为研究人员提供了一些新的见解，后者能通过应用数据库，尤其是通过参考表演方式，而将这些见解融入流行娱乐。

关键词：杂耍表演，基思 - 阿尔比剧院，数字人文学科，流行乐，叮砰巷，表演，进步时代，大众娱乐

· · · · · · · · ·

Vaudeville was the United States' first mass entertainment. It offered a reasonably old form of entertainment—the variety show—cleaned up for a family audience. Vaudeville was the first popular entertainment to draw audiences from all classes, age groups, and regions, and it was the first to attract as many female spectators as male. According to B.F. Keith, one of the industry's leading entrepreneurs, vaudeville audiences were not only "the young men, the men-about-town, and all sorts of men—who used to enjoy the old-time variety theatre. But men, women, and children of all degrees; in short, people in the fullest and most wholesome American sense of the word."[1] At its peak, in 1910, there were 1,600 vaudeville theaters in the United States, located in every region of the country. Roughly, five million Americans attended vaudeville shows every week.

Vaudeville also differed from earlier forms of amusement in the way the business was organized and consumers enjoyed it. Local and regional chains of variety theaters were first created in the 1870s, and vaudeville (as a way of organizing variety entertainment) grew from those beginnings. To deliver variety shows nationally, theater entrepreneurs organized chains of theaters which consolidated bookings. They also organized cartels to divide territory, fix prices, and prevent rivals entering the industry. But vaudeville did not become popular just because it rested on a national distribution system. It grew because, in the late 1890s, the variety show caught on and became what people at the time called "a craze." In its golden age, between 1900 and 1912, it was not uncommon for hundreds of people to queue up to see a vaudeville show. They did so because it was in vaudeville that they saw the latest fashions in clothing and coiffure, heard the newest songs from Tin Pan Alley composers, and laughed at the freshest jokes. The "headliners" vaudeville featured were the first entertainment celebrities, whose homes, salaries, romances, exercise, and eating habits were as important to consumers as their acts. As popular celebrities, vaudevillians helped create a modern style for Americans living in a rapidly urbanizing and industrializing society.

This article is intended to demonstrate the value of an extensive online research database, *vaudevilleamerica.org*. It aims to provide readers with information both on how to research vaudeville and on what kinds of information the database contains. The database comprises reviews taken from newspapers, the trade magazine *Variety*, and the Keith-Albee theater-manager's books that have been digitized by the University of Iowa. The reviews that have been collected in the database were chosen because they offered information on the type of performance, the content of the act, and/or the audience's reaction to it. Each entry contains the name, date, city, theater, and performance type along with a transcription of the original review. Users can quickly access this information using any of four different methods: performance name, type of act, theatre, or keyword search. With the performance search function, the acts can be further sorted by year, performance type, or location of theatre. The keyword search function will bring up any review with that word in the title or content of the review. The variety of search methods allows the user to tailor the database to their research goals.

There are over 80 different performance types listed in the database, which captures some of the best known and most obscure acts that appeared in vaudeville. It is especially interesting to trace the novelty acts that were used to generate interest in a bill. The Salambos, for example, was billed as an electrical novelty act. They used electricity to create trick effects and gave a demonstration of wireless telegraphy—a technology that had only been around for seven years in 1902. Tracing the history of the act tells us something about the rate of diffusion of new technologies. After a performance in New York, for example, the manager reported "it is about the same sort of act that they did in this country about five years ago, but is valuable because it is a novelty. They introduce several new effects in it and the audience was deeply interested from start to finish."[2] We may assume that the novelty of an act like the Salambos, several decades after the introduction of electricity, would make it tiresome to audiences. In fact, a Boston manager felt that while the troupe offered was "an interesting trick exhibition," their act "it is not worth big booking." But this was not because of over-familiarity with electricity, as the manager believed "the majority of people cannot attain the proper understanding of what they are witnessing."[3]

Location was an important factor in how an act was received by an audience. The material would sometimes contain geographic quirks that only appealed to some patrons. Certain subjects or performances types could be received differently in different cities. Within the database, the acts can be sorted by city, which allows one to see how geography affected audience responses. The Song Birds was a satire on the opera war in New York with characters based on Oscar Hammerstein, Enrico Caruso, and Nellie Melba that toured the circuit in 1909. It received rave reviews in Brooklyn, where one manager exclaimed: "It is enjoyable from the rise to the fall of the curtain. A production better suited to vaudeville has yet to be placed on a stage, and although the story is local, centering in the rivalry of the grand opera impresarios, the comedy can scarce fail anywhere."[4] Despite this assessment, Song Birds did not appeal to all vaudeville audiences. The act received a less enthusiastic response in Cleveland which was blamed on the fact that "the fore part of the act consists mostly of New York local stuff, and I do not think the general Cleveland Audiences understand it; at least they did not seem to this afternoon."[5] However, audiences in cities closer to New York, including Providence, Boston, and Philadelphia, raved about the performance. The manager at Keith's in Philadelphia wrote, "I could not conceive of a vaudeville travesty constructed on more popular lines. The hits were applauded and the musical numbers got big hands."[6] The success of the Song Birds shows us both that opera appealed to turn-of-the-century popular theater audiences, even though some found its New York references perplexing. This also tells us that vaudeville audiences in the area around Manhattan were sufficiently familiar with the character at the Metropolitan and Manhattan operas to find their caricature amusing.

Taste did, however, change over time and this can be traced in the reviews. During the war years, for example, patriotic and political material became popular with vaudeville patrons. The singer, Nora Bayes, struggled to win over her audience during a 1915 performance in New York until she sang "'We'll Celebrate the End of the War in Ragtime' that has a kick in its final line that will not fall down anywhere while Germany is keeping Woodrow on the pan."[7] But, politically charged material did not always go over well with audiences looking for an escape. This was especially true for American audiences who had endured two years of war, watched as Europe struggled to rebuild and witnessed a Communist Revolution in Russia. Singer Blanche Ring had to cut her once popular patriotic tune "Bing, Bang, Bing'em" for a performance in 1919 in favour of "an audience song which doesn't go as powerfully, but which is more suitable to entertainment of folks who pay to be amused, not harangued."[8] Similarly, when Milt Collins appeared at Keith's Providence in 1920, his comedy monologue secured some laughs with the audience, but the manager was "afraid that some of his material is dangerous politically."[9]

Managers' reports and reviews in the trade press allowed theatres to track the development and sustainability of every act. Searching the database by the name of a specific act and sorting it by year can reveal how an act evolved over the course of its run. The Sunny South, to consider just one example, was billed as a comedic dancing and singing ensemble comprised of a group of 10–12 African-American men and women. An early performance in Trenton in 1904 received praise from both the audience and the manager. Set on a plantation, "the act is set off very prettily with exceptionally appropriate and artistic scenery in keeping and in character with this offering. 'The Sunny South' is a good act, away from the ordinary vaudeville offering and goes good here."[10] The act continued to live up to expectations during performances in Buffalo and New York City the following year.[11] But over time, the act lost its appeal, sometimes as personnel changed, and sometimes because the audience simply grew tired of the act. This points to the fact that vaudeville audiences were made up of repeat customers, who generally went out to a show every week. While performances by the Sunny South in 1906 still went over well in Philadelphia and New York, in Cleveland, the manager complained that they were not as good as previously: "had these people billed as fifteen colored comedians, singers and dancers. In the first place there are not fifteen, but ten, to continue in error, they are not comedians, and they can't sing. Their dancing is excellent, in fact it is the whole act. Their opening was weak, and scores in the audience left the theatre. Their rapid-fire dancing at the finish is the only thing that carries the act. It is not the Sunny South of a year ago by any means."[12]

Even experienced vaudevillians could not rest on their laurels and while one poor showing did not necessarily mean an act was terminated or relegated to a lower circuit, a bad run could be fatal. Mediocre or disappointing acts were often re-booked in the hopes that performers had been able to improve their acts after they had the opportunity to run through it several times while incorporating criticism and feedback. This happened to the Sunny South which, after its poor showing in 1906, returned to the stage in Cleveland the following year and received rave reviews. The manager wrote, "This act without a doubt was the hit of the show. They certainly have improved since the last time they were here, and

I don't know of any act of this kind, that we have ever played, that went as good as this one did to-day."[13] The act continued to delight audiences in the Northeast throughout 1907.

As this example shows, responding to audience feedback was a crucial component when crafting a successful act. The database reveals the important role the theatre manager played as a conduit between the audience's expectations and the success of an act. The manager tailored pieces to suit the tastes of their patrons and would often recommend that performers cut or changed parts of their acts. These suggestions could include shortening the act, cutting out certain elements, or eliminating lewd or offensive material. Filtering performances by the keyword "cut" or "eliminate" will bring up any review that has contained that word. After a poor performance in Boston in 1903, the manager there suggested that comedian Beatrice Moreland alter her material to play to audiences in that city. He complained that "some of her stories were too pointed for use here and we were obliged to cut them, even though they went in Philadelphia and Portland."[14] The success of a bill generally depended on the reaction of the audience rather than on how a manager rated the quality of the acts.

Especially popular in vaudeville were acts that maintained a snappy, upbeat approach. Brander Matthews, who taught drama at Columbia University at the turn of the century, thought "the attitude of the vaudeville audiences toward the vaudeville stage is one of the most interesting ... the vaudeville audience wants its results quick, it wants to a snack of the big feasts in the show business. It wants an acrobat, a knock-about team, some trained animals, then a play, then some dancers, a song, a conjuror, another play, and so on. It is a restless, impatient audience, but it is the most appreciative of them all. There they sit, their show-instincts open to conviction, without any particular art microbe to oppress them."[15] Managers were especially hostile to anything that worked as a drag on a show. Although one Boston audience apparently enjoyed a dramatic sketch put on by Mary Hampton and company in 1903, the manager was concerned that no one had caught "one glaring error" that he felt ruined the moment of an otherwise bright piece—a violin solo in the middle of the sketch. While the solo was there to allow for a costume change, the manager reported "I have modified the solo somewhat but hope by the end of the week to eliminate the entire thing and in its place introduce some real lively stage business. I can't for the life of me see how this sketch could have gone along with this glaring error being allowed to run so long. Possibly it has not been over the circuit, if it has I should like other opinions of it."[16]

To be successful in this type of fast-paced theater, players learned to fix attention on themselves. Their goal was to establish some kind of connection that might transcend even weak or old material. Vaudevillians came to term the method they used to secure spectator attention the "direct appeal." Media scholar Henry Jenkins described this as a kind of "affective immediacy," a bond of fellowship created between audience and performer. According to Caroline Caffin, a contemporary observer, it was the casual geniality of the vaudeville house, "that feeling of good-fellowship," that made audiences attentive. The audience "loves to be on confidential terms with the performer, to be treated as an intimate. It loves to have the actor step out of his part and speak of his dressing-room, or hint at his salary, or flourish a make-up towel."[17]

Naturalness of manner was considered essential to success in vaudeville. Spectators responded most positively to those performers who behaved like they were not acting and whose words and movements "seem to break out spontaneously." Recognizing this, performers often talked to the audience during their acts, though managers urged them not to single out individuals. The singer and comic, Maud Dunn, after cracking a joke that did not work, would urge audience appreciation with the line: "think it over." Similarly, Ching Ling Foo, vaudeville's premier Chinese magician, after producing a bowl of rice or a child from under his cloak, would ask the audience in Chinese-American stage dialect: "you likee?" Emma Carus, after singing "None of Them's Got Anything on Me" to a 1908 New York audience, exclaimed: "I'm glad that's over." The audience apparently agreed. Animals that refused to perform were common and trainers had to manage the result calmly as audiences were hostile to those who looked like they were angry. Riene Davies, who had a performing bulldog, would apologize for the animal's "ill manners" and then offer recitations to fill up the time. Kidding the audience was another common trick. Francis Wilson, the comic sketch artist, used to close her performance with the comment: "Ladies and Gentlemen: You have behaved beautifully, you have laughed and applauded with an intelligence that is almost human."[18]

Acting as though one was not the key to vaudeville performance. Many players had to present widely contrasting moods and temperaments in their 15 minutes on stage while making each of those feelings appear genuine. Blanche Ring felt the way to put over a song was "to take the audience into your confidence. Try to make each hearer think that you are singing directly to him or her. All the favorite balladists I have heard have possessed this faculty to a marked degree ... They seem to get right at you ... once a singer gets an audience humming with her, or singing the refrain, then it is easy sailing ... I take a purely animal, or fleshy, pleasure in getting my audience with me." Others spoke of honesty, light-hearted-ness, and an ability to share the pleasure they took in per-forming as critical ingredients. Singer Adele Rowland told a reporter that a performer needed "something" to succeed with audiences. "There are girls, you know, that have real talent—sing well, dance well, look well—who never seem to get anywhere. It must be lack of personality. Perhaps my something is alertness. I'm dreadfully alert, you know." Ap-pearing relaxed but remaining engaged on stage might sound simple, but many described it as hard work. May Robson, a musical-comedy star who tried performing in vaudeville in 1904 soon quit, declaring it much easier to play a part than to act like one wasn't.[19]

The vaudeville database is especially useful for tracing how vaudeville's peculiar aesthetic infused different genres. To choose just one example, what we today recognize as Amer-ican popular music developed in the last decade of the nine-teenth century. Historians have offered a variety of explana-tions for why modern popular music emerged in this period. For those who describe popular music as a business, the pre-cipitating cause was the growth of commercial song-writing and publishing, industries centered on 28th Street in New York (Tin Pan Alley). For musicologists like Eric Wilder and Peter van der Merwe, the development of a style with Afri-can-American characteristics—a bluesy feel and syncopa-tion—was critical.[20] Less well documented is the influence of performance on the character of popular music and, in particular, of vaudeville, as the medium through which main-stream music was disseminated. The discussion below will show that vaudeville was a venue whose performance culture strongly influenced the development of modern commercial music.

In the early twentieth century, popular musicians did not appear in concert halls and there were few large auditoria. Those wanting to see a performer or hear the newest compositions could go out to a restaurant or nightclub with a floor show, or attend an operetta or musical comedy, but those were expensive options and not widely available. New music could be heard in the sheet music sections of department, five and dime, and music stores, but there was nothing exciting about hearing songs auditioned in that way. Vaudeville was consequently the destination of choice for those wanting popular musical entertainment: it was reasonably inexpensive, available coast to coast and it offered the thrill of live performance. Because of this, vaudeville was instrumental in disseminating the new popular music of the early twentieth century, Tin Pan Alley tunes especially, but also ragtime, blues, and, to a limited extent, jazz. Singing acts made up roughly a quarter of all vaudeville performances and they became increasingly important as time went on. Between 1902 and 1906, 15% of all acts featured singers; over the next five years, that number jumped to 25% and from 1912 to 1922, it stood at 36%. The steady concentration on singing evidenced vaudeville's role as the primary venue for listening to live popular music.[21]

With well over 10,000 entries in the database, singing was one of the most popular acts on vaudeville. About one-third of all vaudeville singing acts featured a solo performer singing with an accompanist. These kinds of act remained popular because of their simplicity and wide range of appeal. Singing acts generally required little set up or props, so they could be played in front of the curtain while stage crews set up the back for a more complicated act. But despite their simplicity, singing acts were, with comedy skits, the most popular of all vaudeville acts. Song selection was crucial to performers like ragtime singer Blanche Ring. While performing at the Colonial in New York City in 1906, she was "saved by her final song 'Waltz Me Around Again Willie.' The house joined in after applauding the first verse. She is badly in need of a catchy number."[22] Ring's final song selection became popular with the Colonial crowd "who yelled their heads off on it" and forced her to repeat it five times at another performance three years later.[23]

In the late nineteenth century, volume and clarity of diction, rather than personality or character, was considered most important in rendering songs in the popular theater. Singers who sang "tough" songs, impersonating working-class characters, or "coon" songs, impersonating African Americans, were especially popular. Because vaudevillians had to project their voices to the top balconies of theaters seating 2,000 or 3,000 people, their songs were often called shouts. Clear diction was critical in shouting because popular song in the late nineteenth century was a form of story-telling, and the most popular featured a clear narrative. Leading shouters, like May Irwin and Sophie Tucker, were known for singing loud, not well. "Most everyone understands ... songs," a critic commented, "but the talent couldn't quite make out whether Sophie [Tucker] was trying to sing or to break a ceiling rafter with her voice," while another reviewer described Tucker's voice as a combination of a fog horn and a steam calliope. Emma Carus, another popular shouter, was said to sing "with the softness of a salute from a warship." Falling back on the conventional metaphor for attributes that seemed un-feminine, journalists often described female singers' voices as masculine. Many of the most popular were contraltos and they were called female baritones. At the same time, because they were females, it was not considered proper for them to be too emotionally involved in the performance, especially when they were depicting the urban poor or racialized characters. Singers like Tucker and Carus tended to perform in one place on stage, moving little and using their faces and hands for emphasis. They laid emphasis on telling a musical story clearly and loudly so that even those in the back of the house could hear their words.[24]

Around the turn of the century, however, the direct appeal began to change the way singers performed and, as it did, to transform popular music. The growing emphasis on the performer inspired composers to make their work less narrative and more personal. Instead of songs telling stories about others, composers increasingly used the first person. Singers who were selling their personalities naturally presented the music as expressing their own feelings. This encouraged publishers to link vaudevillians more fully to the songs they produced and after 1900, they were paying them to have their pictures on sheet music covers. The song-writer, Irving Berlin, who was just emerging as one of vaudeville's premier composers, said that it was no longer necessary to tell a story in songs and he wrote lyrics in the first person, so that the singer "talks directly to the auditors."[25] This change reflected the growth of celebrity, personality, and a vaudeville performance culture that rested on the "direct appeal." Female singers, one vaudevillian explained, used to "depend upon tonnage to put them across. Those days have slipped into the discard. Now patrons want to see and hear [performers] ... who can sing."[26] Authenticity was achieved by "naturalizing" the delivery and making the song more personal and this individualization, paradoxically, enhanced the song's marketability. All this resulted from the critical shift in the singer's role from storyteller, where the real identity of the performer was erased, to a melding of the performer's emotions with those of the character in the song.

Among the first to deliver songs in a personal way was Ohio-born Clarice Vance. Originally known as a "tough girl" who stomped onto the stage and sang in a stentorian way, "hard, loud and faultless in articulation," in 1900, Vance tried a more subdued approach. At Keith's Bijou in Philadelphia, Vance surprised audiences with a performance of a popular song free of shouting. She was one of the earliest singers to shift attention to her vocal quality, her crisp diction, and lyricism. Her lightened, sweetened sound did not excite the gallery as it did when she bellowed a story, but she claimed to be more satisfied with her work. "I find my audience enjoy the quiet, modest way in which I sing my songs more than they do the blustery, knockabout shouting style generally used in the rendition of coon songs," Vance explained. In her view, the new more personal songs, which she called "ragtime" "should be sung on the stage like they would be in the parlor." Similarly, singer Nora Bayes proved a big hit with vaudeville audiences with her "forward," highly personal approach to song, something more suited, one manager initially thought, to a club or cabaret. Her style was "not particularly pleasing to an older theater goer," a manager explained, when she broke into vaudeville in 1904, but she worked in a "gingery way" and gained "really good applause." [27]

As singer Blanche Ring made clear, the new style evolved because of the need to express one's personality in vaudeville. It became more important to convey intimacy and to draw audience attention to the stage than to make sure everyone heard the words of a story. In fact, words became less important than the feelings being conveyed. In the variety theater you have to "give it to them plainly. Give it to them so that they must get it whether they are listening or not," she told *Variety* in 1909. People often asked her how she was able to "swing an audience along?" Ring said the answer was getting "the gladness in circulation by being glad yourself through and through." As syncopation and ragtime's energy infused romantic, sentimental, and comic songs, it seemed to modernize traditional musical genres. Not surprisingly, rhythm became an instrument in the direct appeal as singers moved with the music and tried to appear more involved in it. According to singer Adele Rowland, the way to put a song over in vaudeville was by using "a direct appeal ... the slightest assumption of insincerity or affectation is fatal." Any artist who, when singing, would "clinch her heart, shut her eyes, or otherwise prove herself devoid of real feeling ... would exit from vaudeville." The increased focus on the star performer was the essence of the thing to Nora Bayes: "you have to make them [the audience] forget themselves. If you can set them to thinking about *your* blues instead of their own, they are taken completely out of themselves ... [then] you are really entertaining them," she explained.[28]

In singing, as in other vaudeville acts, direct appeal brought the issue of performer personality to the fore and entertainers had to make themselves seem likeable or appealing. Nora Bayes, for example, employed subtle devices to sell herself to audiences, even though a reviewer in Variety dismissed it all as "simplicity itself," for no matter what she sang "it is the individuality of the entertainer herself that carries her offering." Caroline Caffin was more astute and saw the craft in the performance. She dissected Bayes' method, observing her efforts to disarm the audience by acknowledging it when she came on stage, with a sideways glance, followed by "a dimpled smile" and then a shy downward look, "as though she would hate to think you might not like her." Then, reassured by the applause, the performer faced the audience and offered "a curving smile" pursued by a sudden upward glance "to see if you caught the curving smile which followed your applause." Bayes' smiles, Caffin wrote, were offered "with an archness which flatters you that she is confident you can see the humor as well as she can" and her songs were rendered "so simply and naturally that it is hard to catch the artifice." The popular singer's personality, a comedian remarked, was the yeast that raised her dough, proof of the skill with which she concealed her preparation.[29]

Vaudeville stars like Nora Bayes appear frequently in the manager's reports. Using her name as a keyword search brings up over 50 entries. From here, you can break down her performances by year, which allows one to see how her routine or its reception changed over time. In one of her earliest performances in 1903, she arrived late to Philadelphia causing a delay but lived up to the praise she had previously received in Providence. The manager reported, "She has a way of talking and acting her songs after the style of Edna Wallace Hopper, and although some of the more conservative in the audience might raise objections to her 'drunk' song, she possesses the cleverness to carry it artistically."[30] By 1905, she was considered a "singing comedienne," so important was her style; in Boston, the manager reported "her dialect is excellent and she appears to have lost considerable of the freshness that characterized her initial appearance here. She receives two and three curtain calls."[31] A Palace Theatre review emphasized that "Lyric and melody are of secondary consideration to the usual Nora Bayes routine, the principal's personality, delivery, and stage tact constituting the value proper and she seems to have those three essentials in abundance right now, more so than ever. She walked off with all honors."[32]

Because of the strong presentation of personality in song, the direct appeal made vaudevillians easy subjects of impersonation. Well-known acts and performers like Bayes were subject to imitation. Some performers faithfully followed the formula of a popular act in the hope of emulating its success. Others hoped to capitalize on the notoriety of vaudeville celebrities. A keyword search reveals that Bayes' name appears frequently in other female acts where her style of personality was imitated. Cecilia Loftus, Belle Blanche, and Madeline Livingston all used impersonations to great effect in their performance. Not all entertainers were as successful, however. In 1906, Cecelia Weston sang at the 58th Street Theatre in New York during which she reportedly made "the most of her hit with Nora Bayes' song, whom she does not credit."[33] The following year, she continued to mimic Bayes' performances but was unable to match her success. Personality was apparently crucial. After performing at the Alhambra, the manager noted Weston "sings Nora Bayes nonsense songs and other novelty items [but] lacks cleverness. Extremely tiresome."[34] Singer Daisy Dimond also used some of Bayes' material, but it did not go over with the audience. The manager at Keith's Cleveland in 1905 reported, "She is singing one of the songs sung here by Nora Bayes. Miss Bayes made a big hit with it, and this woman didn't."[35] Material was only one part of an act, for performers like Bayes part of their success stemmed from their ability to make a song reflect a personality and in doing so to connect to their audience.

The emphasis on communicating personality or individuality grew as the supply of variety artists increased and the public looked for singular elements in a performance. Popular song provides a good illustration of the unfolding relationship between self and performance as singers personalized what had traditionally been a form of story-telling. Although songs continued to express sentiments and described characters that were not the performer's, singers in vaudeville wanted to sound like the music was an outpouring from their own soul, to make the content seem authentic and reflexive.

The transformative relationship between vaudeville performance practice and popular song is only one of the many subjects that can be studied using the database *vaudeville america.org*. Our hope, in making the material accessible to researchers, is that it will inspire new research into popular entertainment, audience sensibilities, and American tastes. Mobilizing knowledge, and making it widely accessible, are mandates of the Social Sciences and Humanities Research Council of Canada which generously funded the *vaudeville america.org* database. Its funding supported the research of a dozen contributors to the website. We hope the existence of this new research tool will encourage researchers to ask their own questions and explore the links between the tens of thousands of reviews that are now available. Whether your interest lies in locating an ancestor who performed in vaudeville, documenting the history of roller-skating or stand-up comedy, or exploring gender or ethnicity on stage, we hope you will find a useful resource in *vaudevilleamerica.org*.

NOTES

1 BF Keith, "Selecting Vaudeville Acts," *New York Times*, 10 January 1904.

2 Manager Report, "1902, The Salambos, New York City," University of Iowa, *Keith-Albee Vaudeville Collection*, Manager Reports, 2 September 1902–3 September 1903. Accessed from http://vaudevilleamerica.org/performance/the-salambos-2/

3 Manager Report, "1902, The Salambos, New York City," University of Iowa, *Keith-Albee Vaudeville Collection*, Manager Reports, 2 September 1902–3 September 1903. Accessed from http://vaudevilleamerica.org/performance/the-salambos-3/

4   Manager Report, "1907, The Song Birds, Brighton Beach Music Hall," *Variety*, 7:3 (20 July 1907). Accessed from http://vaudevilleamerica.org/performance/the-song-birds-2/

5   Manager Report, "1907, The Song Birds, Keith's Cleveland," University of Iowa, *Keith-Albee Vaudeville Collection*, Manager Reports, 23 September 1907–12 March 1908. Accessed from http://vaudevilleamerica.org/performance/the-song-birds-7/

6   Manager Report, "1907, The Song Bird, Keith's Philadelphia," University of Iowa, *Keith-Albee Vaudeville Collection*, Manager Reports, 4 February 1907–9 September 1907. Accessed from http://vaudevilleamerica.org/performance/the-song-birds-6/

7   Manager Report, "1915, Norah Bayes, Palace, New York," *Variety*, 40:3(17 September 1915). Accessed from http://vaudevilleamerica.org/performance/norah-bayes-3/

8   Manager Report, "1919, Blanche Ring, Majestic, Chicago," *Variety*, 53:13(21 February 1919). Accessed from http://vaudevilleamerica.org/performance/blanche-ring-7/

9   Manager Reports, "1920, Milt Collins, Keith's Providence," University of Iowa, *Keith-Albee Vaudeville Collection*, Manager Reports, 13 September 1920–8 December 1921. Accessed from http://vaudevilleamerica.org/performance/milt-collins-3/

10 Manager Reports, "1904, The Sunny South, Trent Theatre, Trenton," University of Iowa, *Keith-Albee Vaudeville Collection*, Manager Reports, 28 November 1904–28 August 1905. Accessed from http://vaudevilleamerica.org/performances/?fwp_performance_name=the%20sunny%20south&fwp_performance_year=1904

11 Manager Report, "1905, The Sunny South, Shea's, Buffalo," University of Iowa, *Keith-Albee Vaudeville Collection*, Manager Reports, 28 November 1904–28 August 1905. Accessed from http://vaudevilleamerica.org/performance/the-sunny-

south-3/; Manager Report, "1905, The Sunny South, Keith's Union Square, New York," University of Iowa, *Keith-Albee Vaudeville Collection*, Manager Reports, 4 September 1905–23 April 1906. Accessed from http://vaudevilleamerica.org/performances/?fwp_performance_name=the%20sunny%20south&fwp_performance_year=1905; Manager Report, "1905, The Sunny South, Keith's New York," *Variety*, 1:2 (23 December 1905). Accessed from http://vaudevilleamerica.org/performance/sunny-south/

12 Manager Report, "1906, The Sunny South, Keith's Cleveland," University of Iowa, *Keith-Albee Vaudeville Collection*, Manager Reports, 30 April 1906–4 February 1907. Accessed from http://vaudevilleamerica.org/performance/sunny-south-3/

13 Manager report, "1907, The Sunny South, Keith's Cleveland," University of Iowa, *Keith-Albee Vaudeville Collection*, Manager Reports, 4 February 1907–9 September 1907. Accessed from http://vaudevilleamerica.org/performance/sunny-south-5/

14 Manager Report, "1903, Beatrice Moreland, Keith's Boston," University of Iowa, *Keith-Albee Vaudeville Collection*, Manager Reports, 2 September 1902–3 September 1903. Accessed from http://vaudevilleamerica.org/performance/beatrice-moreland-3/

15 Brander Matthews, "Why Everyone Loves to Go to the Theatre," *New York Times*, 2 June 1907.

16 Manager Report, "1903, Mary Hampton and Co., Keith's Boston," University of Iowa, *Keith-Albee Vaudeville Collection*, Manager Reports, 2 September 1902–3 September 1903. Accessed from http://vaudevilleamerica.org/performance/mary-hampton-and-co/

17 Henry Jenkins, *What Made Pistachio Nuts? Early Sound Comedy and the Vaudeville Aesthetic* (New York: Columbia University Press, 1992): 61; Caroline Caffin, *Vaudeville* (New York: Scurfield, 1914): 21.

18 Henry Evans, "Adventures in Magic, the Chinese Question,"

The Sphinx (18 September 1919): 160-61; "Massey and Kramer," *Variety*, 28 April 1906; "Emma Carus," *Variety*, 19 September 1908; "Riene Davies," *Variety*, 1 January 1910; "The Passing Show," *The Times* (Washington), 4 November 1900.

19 "Vaudeville No Refuge," *New York Herald*, 9 October 1921; New York Public Library, Billy Rose Theater Collection, MWEZ + n.c. 19,064, Blanche Ring Scrapbook, clipping: *San Francisco Examiner*, April 27, 1911; "Adele Rowland," *Chicago Daily Tribune*, 2 May 1909; "May Robson in New Comedy," *New York Tribune*, 5 September 1905.

20 David *Suisman, Selling Sounds: The Commercial Revolution in American Music* (Cambridge: Harvard University Press, 2009); Alec Wilder and James Maher, eds., *American Popular Song: The Great Innovators, 1900–1950* (New York: Oxford University Press, 1972); Peter van der Merwe, *Origins of the Popular Style: The Antecedents of Twentieth-Century Popular Music* (New York: Oxford University Press, 1989).

21 Calculated from data in website. Accessed from http:// vaudevilleamerica.org/performances/

22 Manager Reports, "1906, Blanche Ring, Colonial, New York City," *Variety*, 4:3(19 May 1906). Accessed from http:// vaudevilleamerica.org/performance/blanche-ring/

23 Manager Reports, "1909, Blanche Ring, Colonial, New York City," *Variety*, 13:9(2 June 1909). Accessed from http:// vaudevilleamerica.org/performance/blanche-ring-2/

24 New York Public Library, Billy Rose Theater Collection, MWEZ x n.c. 21,061, Ned Wayburn Scrapbook, clipping: "She Is a Burlesque Queen 'Bouncing,'" *Evening World*, 3 November 1911: Sophie Tucker Scrapbook, clippings: Show World, 29 September 1909; *Evening Telegram*, 12 October 1909 and Vancouver Paper, 4 July 1910; Sargent Papers, clipping: "Campbell Is Shy."

25 Irving Berlin, "Words and Music," *The Green Book Magazine*, 14:1(July 1915): 104-5.

26 "In the Spotlight's Rays," *Cincinnati Enquirer*, 9 November 1924.

27 "Clarice Vance," *San Francisco Call*, 18 April 1899; "Amuse-ment Notes," *Philadelphia Inquirer*, 22 April 1900; "Clarice Vance," *Newport Daily News* (RI), 14 July 1903; "Miss Clarice Vance," *Indianapolis News*, 7 November 1903; "Vaudeville at the Grand," *Indianapolis Journal*, 10 February 1903; "How to Sing a Ragtime Song," *Detroit Free Press*, 27 January 1907.

28 "Blanche Ring," *Variety*, 11 December 1909; Blanche Ring, "How to Put 'Em Across," *The Green Book Magazine*, 8:1 (July 1912): 45-47; "Popular Air Has Appeal," *Los Angeles Times*, 20 July 1924; Nora Bayes, "Why People Enjoy Crying in a The-ater," *The American Magazine*, 85:4 (April 1918): 33-35.

29 Caffin, *Vaudeville*, 27-29; "Nora Bayes," *Variety*, 11 March 1906; "How to Make a Hit in Vaudeville," *Broadway Weekly*, 28 September 1904.

30 Manager Report, "1903, Nora Bayes, Bijou, Philadelphia," University of Iowa, *Keith-Albee Vaudeville Collection*, Manager Reports, 21 September 1903–14 March 1904. Accessed from http://vaudevilleamerica.org/performance/nora-bayes-13/

31 Manager Report, "1905, Nora Bayes, Temple, Detroit," Uni-versity of Iowa, *Keith-Albee Vaudeville Collection*, Manager Reports, 28 November 1904–28 August 1905. Accessed from http://vaudevilleamerica.org/performance/nora-bayes-16/

32 Manager Report, "1915, Nora Bayes, Palace Theatre," *Variety*, 41:5 (31 December 1915). Accessed from http:// vaudevilleamerica.org/performance/nora-bayes-12/

33 Manager Report, "1906, Cecelia Weston, 58th Street, New York," University of Iowa, *Keith-Albee Vaudeville Collection*, Manager Reports, 21 September 1903–14 March 1904. Ac-cessed from http://vaudevilleamerica.org/performance/cecelia-weston/

34 Manager Report, "1905, Caecilia Weston, Alhambra, New

York City," *Variety*, I:1 (16 December 1905). Accessed from
http://vaudevilleamerica.org/performance/caecilia-weston/

35 Manager Report, "1905, Daisy Dimond, Keith's Cleveland,"
University of Iowa, *Keith-Albee Vaudeville Collection*, Manager
Reports, 28 November 1904–28 August 1905. Accessed from
http://vaudevilleamerica.org/performance/daisy-dimond/

Book Review

· · · · · · · · · · · · · · · · · · ·

Split Screen Nation: Moving Images of
the American West and South. By Susan
Courtney. Oxford University Press, 2017.
329 pp.

ISBN: 978-0190459970

Reviewed by James Altman

University of Nevada, Las Vegas

Susan Courtney is a noted scholar of numerous aspects of
American film culture. In *Split Screen Nation: Moving Images of the American West and South*, she examines the underlying ideologies, preconceptions, misconceptions, and
mythos that combined, during the Cold War, to give "The
Screen South," and "The Screen West" enduring cinematic
reputations. As Courtney reckons, "The Screen South," is
inexorably encumbered by its antebellum past, simultaneously ashamed of it, and nostalgic for it. "The Screen West,"
by contrast, in having, essentially, no meaningful past, waits
eternally empty, open, and pliable. Her scholarly goal is not
to venerate, or to denigrate the screen depiction of either region. Rather, this thought-provoking study wishes to unravel
why these "screen regions" are depicted as they are, how they
influenced popular culture in their time, and how, and why,
they continue to resonate in popular culture today.

The book contains four chapters. Each, ostensibly, focuses
either on one of the "screen regions," some aspect of inter-
play between them, like the function of Southern characters
in westerns, and/or the role of local and national landmarks
in mythmaking. Practically speaking, however, insights and

observations recur and coalesce freely between chapters like a film montage. At every turn, new, unexpected, connections and divergences between the Southern Gothic, Westerns, the Civil Rights Era, The Cold War, propaganda, and mass entertainment reveal themselves. From acclaimed adaptations of Tennessee Williams plays, to Cowboy heroes like John Wayne and Tex Ritter, to home movies and publicly produced "informational" pieces promoting everything from bus tourism, to the necessity of learning first-aid, *Split Screen Nation: Moving Images of the American West and South* draws together not only the myriad themes present in Cold War era film, but provides much useful insight on some of its perspective on wider American popular culture then and now.

The first scenes in the montage, and expertly analyzed, are provided by travelogues sponsored by companies like Ford and Greyhound. Films like *America for Me!* and *Freedom Highway* encourage Americans to see the whole of the country by bus or automobile caravan. They contain a cross-section of typical middle-class white America at the time with characters representing blatant regional stereotypes, such as the timid New England schoolteacher, the brash Texas cowboy, and the wide-eyed Midwestern farm boy. All are zealously patriotic, or become so after coaxing from their fellow travelers. These films typically make virtually no mention of minorities, or of the changing face of America. They are, in effect, a sort of "squeaky clean" picture of what Middle America thought of itself. Feature-length home movies, notably *Family Camping*, add to the "Leave It to Beaver" motif, celebrating the nation's landmarks, such as the Lincoln Memorial, while consciously avoiding the Deep South, and the struggle for civil rights. While insightfully analyzing each film, Courtney asks us to consider why patriotism and mythmaking appear so inexorably intertwined, and what that means for any society, in any era.

As the focus shifts to "The Screen South," *Gone with the Wind*, *A Streetcar Named Desire*, and *Cat on a Hot Tin Roof*, receive much enthralling discussion, not only for their cinematic achievements, but also for their role in marking the South the ultimate repository of America's transgressions, racial and otherwise. For Courtney, Hollywood's characterization of Southerners as uber-racist, sexually perverse, mentally unstable, and savagely violent, allows the rest of the nation to imagine itself, comparatively, blameless. Strangely, *To Kill A Mockingbird*, receives little mention, beyond the idea that it is, somehow, "much less blatantly Southern" than the others mentioned here. Moreover, no explanation of, or evidence for, this supposed "difference" is presented.

"The Screen West," by contrast, comes across as a, virtual, lump of clay, waiting for rugged pioneers to sculpt it in a way more racially mono-cultural, more individualistic, more patriotic and, thus, more "American" than "The Screen South" could ever be. Westerns like "The Big Trail," "Stagecoach," "Rio Bravo," and "Big Jake" endlessly showcase the Cowboy hero's triumph over an unforgiving landscape devoid of civilization, hostile natives, and unscrupulous Southerners seething over the Old Confederacy's defeat.

Those interested in the evolution of film, filmmaking, and onscreen storytelling will find *Split Screen Nation: Moving Images of the American West and South* a treat to read. Those interested in film's ability to shape cultural attitudes will also find the book intriguing.

Book Review

· · · · · · · · · · · · · · · · · · ·

Sounds of Origin in Heavy Metal Music.
Edited by Toni-Matti Karjalainen. Cambridge Scholars Publishing, 2018. 195 pp.

ISBN: 978-1-5275-1170-5

Review by Heather Lusty
University of Nevada, Las Vegas

For decades, the slim body of scholarship on heavy metal music has been predictably and uninspiringly focused on fans, centered on questions like: Who listens to heavy metal? Why do they enjoy such aggressive music? Should we treat them like "regular people?" Does metal exclude women? While much of the superficiality of this approach lies in the interests of sociology itself, scant few other academic fields have willingly entered the foray of music scholarship since the "established" comprehensive surveys of Denna Weinstein and Robert Walsam's 1980s studies. Yet the diverse body of heavy metal genres, concepts, and focus invite serious scholarly attention that is just beginning to blossom.

One such example is Toni-Matti Karjalainen's new edited collection, Sounds of Origin in Heavy Metal Music, a natural outgrowth of the Modern Heavy Metal Conference (MHMC) Karjalainen founded in Helsinki in 2014. Every year since its establishment, MHMC draws more than 150 scholars from around the world, as far away as Brazil and the Philippines, and invites the genuine interest and participation of industry and media as well. Having had the pleasure of attending 2018's symposium in Helsinki, I can attest to the wide breadth of creative approaches international scholars bring to the heavy metal studies scene. This collection reflects the theme of 2017's MHMC, "Music and National Identities," which coincided with Finland's independence centenary. The essays reflect both the dynamic inter-connectivity and the unique national flavor of heavy metal around the globe.

Toni-Matti Karjalainen's contribution, "Tales from the North and Beyond: Sounds of Origin as Narrative Discourses" opens the volume with a fascinating look at the use of country-of-origin references in media coverage, which often cherry-pick nationally-flavored phrases and stereotypes that usually do not accurately reflect the music (15). The chapter showcases Finnish metal, and provides copious examples of generic narratives that claim a natural affinity of Finnish musicians to "natural and mental landscapes, [and] the "northern" dimension" of a snowy, despondent, strongly Romantic ideal of Nordic melancholy — a consistent depiction of the Finnish metal scene, despite its impressive diversity of sound and construction. Karjalainen notes that the place-bound annotations and accompanied "narratives of origin" often have little to do with the musical content or style of the band/album being reviewed; yet these descriptions often create meaningful and vivid associations in the reader (3). Prefabricated narratives link historically shaped genres and locational styles, which may help metal-conscious readers of magazines to contextualize the band/album within the larger map of metal sub-genres. Karjalainen examines a wide body of metal-centered media to illustrate this stereotypical narrative, juxtaposing bands, scenes, sub-genres, and other identities and characteristics that make up the "sounds of origin" in Finnish metal with the generic "frozen tundra" references that have little to do with the sounds or foci of Finnish music generally (although it may fit a smaller, select group of Finnish metal bands).

A cluster of chapters focus on the influence of Norwegian black metal in other cultures, highlighting the local and regional influence on constructions of narrative and aesthetics. Baptiste Pilo's "True Norwegian Black Metal: Nationalism and Authenticity in the Norwegian Black Metal of the '90s" explores the search for authentic Norwegian identity in the first wave of Norwegian black metal bands, emphasizing a desire to understand Norwegian culture as separate from that of contemporary European countries. This chapter admirably delineates the shortcomings of the initial categorizations or observations (and pearl-clutching) over the interest in distinct national identities in certain metal subgenres. Pilo cites Jean-Luc Chabot's observation that "nationalism suffers from an imprecision of meaning and an ambiguity of use" (quoted in Pilo, 42), suggesting that "the nationalism of black metal is not patriotism [... nor] constitutive nationalism [... but] closer to a political nationalism, placing the interest of the nation above other interests; even if no band is committed to apolitical party [... [T]he nationalism of the Norwegian Black Metal actually is anachronistic since it is deeply anchored in the national romantic idea of the nation" (Pilo 42). There are three types of authenticity presented: expression, experience, and execution, which Pilo links to the authenticity of the "metal underground," the pre-Christian heritage of the Vikings, and the political nationalism stances and aesthetic choices glorifying national heritage (44). National authentication is approached by musicians in myriad ways that cannot be shaped into a single lump of clay. This essay gives scholars a fresh approach to the complexities of "national identities" in heavy metal, which to date have been largely painted in black and white.

"Songs of Darkness: Identities in Italian Black Metal"—by Tommaso Frangioni, Filippo Masina, Giulio Pieroni, and

Mario Venturella—reflects the initial findings of a larger study focused on the appropriation and adaptation of the Scandinavian black metal narrative in Italy. Although the field of Italian black metal is strikingly diverse, with at least five distinct branches—first wave (using both its grammar and symbolic/colloquial apparatus), NSBM, elitism inspired by the writings of Julius Evola, regionalism, and those drawing fully from Italian national culture)—they share similarities inherited from the Scandinavian model, including heritage and anti-establishment themes, pre-Christian origins, and conflict with the country's Catholicism and bourgeois morality (44). All of the branches appropriate various elements of Italian history and culture "congruent with the aspects they intent to promote: feelings of misanthropy, nationalism, elitism, and rejection of modern bourgeois society [...]" (45). The authors highlight the importance of understanding the function of adopting aspects of culture and heritage to form distinct identities through symbols, costumes, and historical memory—these comprise the foundational approaches to understanding imagined communities established by Benedict Anderson in the early 1980s.

Gianluca Chelini's chapter, "Javanese Black Metal: Towards a Definition of Post-Heritage Music," highlights the rapid growth of black metal-influenced local music in Java. A unique fusion of local musical traditions, literary influence, and cultural traditions (including philosophical concepts from Hindu and Kedjawan) highlight the process of what Chelini terms "heritagisation" in the Javanese metal scene (98). The radical changes in the social and political scene in Indonesia over the last two decades is reflected in the local metal scene, most notably in its hybrid nature, incorporating lively national debate on the values and significance of local traditions (97). Chelini discusses two distinct strands of Javanese black metal; the first she terms "Black Metal for a New Java," in which musicians have commodified adat (Adat istiadat (rituals) are practices deriving from pre-Islamic elements outside the teaching of Islam). The other strand Chelini describes as a touristic culture and heritage mentality. Citing anthropologist Michael Picard's work evaluating the importance of the economic value of culture and its importance to the cultural identity of an island people, Chelini notes that the Balinese developed an awareness of "culture" that has influenced the incorporation and monetization of local sounds, tales, and identity in the music scene.

The chapters remaining reach across the oceans—Joseph Norman's chapter, "From the Bogs of Aughiska: Dark Ambient, Folklore, and Irish National Identity" presents the links between "Heritage Black Metal" and the distinct culture of the West Country—heritage, history, politics, landscape, and folklore. Drawing on the history and heritage of Ireland, and County Clare specifically, Norman connects the musical output of founder Conchur O'Drona's Bogs project to the Irish Gothic tradition of the Weird, the uncanny, and the sublime. Although full of idiosyncrasies and contradictions, these reflect the tensions between black metal elitism and nihilism, and folk populism and optimism. Noting that Biddle and Knights[1] have argued for the nation as "a crucial but ambivalent category for understanding how cultural texts and practices function in the construction of personal and collective identities" (quoted in Norman, 118), Norman's project connects personal experience to broader regional and national concerns, "using heritage to knit the Irish extreme music scene together, and to help disseminate that island's culture and history to the broader associated with such musi-

---

1 Biddle, Ian, and Vanessa Knights, Eds. Music, National Identity and the Politics of Location: Between the Global and the Local, Routledge, 2007.

cal scenes" (Norman 118, 136). O'Drona's incorporation of tales and legends, local myths, and folk traditions in his music play a powerful role in the preservation of County Clare culture and identity.

Matt Sage and Caelli Jo Brooker explore the "Manifold Intensities: Musical Identities in Contemporary Antipodean Metalcore and Post-Hardcore" in their chapter, focusing on performance authenticity in Australia's national music scene. The meteoric rise of the metalcore and post-hardcore subgenres reflect the inclusiveness and diversity of the Australian local scenes. The contrasting extreme and melodic vocal techniques exemplify the subgenre. Intense live performances are characterized by energetic mosh pits and anthemaic crowd accompaniment. Amanda DiGioia's chapter ends the collection, looking at the heavy metal scene in a tiny sliver of New England. "Love Breed or Hate Haven? Localized Narratives of Identity in Heavy Metal Scene of New Haven, Connecticut" utilizes fan and musician interviews to explore the music scene on the East Coast. DiGioia finds that New Haven residents' shared identity of civil rights (in a culturally pluralistic community) puts them and the local music scene in opposition to the general political climate of the United States. DiGioia also highlights the prominent visibility of marginalized groups and the inclusion of gender racial "others" in the scene.

Karjalainen's "Epilogue" nicely ties together the complex negotiations on national and local identities in in the heavy metal scene, observing that the contradictions and paradoxes therein can be traced back to complex questions of authenticity and authority (192). The strengths of this collection are numerous, but the sheer breadth of focus emphasizes the underserved local scenes and under-explored approaches to contemporary music studies. As heavy metal completes its fifth decades, now arguably more popular than any other global music genre, the local narratives at the core of some of the earliest metal bands (Black Sabbath, Iron Maiden, Primordial, Venom) are still at the core of local and national scenes. Indeed, heavy metal is truly the music of the people in a world gone mad.

Book Review

· · · · · · · · · · · · · · · · · · ·

Flavors of Empire: Food and the Making of Thai America. Padoongpatt, Mark. University of California Press, 2017. 270 pp.

ISBN: 978-0520293748

Vibrator Nation: How Feminist Sex-Toy Stores Changed the Business of Pleasure. Comella, Lynn. Duke University Press, 2018. 294 pp.

ASIN: B074TCX2HZ

Reviewed by Jarret Keene
University of Nevada, Las Vegas

I don't believe it's an overstatement to say that the Interdisciplinary, Gender, and Ethnic Studies department at the University of Nevada, Las Vegas, offers one of the most progressive and productive collections of cultural scholars and social historians in all of higher education. From Dr. Erika Abad (who teaches a class on the Lin-Manuel Miranda musical *Hamilton* with an eye toward Latinx presence in pop culture) to professor Tim Gauthier (currently writing a book and publishing articles devoted to issues of community and immunity in the Robert Kirkman graphic-novel series *The Walking Dead*) to three-time National Poetry Slam champion and creative scholar Javon Johnson (co-editor of *The End of Chiraq: A Literary Mixtape*, just out from Northwestern University Press), the list of accomplishments by these writers and thinkers leaves me in awe and suffering from a case of impostor syndrome mixed with, well, envy.

And then there's the outstanding quality of the research itself, as confirmed in two recent books. First, Professor Mark Padoongpatt tells, for the very first time, the fascinating story of how Thai food gradually spiced up the limited culinary options in the suburbs with *Flavors of Empire: Food and the Making of Thai America* (University of California Press, 2017). Beginning with an examination of the U.S. empire in Cold War Thailand, Padoongpatt relates how "foodways emerged as the key site for constructing Thais as an exotic neocolonial subject." It all began, naturally, with the efforts of federally funded social scientists, assigned the task of calculating the country's potential in benefiting Western interests. Indeed, no stone is left unturned, Padoongpatt noting the Stateside impact of the 1951 Rodgers and Hammerstein musical *The King and I*, arguably the most serious postwar representation of Thailand, which arrived in the form of a Twentieth Century Fox movie starring Yul Brynner and Gertrude Lawrence. Moreover, there's no shying away from transactions involving Thai sex workers and U.S. servicemen in Bangkok, conducted under the guise of "R&R trips," or from patriarchal exploitation of women's bodies, which were deemed "beautiful" and "exotic":

> Journalist Lloyd Shearer expressed these views in the 1968 Parade Magazine article, "Thailand is a Man's World—and the G.I.'s Like It." Shearer described Thai women to readers as "in the main, lovely creatures of delicate beauty." He also said Thailand's Queen Sirikit and her physical beauty was a prime "reflection of the country's enchanting young women" because she was "petite, demure, shapely, reserved."

When the young men left the military to join the workforce, they needed a place to vacation. Thus, the Thai tourist infrastructure got underway. But Padoongpatt isn't content to make this simply a story of a nation -mining another, more feminized (and exotic) country; he has a sensitive, nuanced touch, especially when articulating the influence of, say, forgotten cookbook author Marie Wilson. It was Wilson, along with fellow culinary adventurer Jennifer Brennan, who, as Western women, "became experts on Thai ingredients, cooking methods, equipment, and the kitchen." In their cookbooks, they presented a fantasy of Thailand to U.S. consumers—an extension of colonial behavior that enabled white women to establish culinary authority. Still, Wilson and Brennan encouraged readers to superficially acknowledge the beauty of another country, another culture, a food different from American (and Anglo) fare.

Even more fascinating is Padoongpatt's telling of how the Bangkok Market in Los Angeles introduced Thai foodstuffs to the U.S. His description of Thai immigration to the States, in the wake of the 1965 Immigration Act, informs us that Thais in L.A. adopted the slang term "Robin Hoods," referring to those outside of legal status as being noble outlaws. Padoongpatt doesn't sugarcoat the reason why the illegal immigration of Thais was often overlooked; he cites a U.S. consular official who told the *L.A. Times*: "Why worry about 10,000 Thais when there are 600,000 Hispanics coming across the border?" Chapter Three ("Too Hot to Handle?: Restaurants and Thai American Identity"), meanwhile, digs deeply—and *throughly*—into the journalistic coverage and culinary criticism aimed at Thai restaurants and food festivals, and how these intersected with the white imagination and its inherent biases. Finally, Padoongpatt delves into the delicious history of Thai Town, the "77th Province, and how culinary tourism works in the (late-)capitalist forge of the City of Los Angeles. He examines everything: menus, ribbon-cutting brochures, city-planning agendas. After sopping up the concluding chapter ("Beyond Cooking and Eating"), one is left with an obvious, unresolved question: Why doesn't Padoongpatt have a Netflix series where he takes viewers on a real (and visual) tour of the impact of Thai people and culture in America?

Dr. Lynn Comella is the more polished writer, having slugged it out in the deadline-trenches for print outlets as varied as *Forbes* and weekly culture magazine *Vegas Seven*. Her celebrated book, ***Vibrator Nation: How Sex-Toy Stores Changed the Business of Pleasure*** (Duke University Press, 2018), is a riveting account of how feminist-owned shops challenged and changed our collective notion of social activism, sex-positive retail, and women's intimate lives. Twenty years in the making, it's far and away the best and most important tome devoted to the issues of gender and power and capitalism in recent years. Furthermore, it's just plain *fun* to read.

Vibrator Nation opens with a remarkable scene—a 1973 conference on female sexuality organized by NOW, the National Organization for Women, held in a public school on Manhattan's Upper East Side. There, pioneering sex educator Betty Dodson knocked down the gate that stood between women and their own sexual liberation and pleasure by offering a slide show projecting a diversity of women's vulvas. But what might have easily been a media circus ended up as something very different—an empowering "speak-out." As Comella states

> Borrowing from the tradition of feminist
> consciousness-raising, in which women

shared their personal experiences as a basis for political analysis, a number of women took turns on the microphone to talk about their sexuality. While Dodson joked about her vibrator, others spoke candidly about open marriage, swinging, bi-sexuality, childhood sexual abuse, and heterosexual power dynamics. They shared stories about sexual exploration and expressed frustration about the sexual double standard. "I am thankful to the people in the women's movement and in the gay movement who have paved the way to loosening the shackles on sexuality," said one speaker.

Indeed, how the pins and bolts of those chains were unlocked over time has never been more eloquently and intriguingly recounted as it is in this book. From the early retail efforts of Dell Williams—who founded the first sex-toy business after a disappointing attempt to buy a massage device at Macy's—to calligraphy project-cum-sex manual, *The Playbook for Women About Sex*, written and published by Good Vibrations founder Joani Blank, the story of sex toys is far and way more compelling then, for instance, the history of comics shops or "head" (cannabis-culture) shops. Comella is the perfect guide, explaining to readers how feminist sex-toy retailers brand and market their products with an eye toward activism.

The narrative isn't confined to Pacific Northwest; the author investigates seedier stores, like A-Action Adult Books in Downtown Las Vegas—situated a few blocks from this reviewer's house and a place too sketchy for me to consider frequenting. In A-Action, Comella articulates the reason why many sex shops, as women-friendly spaces, have a long way to progress:

> This was a business that traded in sexual opportunity, not sexual information. The video booths were the main event, the real selling point, and, most likely, big money-makers. And while the clerk was chatty and friendly—even describing in unsolicited detail his experience using a penis pump—the business's male customers (and they were all men) gave me quizzical looks, seemingly unsure about to what to make of my presence. Who was I and what was my purpose? Was I sexually available? And if not, why was I there?

Comella contrasts this sleazy Sin City joint with the classier design and progressive credo of respectable retailers like Babeland (Seattle) and Good Vibrations (San Francisco). It's an approach that has paid off, elevating sex shops—at least in those parts of the larger Trump-ravaged country—from the province of "dirty old men" and making them a comfortable place for landlords, the community, and shoppers themselves. Other absorbing parts of the book—like "Retail-Based Sex Ed," for example—introduce us to the pioneering roles of Good Vibrations staff sexologist Carol Queen, while other sections show us what happens when a feminist sex-toy shop undergoes a change of ownership, moving from co-op status and into a corporate direction. Comella chronicles it all with care and precision; the result is a must-read, a fascinating story about the mainstreaming of women's sexual pleasure and how feminist sex-positive retailers made the world a better and more informative place for women (and men and everyone else) to live our sexual lives without having to be embarrassed or degraded. Comella (and her department colleague Padoongpatt) deserve serious acclaim for rendering once-hidden struggles to bring exotic and erotic concepts into the suburbs, and to the American public's attention.

Contributors

James Altman serves as Academic Support Specialist for the Academic Success Center (ASC) at the University of Nevada, Las Vegas. His research interests include Modern and Contemporary Literature, Modern and Contemporary Poetry, Popular Culture, and how best to implement assistive technologies to aid student learning. He has published both scholarly and creative work. He is a book reviewer for the Journal of American Culture (JAC).

Marcus Axelsson graduated from Stockholm University with an MA in Translation Studies in 2011 and later on earned a PhD in Scandinavian languages from Uppsala University in 2016. Since 2017, he works as an Associate Professor at the Department of Teacher Education at Østfold University College in Halden, Norway. He carries out research within the fields of Translation Studies, the Sociology of Culture and Scandinavian Studies. He focuses mainly on the export and translation of literature for children and young adults.

Daryl Malarry Davidson is an afficionado of classic movies who is pursuing an interdisciplinary PhD in screenwriting studies at Ohio University. Earlier versions of his and Marc J. Olson's limited-series teleplay, *Fool-Court Press*, received honorable mention from two *Writer's Digest* Writing Competitions and the Charleston International Film Festival. The farce deals with an egotistical, white professional basketball player who feels so unappreciated that he issues a challenge: the top five white players, he tells the media, could beat the top five Black players. Davidson earned an MA in screenwriting & film studies and an MFA in screenwriting from Hollins University.

Nanette Hilton's writing and artwork is published in travel and trade magazines, literary and scholarly journals, and as instructional manuals. She holds a degree in Writing and teaches English Composition. When not creating, Nanette may be found cycling the Mojave or enjoying time with her husband and their five daughters.

Kathy Merlock Jackson is Professor of Communication at Virginia Wesleyan University, where she teaches courses in media studies and children's culture. She is the author of over a hundred articles, chapters, and reviews and has published nine books, four of them on Disney-related topics, and one, most recently, on *Shapers of American Childhood*. She is the former editor of *The Journal of American Culture* and Vice President/President-Elect of the Popular Culture Association/American Culture Association.

Jarret Keene teaches ancient literature and creative writing at the University of Nevada, Las Vegas, where he also coordinates the World Literature Second-Year Seminars. He is currently hard at work on a book devoted to the authorship of legendary comic-book creator Jack Kirby.

Heather Lusty is an Assistant Professor in the Honors College at the University of Nevada, Las Vegas. She works on modernism, nationalism and identity, and architecture. She has edited a collection of essays on James Joyce and D.H. Lawrence entitled *Modernism at Odds* (UP Florida, 2015), and a collection of Lawrence's stories, *The Border Line: D. H. Lawrence's Soldier Stories* (Palamedes Publishing, 2018). She is currently working on a manuscript examining performance in heavy metal music.

David Monod is a professor of history at Wilfrid Laurier University in Waterloo, Ontario, Canada. His most recent book is *The Soul of Pleasure: Sentiment and Sensation in Nineteenth-Century American Mass Entertainment.* He has recently completed a book manuscript on the history of vaudeville.

Brian A. Mosich attends the Boyd School of Law. Described by friends as: More than you expect, loyal, straightforward, open-minded, kind, an instrument of chaos, challenger, amusing, reliable, The Ashbringer, a master at problematizing anything, stoic, strategic, philosophic, perplexing, concise, unfathomable, methodical, a puzzle solving wizard, and [damn] 37.

Scooter Pégram is the director of the French programme at Indiana University Northwest, where he is also Associate Professor of French and Minority Studies, and is member of the faculty in Women's and Gender Studies. A sociolinguist by training, Dr. Pégram has published numerous articles on subjects encapsulating youth of colour across North America and France on topics such as identity, acceptance, racism, integration, gender and language. Currently, Dr. Pégram is researching the intertwining topics of resistance, racism, gender, language, and identity as manifested via the medium of French-language hip-hop music.

Lyndsay Rosenthal recently completed her SSHRC-funded PhD dissertation at Wilfrid Laurier University.

Daniel Ferreras Savoye is a professor of French and Spanish literatures and Cultural Studies at West Virginia University. His work on marginalized authors, comic books, detective fiction, popular culture issues and critical theory has appeared in *Hispania, French Literature Series, Ángulo Recto, Lectura y signo, The Popular Culture Review* and *La tribuna.* He is the author of *Lo fantástico en la literatura y el cine* (ACVF, 1995/ 2014), *Cuentos de la mano izquierda* (Silente, 1999), *Amor 3.1* (Biblioteca del Laberinto, 2010), *The Signs of James Bond* (McFarland, 2013) and *Beyond Literary Studies* (McFarland, 2017).

Tammy Wahpeconiah is a professor and interim chair of English teaching courses in American, American Indian and Ethnic American literatures at Appalachian State University. She earned her B.A. from the University of Miami and her M.A. from Michigan State University. She received her Ph.D. in American Literature from Michigan State University. Her research interests include early American Indian writers, contemporary American Indian literature, Ethnic American literature and science fiction and fantasy. She has published a book entitled *This Once Savage Heart of Mine: Rhetorical Strategies of Survival in Early Native American Writing* focusing on the writings of Joseph Johnson and Hendrick Aupaumut, as well as articles on Sherman Alexie, William S. Penn, and Ted Chiang.

Graeme John Wilson was born in the United Kingdom but raised in the United States; a dual citizen of both countries, he is currently pursuing his Ph.D. in Media and Communication at Bowling Green State University in Bowling Green, Ohio, where he works as a teaching associate. In December 2017, Graeme received a Graduate Certificate in Women's Studies from the university. He will graduate with his PhD in 2019. Graeme's specific research interests lie in the visual representation of gender and racial identities in popular narrative media. Graeme has presented his research at various conferences, including the Broadcast Education Association (BEA), National Communication Association (NCA), and Popular Culture Association (PCA) annual conventions.